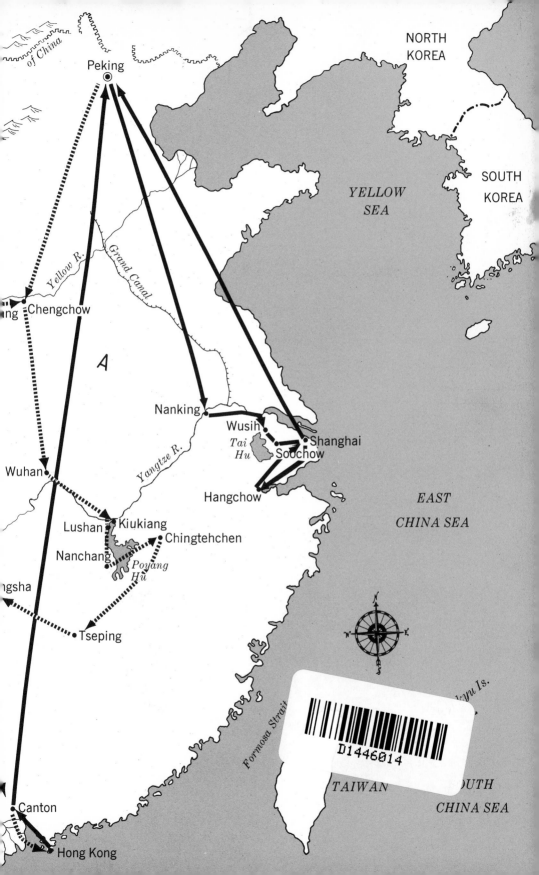

NORTH KOREA

SOUTH KOREA

YELLOW SEA

...of China

Peking

...ng Chengchow

Yellow R.

Grand Canal

A

Wuhan

Yangtze R.

Nanking

Wusih

Tai Hu

Shanghai

Soochow

Hangchow

Lushan Kiukiang

Chingtehchen

Nanchang

Poyang Hu

...ngsha

Tseping

EAST CHINA SEA

Canton

Hong Kong

Formosa Strait

TAIWAN

...yu Is.

...OUTH CHINA SEA

The East Is Red:

The View Inside China

by MASLYN
WILLIAMS

William Morrow & Company, Inc.

NEW YORK 1967

915.1
W

Published simultaneously in Canada by George
J. McLeod Limited, Toronto.

Printed in the United States of America.

Library of Congress Catalog Card Number
67-29845

For Ruth

PREFACE

THIS account of recent travels in China covers a period of roughly three months, during part of which time the writer traveled the conventional tourist route with a group of Australian excursionists, enjoying semiofficial courtesies, but afterward went as a single visitor, accompanied only by interpreters, to places less frequently seen by outsiders since China became a Communist nation.

For purely literary reasons this account does not follow the itinerary of travel in strict continuity. Visitations, events, and conversations have been arranged in an order which, to the author, seems to permit of a more sensible presentation of developing impressions. And because some part of the tourist track has recently been well raked over by other literary visitors, much purely informational material, readily available in other publications, has been altogether omitted.

Also, for reasons of discretion some of the characters have been slightly disguised. Otherwise this account is as accurate as diligent study, earnest observation, and honest intent are able to make it.

Maslyn Williams

Ordos Desert

Great Wall

Yellow R.

C H I N

Yangtze R.

Tung

BURMA

FIRST JOURNEY
SECOND JOURNEY

Pearl R.

NORTH
VIETNAM

LAOS

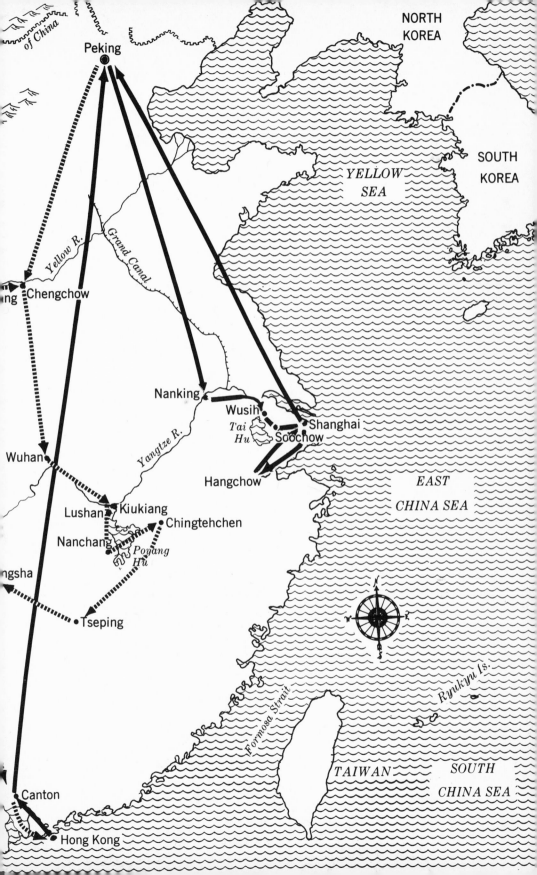

of China

Peking

NORTH KOREA

SOUTH KOREA

YELLOW SEA

Yellow R.

Grand Canal

Chengchow

ng

Nanking

Wusih

Tai Hu

Shanghai

Soochow

Wuhan

Yangtze R.

Hangchow

EAST CHINA SEA

Lushan

Kiukiang

Chingtehchen

Nanchang

Poyang Hu

ngsha

Tseping

Formosa Strait

Ryukyu Is.

TAIWAN

SOUTH CHINA SEA

Canton

Hong Kong

Chinese Names

THE system of Romanization used, by my advice, in this book is that used by most Western newspapers and in Chinese foreign-language publications. It follows roughly the Wade-Giles system except that apostrophes and umlauts are omitted. Thus Wade-Giles distinguishes between the aspirated *ch* sound in ch'ang and the unaspirated *ch* sound in chang which is in fact very close to the English *j* sound.

It is understood, then, that the system used in this book will not meet with the approval of every reader because it does not make such distinctions as these. Nevertheless, most people are probably more familiar with this more simple system.

For place names the standard postal Romanization has been used.

C. P. Mackerras
Recently of the Peking
Institute of Languages
and now of the Department
of Far Eastern History,
Australian National University.

Part
One

Let us look at the earth around us.
What is happening under our eyes within the mass
of peoples? What is the cause of this disorder
in society, this uneasy agitation, these swelling
waves, these whirling and mingling currents and
these turbulent and formidable new impulses?
Mankind is visibly passing through a crisis of
growth. Mankind is becoming aware of its
shortcomings and its capacities . . . it sees the
universe growing luminous like the horizon
just before sunrise. It has a sense of
premonition and of expectation.

Pierre Teilhard de Chardin
The Divine Milieu

CHAPTER

1

LET us begin with Miss Ping.

I didn't see her at the airport in Peking when I came in the daily plane from Canton, but as I didn't know her then there was no way by which I could have picked her out of the huge, exuberant crowd waiting for our flight to arrive. Even had I been looking out for her it is unlikely that I would have seen her among so many people, because Miss Ping is physically quite undistinguished in spite of her name being Glorious Chrysanthemum, and because she is so dedicated that she does her best to look Communistically anonymous.

In any case there was so much going on at the airport; so much movement that I would never have picked her out of the thousands of people chanting slogans and waving forests of little flags and paper flowers (except for the files of soldiers standing stiffly to one side) and all looking up expectantly, waiting to see the Albanians leave the plane.

It was exciting, this lively crowd of thousands lined behind barriers, shouting, "Long live militant friendship between the people of China and Albania"—so it said in the *Peking Review* two days later—and I felt myself caught up in it, stimulated by the insistent rhythmic sound of the shouting; the thumping of drums, the continuous din of cymbals crashing, the bronze gongs booming out above it all like waves falling on a sea wall in a storm; swirl of multicolored folk clothes with long twirling sleeves and scarves, worn for this gay occasion by men and women from Tibet and Manchuria and the other borderland minorities; and behind them the banks of red banners flanking a huge, hook-nosed portrait of Albania's Chairman Mehmet Shehu.

Thousands of smiling, excited, organized people had gathered to greet him and his fellow delegates from the land of the eagles: China's guests, invited for the May Day celebrations.

They went quickly down the landing steps. Gray, ungainly men smiling widely, showing silver teeth, they strode across the tarmac with coats blowing, going to where Chou En-lai and Chairman Liu were waiting, and girls with sheaves of gladioli. Meanwhile we other foreigners, tourists, and secondary guests watched from the windows and doorways of the plane and saw big-boned Shehu reach out to clasp trim Chou En-lai to his chest and swing his great head first to one side, then the other, laying gray on yellow cheek in comradely embrace.

Somewhere on the edge of all this was little Miss Ping, from Luhsingshe, the State Travel Service which provides guides and interpreters for all foreign visitors.

We saw Chairman Liu step forward, benevolent and bland like Mao Tse-tung, though younger, and taking Shehu's hands, make him three times welcome in the name of the Communist Party of China, the Chinese Government, and the Chinese People, in that order, who, he said, deeply appreciated this visit by representatives of the heroic Albanian people, our blood brothers in the world-wide struggle to oppose the U.S. imperialist policies of death and aggression. Everybody cheered and clapped, and cameramen moved closer. Those of us inside the Ilyushin turned to each other smiling, pleased to be seeing all this.

"We are deeply moved," replied Shehu, "for we feel the hot love of seven hundred million people pouring upon us, a love as pure as the Chinese sunlight, as inspiring as the ever victorious theory of Marxism-Leninism."

A chorus came crashing through loudspeakers:

> Socialism's fine,
> Socialism's grand.
> The standing of the people
> Is tops in socialist lands.

2

But however warm the sun of China's love, the wind was keenly bleak and thick with Gobi grit, and I was cold now, having no jacket, and not altogether sorry when we were let go down along the edges of the crowd into the terminal building, where a group of guides and interpreters, without flowers, waited to take us in tow; tourists from France, teachers from Canada, and a mixed bunch of Australians.

Smiling and gracious, they came forward, separated us into nationalities, then led us with pleasant and gentle gestures into an annex where the rest were put at tables set with savory things and drinks, but we Australians stood waiting while our guides gathered to talk among themselves as if something were amiss.

Then they looked toward the door and we saw a girl come in by herself, embarrassed (it seemed that she had been sent to fetch us from the plane but, being distracted and patriotically taken up in the clamor and commotion outside, had not seen us). Now we all watched her, a glum, dumpy figure in a faded tunic and trousers sagging at the seat. Coming toward us, she peered myopically through thick-lensed spectacles—pale of face, though blushing a little for this present disgrace, with black plaits, sawn off at less than shoulder length and tied with red rag, sticking out stiffly from under a cloth cap. A shapeless girl, uncertain and self-effacing. Her age, she said later, was twenty-three.

So at the airport in Peking I first saw Ping Jung-Chu, or Glorious Chrysanthemum, who later came with me through China as a permanent interpreter, though others with more fluency and detailed local knowledge took over at key places along the way to supplement her inexperience, since she was a junior, not long out of the language institute, and had scarcely finished training. She was not yet good enough, obviously, for group work of any kind but adequate to manage transient passages in the itinerary of an individual visitor of no particular distinction.

I learned in time to like her very much and sometimes, in an excess of sentimental Western affection, called her daughter, which made her cheeks go pink. But that came later.

She sat beside me in the coach going to the city but seemed shy, kept her head down and spoke not much above a whisper, and was tongue-tied when I asked her name and age and something about her family. I should have known that traditional Chinese reticence, stretched to an extreme of self-depreciation by the Communist cult of submergence within the mass personality of "proletariat," must have made my curiosity seem ill-mannered and uncomfortably barbarous to this young and unsophisticated girl whose previous knowledge of foreigners was negligible. She could not yet have discovered that it is the nature of Westerners to be direct, because time and not refinement is our most precious possession.

But I persevered and got her name in my notebook, though she seemed to resent even this familiarity until the head guide, Mr. Feng, leaning back from his seat in front of us, spelled it out for me clearly, watching me write. When I was done, he added with a grin, "You may call her Miss Ping." At this she pouted, embarrassed and displeased, took a paperback from the plastic handbag which she carried, and began to read what appeared to be a textbook, in English.

I tried, briefly, to read over her shoulder, but Miss Ping retreated deeper and there seemed no point in pursuing a one-sided exercise in friendship with this reluctant child. I watched the streets instead. They were busy with the breaking up of crowds of people who had lined the roadside to welcome Shehu and his retinue as they drove in open cars along the wide tree-lined boulevard with Chou and Liu, people who had provided the cheering and the waving of banners and flags. Dense, happy crowds (said the *Liberation Daily*), workers, students, army men, militia, government functionaries, children and students and other Peking residents, who had given our Albanian comrades a tumultuously warm welcome.

Now they were going home or back to the factories, barracks, schools, and kindergartens. Among them were columns of cute, chubby children with pink cheeks and red scarves tied around their necks, walking two-and-two, holding hands with teachers beside them (surely no infants sweeter than these Chinese with their brown button eyes and fat, ambiguous faces). There were students led by youths with red banners, boys and girls in similar blue tunics singing "Workers of the World Unite" as they strode with pride along the wide-pathed footway, under the spring-green trees that line Peking's streets: young poplars leaning away from the

4

touch of the rough and blustering wind; willows swinging and swaying like girls' skirts; and lilac leaning over walls, spreading its scent everywhere (so few cars or trucks and thus no fumes to foul the air).

But because there are so few motor vehicles men and women and young girls do the work of trucks, lugging barrow loads of merchandise and manufactured goods through the streets, trudging between the shafts or tugging on ropes attached to harness hung on their shoulders or slung crosswise over their breasts. A phrase from Han Suyin came into my mind as our bus passed them, one after another, following in the gay wake of the Albanians: generations of Chinese "bent over the earth in constant service."

In the coach we whispered, nudged, and made faces at each other, exchanging flickers of sympathy tinged with disapproval, for it seemed to us inhuman that people should do the work of animals and become beasts of burden, not merely hauling light or reasonable freights, but many straining to the utmost of their strength, with the sinews of their necks stretched tight like strings, and the muscles of their legs and arms sticking out like ivory balls, dragging loads that half-a-dozen men might find difficult to lift.

One of our men, a small-town capitalist and an avid reader of *Time* Magazine (unmentionable in China), was indignant and made no bones about it.

"Terrible, isn't it? Terrible to see human beings treated as slaves in this day and age." He was red in the neck and stammering. "It makes me feel sick to see such things."

Our chief guide, smiling, half stood to speak to us. "You will observe that all the carts have rubber tires on their wheels. Before liberation, when most of the poor people in the city had to work for corrupt officials and reactionary capitalists, the carts had wooden wheels and were hard to pull. The people were paid so little then that it was cheaper to have men pull the carts than to keep and feed horses, and because the workers did not get enough to eat many of them died between the shafts.

"Now under the leadership of the Party, the transportation industry is organized into cooperatives controlled entirely by the workers. All the carts have rubber tires and everyone is paid a just wage, has free medical attention and proper holidays. And as the industrialization of China develops, and we have more motor trucks, most of these people will be absorbed into the automobile industry."

We listened attentively, glad to have this explanation, wanting to be assured that we could go through China without feeling uncomfortable, relieved that what we were seeing was a sign of progress and not of incurable distress or a lack of concern or sensitivity on the part of the regime. So when he had finished we looked at each other again, nodding agreeably. And someone said how well Mr. Feng spoke English, with an accent so beautifully British and better than our own.

Then sudden excitement and all the people in the street were looking up, pointing and laughing out loud. Miss Ping raised her head to look out of the window and seemed satisfied with what she saw. Above the fresh green trees hundreds and hundreds of coloured balloons were rising into the sky from the great square of Tien An Men (The Gate of Heavenly Peace) in the middle of Peking, flying wildly in the wind like birds let loose.

We could hear singing and loud shouts, and a raucous, hortatory voice coming from loudspeakers hung in the trees among the young spring leaves, scattering the sparrows.

Mr. Feng turned around once more to face us. "The comrades from Albania have arrived at the Great Hall of the People."

Later, toward evening, when we had been settled in our rooms at a hotel used exclusively for foreigners, we assembled in the foyer, where Mr. Feng counted us, though with difficulty for some were wandering in and out among other guests in annexes and counters finding new things—picture postcards, views of Peking, guidebooks, packages of striking and delicately designed postage stamps, silk fans, color slides, and other elements of the miscellany and trivia of tourism—while Mr. Feng watched, tolerant, a short, slim middle-aged man with close-cropped hair flecked white, aging early, wearing a tight gray tunic buttoned at the neck (the uniform of senior functionaries and party officials).

He seemed a gentle, patient man, perhaps a little prim, standing quietly in the middle of the huge foyer smiling benignly, accustomed to the childlikeness of foreign visitors arriving for the first time in China. Miss Ping and another assistant, a youth, were close

6

by, both standing deferentially a little apart until Mr. Feng looked at the clock, then clapped his hands sharply and sent them to gather us together.

These were our team, the three of them, Feng, the senior interpreter and guide, with Miss Ping and the young man, Tai, who moved among us and sat in the bus wherever we went, splitting our numbered dozen into groups more easily dealt with in crowds and on minor forays for shopping or sight-seeing.

Then there was a fourth man who spoke no English but came with us everywhere and mixed among us freely, making amiable if limited conversation through the other three. This man, we understood, was not from the Travel Service but from the Chinese People's Association for Cultural Relations with Foreign Countries, the State agency responsible in terms of protocol for our being in China, with whom every detail of our program was discussed each day so that any requests or suggested deviations, either as a group or by individuals, could be adjudicated and, if possible, arranged.

His name was Wang and he was a Party man, a cadre, trained in Communist dialectic; a man to give proper definitions, to make decisions for all of us; the channel through whom we learned the definitive Chinese truth about China, and through whom the relevant Chinese agency could follow and note our physical and spiritual progress on this pilgrimage.

He was standing by the reception desk reading our names in the register and discussing us with the clerk, who, leaning across the counter, ran his finger down the list and spoke our names phonetically, in English (my own became Willimus), identifying us with discreet gestures one by one so that Wang would know who we were.

He seemed, on sight, an easy man to like—fat, affable, with sly humor in his eyes. Now he, too, looked at the clock and came to Feng and spoke, watching while the youngsters mustered us. Then he went outside with us to where the coach was waiting.

"We go now," said Feng, counting heads as we entered, "to a small reception for our Australian friends."

Almost every honest foreigner who visits Communist China from the "free world," armed at all points with historical and

7

contemporary prejudice, will be tempted at an early stage to see something good in changes that have taken place since the founding of the People's Republic in 1949; for normal human creatures respond instinctively to kindness, generosity, and good nature as a dog responds to patting or a cat to having its stomach scratched. This despite the fact that Communists (like most other converts to dogmatic ideologies) tend to offset every good impression by overlaying simple, happy facts with grotesquely unnecessary dialectical explanation.

This at least is what I found and felt, as did my friends and every other foreigner I met and talked with inside China, beginning with this first reception at the restaurant Tien Wen Kuan in Peking.

We were a homely group of tourists of no great political significance, except that some were members of a minor Australian society for promoting friendship with China; and we were all of us surprised by the ceremony and style with which we were made much of by functionaries of the government in this and every other city visited. How elegantly we were fed and given little gifts, my own on this first night of my arrival in China being a miniature model landscape carved delicately in boxwood, with an ivory egret wading in a lake, the whole enclosed in a glass disk hung with tassels of red silk.

The women with us, receiving these things, uttered cries of delight, immediately loving China and everything Chinese. Even our capitalist, a good, magnanimous man, was touched and went round shaking hands with every Chinese with us, including little Ping, explaining that he had no malice in his heart against them as a race but that compassion got the better of him when he saw people suffering like those poor men and women struggling in the streets with heavy carts.

Afterward he asked quietly, sitting next to me at dinner, how much I thought the craftsmen would be paid for making these things, which must be quite cheap to be given away so freely, though they were lovely and it was generous of the Chinese to make such gestures even if they were political and part of the brainwashing treatment.

But I could not help him, having no head for these things. In any case waiters were slipping in and out filling glasses, and our

8

host, getting to his feet, began to give a toast, Feng interpreting:

"The Chinese People's Association for Cultural Relations with Foreign Countries is most happy to welcome friends from Australia. We appreciate that you have come many thousands of miles to see for yourselves how much the Chinese people have achieved since liberation.

"We have this saying, that to see once is better than to hear a hundred times. So we are pleased that you have come to find out for yourselves what is happening in our country instead of listening to filthy lies spread far and wide by the capitalist press which in every country is a lackey of the imperialists."

I think that some of us were slightly shocked by this sudden bluntness, taken by surprise. Yet the words were spoken so simply, without heat or emphasis, that they seemed to have no practical significance, to lack meaning as do many of our own phrases, used daily, become senseless and no more than a component part of conventional conversation. And my rich friend beside me seemed happily untouched, beaming and watching Feng, who continued:

"Before liberation China was a consumer nation exploited by foreigners and their running dogs, the local despots. Now, thanks to the brilliant leadership of the Chinese Communist Party under the guidance of our dear Chairman Mao Tse-tung, China is a producing country, completely independent of all foreigners and revisionists."

The only Communist in our group said, "Hear, hear!" clearly, and settled in his seat, happy to be in this holy city of Peking and ready to listen for a long time to these comfortable liturgical words from the lips of one baptized truly in the red fire of revolution, confirmed in the faith of Marx and Lenin, and now a cadre: a kind of priest, though no believer in fairy tales or God talk.

But the speaker, being a pleasant man with a proper sense of occasion, said that he thought we must be tired after the long day and the journey from Canton. So having made a token comment on American aggression and the iniquity of Soviet and other Splittists, he concluded:

"We hope that your visit to our country will be a pleasant one. That you will feel free to ask questions and to see everything that interests you. And that your visit will promote friendship and understanding between our two countries."

9

At this we all nodded agreeably and grasped our glasses, for this was something we could understand.

Comrade Wang, who had been sitting across from me, expressionless, now smiled and came quickly to his feet to lead the drinking, calling *"Kanpei* [Bottoms up]," carefully clinking glasses all around the table before sinking his drink with one swift lifting of the hand, then smacking his lips and saying with satisfaction, "Very good," so that we all laughed, surprised by this sudden, unexpected discovery of English in him, and were at ease again, and drank and made more speeches at each other, saying that we were certain that all men desired peace and wished to live agreeably together without conflict. Mr. Feng finally begged for a rest and said that Miss Ping must interpret the next speech, at which she flinched and fluttered, saying, "Oh no, no, no, my English is not good enough for this." We said, then, that a deputation should go to the kitchen to congratulate the cook, and that she should lead and speak for it. At this she looked beseechingly at Wang, but he, in good humor, and cheerful with drink, gave approval so that there was no refusing.

In the kitchen we met Chen, a full-fleshed man as smooth and shining as his pots and pans, who smiled and bobbed and nodded and waved his hand in one wide gesture, saying without speaking that we were welcome to inspect his domain. But Miss Ping, anxious that first things should be first, said we should understand that this man Chen was no ordinary chef but also a member of the National People's Congress and so attended the yearly sessions in the Great Hall of the People on the Tien An Men, representing a section of the people of Peking, and had part in electing members of the Standing Committee which governed the country.

She said this earnestly, anxious that we should see and believe that the Government of China is truly a government of the common people; but for my part I had little interest in these conceits, knowing them to be empty in any country and under any system, for the simple people of no nation have any practical power exceeding that of confusedly choosing, from time to time, between one group of autocrats and another.

And in this little Miss Ping seemed no more wise or simple than others of her generation, anywhere, who in this period of universal revolution much search for and find some faith which is relevant to this day and age; some philosophy of profit and loss that takes more cognizance of people than of power; some machinery of politics and economy to replace the dangerously worn-out systems which have brought the human race, at this stage of its intellectual and material development, to the very edge of total self-destruction.

For one finds, in time, that faith in the benevolence and good sense of rulers who are taken on trust at their own arrogant evaluation is unproductive and best left to the young, who must for a time concern themselves with these transitory things and learn through disillusionment that each man is a world within himself, subject to his own laws and governance, that suffering is certain and necessary to personal development regardless of the nature and state of government in any country.

For me, visiting in this Chinese kitchen, Chen the chef was a figure of more significance than Chen the member of the National People's Congress. This first Chen was an artist, a creator, and the second Chen a cipher chosen to give some semblance of verisimilitude to the illusion that "the people" have political power.

And there was the duck in the oven.

A duck of size and symmetry such as I had not seen elsewhere. Not in the kitchens of Prague or Provence or of Amsterdam, where ducks in the oven are treated with a delicate reverence; not in America, where the world's best eating may be done if one knows where to look for it. An astonishing and solitary duck, hung in a cavernous red-brick oven like a golden sun suspended in an incandescent heaven.

"*Kao ya*," said Chen seraphically, standing a little apart, hands crossed on contented belly.

"Peking duck," said Miss Ping, interpreting, "very famous dish of this city. Before liberation only rich capitalists eat this. Now any person can have." She seemed pleased to be able to deliver this justification of her belief in the regime. And in the kitchen, in the presence of Chen the chef and this succulent duck, it seemed justification enough, even for a revolution, that any one of China's millions should now be able to sit at table and share what had previously been the pleasure of despots and foreigners.

It was pleasing, also, to see that Chen kept a god in his kitchen (a crimson image painted on paper), which seems proper for a

11

cook even if Communist, for these things are above politics and a duck as lucious as that hanging in the oven was, I thought, worthy of heavenly protection and the comforts and approval of religion.

The fire in these ovens is fed with local palm wood, which burns with a blood-red glow and without smoke; and the duck is brushed with honey to seal its skin so that none of the juices can escape or are tainted; and water simmers inside the carcass as it cooks. This is the formula for Peking duck, which I discovered in the kitchen of the restaurant Tien Wen Kuan.

As for the creature's graceful shape and astonishing weight, this is achieved systematically by letting the bird grow naturally for forty-five days from its hatching, then stuffing it to capacity through a tube, twice daily, with sorghum and other coarse grains for forty days.

With such practical facts in mind I found it touching to discover that ducks, along with other domestic creatures, crops, and people, have an official birthday in the Chinese calendar—the fourth day of the New Year, following after chickens, dogs, and pigs, and having precedence over cattle, horses, human beings, rice, fruit, vegetables, and barley, all of which have birthdays marked with fireworks, music, displays of paper flowers and other decorations.

Miss Ping said that these festivities were still kept, though more so in the country communes, where many of the older peasants remained simple and more superstitious than city people, but that in famous restaurants like this one the duck's day was kept with some ceremony for the sake of entertainment.

This gave me comfort, and leaving the restaurant, I felt reassured that the simple good sense of man will always hold its own in the face of any transitory mania, and will ultimately prevail against warped and fanatical forces which seek, from time to time, to fix it firmly in an ideological vice, and hammer it into a stylized state of submissive bliss, forgetting that man, the creator, is above and beyond all fixed systems and one with whatever god there is.

So I shook Chen's hand and said. *"Henhao* . . . very good," and we parted, laughing, with Miss Ping leading me and my friends through a laneway of kitchen assistants and second cooks in white suits, who were clapping and nodding their pleasure and approval.

So ended our first day in Peking.

12

CHAPTER

2

MOST tourist hotels in China have a sitting room on each floor furnished in nineteenth-century fashion with solid sofas, settees, and deep armchairs draped with antimacassars; a rather stolid décor derived from Russia along with much of Peking's early post-liberation architecture. The pictures and brocades which decorate these rooms are traditional and depict intimate, simple things in Chinese style: a kingfisher, suspicious kitten, a man carrying a plow, plum trees in blossom on a mountain. Two other objects, a short wave radio and a television set, symbolize, in part, China's present metamorphosis and partial capitulation to the universal standards of modern civilization.

It was in one such room, soon after daybreak, that I found an elderly man bent over the radio searching for the Voice of America.

His reply to my "Good morning" was slightly accented and I guessed him to be from the northern part of Europe, though fluent in English. Years ago he must have been tall and formidably built, but he was now bent a little and slackly fleshed and had only sparse hair and a straggly white moustache. His fingers, twisting the controls of the radio, were long and slender like a spider's legs. He said that he was trying to get the morning news from Manila.

"It will make me unhappy, but if I let myself be irritated exclusively each day by Chinese propaganda I will become angry with them and my vacation will be spoiled. So I listen to the Americans whenever I can as a counterirritant."

He continued to speak without looking at me.

"I have the disadvantage in this matter of knowing the Chinese language, and for me there is no escape from the babble that goes on all day. And I know that the Chinese are not as stupidly naïve as their own propaganda and publicity would make them seem to be. I taught here for many years in the university and I know that they are an intelligent and very sensible people. And this, I am sure, must be true also of the Americans in spite of what they say, otherwise the world is doomed to go back to the dark ages."

He was silent for a minute or two, listening. Then he switched impatiently to another band and began the search again, twirling the knobs swiftly, chopping voices into little meaningless hiccuping pieces, a scatter of overlapping snatches of Spanish, Japanese, Thai, French. He hesitated for a few seconds over an unmistakable fragment of innocent Australian carrying horse-race results to the boys in Vietnam.

Then he whispered, more to himself than to me, as the syllables slipped through his fingers, "Words, words and words. Where do they come from? Who dictates what must be spoken? It is the devil." He spoke sharply. "He makes good use of this machine with his thousands of servants scattering idiot lies and the seeds of hate and violence and all kinds of confusion and misunderstanding among the ignorant." He looked at me. "Yet people say there is no Satan! How should ordinary people create so much evil out of their own heads without his help?" He shook his own head angrily. "Oh, the wickedness of it."

I laughed, not at what he had said, but because he seemed so comically indignant, peering over his glasses at me and saying "wicked" with a "vee." So then I nodded, too, and said, "Yes, sir, you are right, and if every radio in the world could be silenced there might be hope for us, though the unaccustomed quietness might be even more frightening. We would have to begin thinking for ourselves and make our own speeches, and might find that we had nothing sensible to say."

He grunted and switched off the set. "I have missed the news now, but maybe just as well. It's never good these days. Better not to listen."

14

We stood, the two of us, strangers to each other but brothers, dissimilar men though of common kind—understanding that we shared with one another and with tens of millions of other people the disquiet, the apprehension edging on despair, the worry of not understanding what is happening to mankind; conscious that behind the haze of ignorance and fabricated fear and hate which hides one nation from another there is a common longing for love, a dumb reaching out for understanding, an urgent search for some simple truth to which we are all still blind: a truth still obscure, that will save us if only we can find it.

As we stood we could hear music, faintly, floating over the city from loudspeakers on the high tower of the radio station. A huge choir was singing:

"The east is red from the rising sun,
In China appears Mao Tse-tung.
He is our Guide,
He leads us onward to build a new China."

Below us in the courtyard, young men played basketball. We could hear their voices mixing with the music as they called to each other anxiously, and the umpire blowing his whistle. Buses slid (silently from this height) along the wide streets between trees unhindered, with no other vehicular traffic to dispute with them this early, though even at midday there are seldom more than a dozen cars and trucks to be seen at any time.

We went walking for a while in the streets before breakfast, and as we went we gave each other as much knowledge of ourselves as would seem to meet the requirements of courtesy.

He said that he held the Chair of Oriental Studies in a European university. He had come back to China after twenty years because much had been done since liberation to uncover and study a great many sites of considerable historic and antiquarian interest. In Peking and other cities where old buildings have been razed to make room for new housing, factories, and national buildings, the excavation of foundations has led to many discoveries of interest to archeologists. In remote places where dam building and major mining works have been undertaken for the first time, paleontologists are making exciting finds. All this, he said, is meticulously documented by Chinese scholars and published

15

widely so that scientists and academicians in all parts of the world are now anxious to come to China.

He, with a sabbatical in hand and friends among Chinese scholars (some of them former pupils), was fortunate, and more so (in spite of his irritation with the radio) because he had the language and a knowledge of where to go and what to look for, which made me envious. Then comparing itineraries, it seemed that our paths would run parallel much of the time and occasionally cross, so that often I might have advantage of his knowledge and experience.

We went a little way along a wide avenue, then, turning into a walled side street, saw a cluster of schoolchildren grouped together, looking up at a billboard on which a text was written in huge red script.

We stopped to watch.

One of them, a keen, clean lad, neat in flannel shirt and corded pants with a red scarf round his neck, was reading the text out loud while the others listened. Then at a signal from his hand they repeated it together in singsong unison, insistent, keeping cadence. Seeing them, I also saw myself, a child of similar age, standing with other lads before an altar at Mass, ecstatically chanting with high heart slabs of beatific liturgy, feeling totally alive, virtuous, and worthy (having got up from bed early, before others of the household were astir), and glad to be let take part in this dialogue with God, the unknown and unknowable. And I was suddenly sorry for lost innocence.

"What does it say?"

The professor seemed amused at my earnestness and, peering at the billboard, read:

" 'We are the children of the revolution, sons and daughters of people who were oppressed. We will make ourselves strong with the thinking of our great leader, dear Chairman Mao. We will follow him through storms. We will learn to remove mountains. We will learn to swim by swimming, and learn to be true revolutionaries by making revolution.' "

I said I thought it strange to see so many of these huge inscriptions set up everywhere and treated with such apparent reverence. To this he answered that one must try to understand the unique place occupied by calligraphy in Chinese culture. Handwriting, he explained, is one of the ancient and superior arts and a means of personal expression that combines, in a manner unknown to the West, the arts of both poetry and painting; and each Chinese character projects not only some sentient impression, but also suggests a related sound and action picture of the thing or matter under discussion.

"It is a somewhat complex subject to discuss during a morning walk," he said "and on an empty stomach, but to put the matter briefly, I might say to you that whereas our kind of writing is the quick stringing together of fixed symbols to convey sense, in which legibility and the choice of words are the only significant factors, these Chinese symbols or ideograms, as they are called, convey a series of pictures accompanied by a supersensory sound track, and that they reflect the character and individual sensitivity and expressiveness of the person who paints them.

"Chinese calligraphy is not, then, simply writing but a unique form of imaginative self-expression. A poster full of ideographs holds more interest for a Chinese than does a statue of a person, or a photograph, in somewhat the same way that a comic strip tells us more than a still picture does.

"This is why, for example, many of the most treasured monuments in China are simply stone tablets inscribed with the sentiments of some ancient scholar or king in his own handwriting, as in the case of the famous Tang emperor Tai-tsung, who lived very early in the seventh century, and whose calligraphy is still reproduced in junior school textbooks as a model for the children to copy. It is also why the classical statements of Mao Tse-tung are so frequently displayed in his own handwriting, which is regarded as being particularly artistic and expressive, and worthy of a great and wonderful leader."

We moved away and as we went he said, "Only those who knew China in the old days can evaluate what has happened in these past seventeen years. What changes have been made, what progress. And only within the perspective and against the background of history can any sensible judgment be made about China today. Most other assessments are based on simple ignorance, fear, self-interest, prejudice, and a lack of understanding."

Then he stopped and fixed me firmly over his glasses.

"Not that I agree with all that is happening here right now. But then I don't agree with all that is taking place in Europe or in America; and I don't suppose that you are satisfied with everything that happens in Australia?"

"No," I said, "I'm not. Though so far we are still able to disagree with our government."

"I hope that you will be able to say that in a year or two."

He looked past me at the people in the streets, the streams of bicycles, the buses going by—gray streets, gray sky, and people in blue tunics, caps, and cloth shoes.

"Picasso—the blue period."

I liked him and was glad that I might see him sometimes during my visit. A balanced man, knowledgeable, tolerant and wise, with no hate in his heart. No fear, either, except the fear that madness might overtake and destroy us all before we learn how to utilize the fruits of our own genius.

Later that day, when our party was taken forty miles into the mountains northward from Peking to see the Great Wall, he came with us, he and his wife, who was motherly, and we sat in the embrasure of one of the watchtowers out of the bitter wind.

"It blows from the Arctic, over the steppes and the desert, and in winter will freeze a weak person to death; indeed, a million men and women are reckoned to have perished while the wall was being completed. These were slave laborers taken in the wars between the Chin king, who first united China two hundred years before the time of Christ, and the other six kings he defeated to achieve this.

"This wall was then the limit of civilization—the far edge of the world from the Chinese point of view: In some ways they still think like this. Beyond this point there was a desolate, empty world with no birds or beasts. A place of bleached bones out of which there came from time to time hordes of brute barbarians to rob and rape and lay waste the farmlands of northern China.

"This was why they built the wall. In sections at first, to protect the northern kingdoms and minor states. Then, after the Chin victory, the segments were joined to make a whole which stretched from the sea for seventeen hundred miles far into Turkestan on

18

the edges of the ancient kingdom of Samarkand, closing China off from the rest of mankind."

He talked on quietly, almost to himself, as the vast panorama of China's history unwound within his mind, while I listened and his wife knitted and watched fondly as a contented woman watches a clever child. As we sat, looking at the furrowed landscape, hundreds of holidaymakers from Peking and other cities and communes clambered, climbing past us, up the many steps toward a fortress on a high peak beyond which the wall went winding like a giant snake along the mountaintops to be lost in cloud.

The young were laughing, exchanging chaff, challenging each other to go faster, to race one another to the top, where their friends waved from among the crenellations and called encouragement. But the elderly went carefully, sons and daughters at each elbow holding and helping them, because the way along the wall is steep and its cobbled stones are worn smooth with the traffic of two thousand years. Among the elderly there were a few aged ladies tottering gamely on miniature feet. These and other old ones stopped for breath in sheltered places and posed in tight family groups for photographs taken by their children, not waiting to make the high tower at the top.

As always in these situations one discovers much, realizing more and more how this world is all of one piece, its history and its people; learning how nations are shaped by successive events to become the way they are, though one learns only by seeking out the things that lead to understanding.

So, sitting on the Great Wall in a rough spring wind with this scholar, hearing him speak about the Chinese, I began to learn a little of their history. How, for a thousand years, they were isolated and cut off from any communication with other civilizations —walled in by the Himalayas in the west, by the nomads of the northern steppes and deserts, and beyond these by the Huns. Small wonder, then, that the Chinese of those times, so enclosed, felt that they alone of all people of the ancient world were dignified and civilized.

"In those times," the professor said, "the forts and castles spaced along this wall to guard the passes into Peking and other cities were garrisoned by colonies of soldier settlers who were given the use of farmlands round about in return for their services to the emperor." He lifted a finger westward. "No doubt, today, the People's Liberation Army is somewhere out there in Sinkiang where the Wall ends, guarding the border between China and Russia, ready to keep out the traitorous revisionists of the U.S.S.R."

Mr. Feng went past with some of our party; then Miss Ping came by with others and stopped for a moment while one of them took a photograph. We could hear her tell them, while they stood smiling at the camera, "In the old days before liberation many peasants, workers, and soldiers died to defend this wall against enemies and to keep it mended to protect the rich kings and wealthy warlords. Now it is a national monument belonging to the people and, as you can see, everybody can come here to enjoy the scenery and make picnics."

The professor shifted his position, easing himself and wrapping his scarf higher about his neck while his wife watched, hand held ready to help if necessary.

"The patterns of history change and interweave like pictures in a kaleidoscope, repeating themselves in similar shape again and again; and though the areas of critical activity shift as the wheel of time spins and turns, what happens in any age and place is familiar, has been affected by something that occurred earlier, and will affect, in turn, what is to come.

"Mankind is a unity, complete and indivisible, and has been so from the beginning despite natural barriers. But our developing technology and means of communication have brought the clans and tribes and nations closer together age by age, for good or ill, so that all mankind must ultimately and perhaps quite soon become one people, sharing a common end."

He spoke without deep feeling, almost casually, as one for whom such theories no longer had significance, and his interest seemed keener in little things. He said, for instance, that recent excavations in Central China had uncovered a number of third-century sarcophagi which were decorated with hunting scenes, and that some reports, describing the horses' harness, implied that it was fitted with stirrups.

Then, seeing me clearly mystified with this seeming triviality,

he said that no museum in Europe contained evidence that stirrups were in use earlier than the sixth century, and consequently
if these rumors were true, it was historically interesting because
the stirrup was essentially a military invention designed to give
bowmen steadier and better control when aiming, and that this in
turn might be connected with the earlier Chinese invention of the
mechanical crossbow, which revolutionized warfare and was the
beginning of an inventive thread that links the primitive bow and
arrow with today's nuclear weapons.

"History and politics have always grown together from the
muzzle of a gun, inseparable, entwined, and will continue to do
so until mankind is finally civilized or annihilated."

His wife, unimpressed by these speculations, said that it was too
cold to sit there longer, and too much for either of them to climb
higher, so they should go back down to the parking lot, where
there was a restaurant, and wait there for the others to return.

I went with them, having no wish to go higher. I was anxious,
rather, to gain from this acquaintance all the promise that it
offered, for listening to him, I could measure the depth of my own
ignorance, and knew that it would be foolish to miss anything he
might say.

We ate together, waiting for the others, talking much at random, and he mentioned many things, of which I remember some
and some forget.

He spoke much about Chin, the king who completed the Great
Wall, then took his soldiers out of skirts and put them into
breeches so that they might ride unhampered into battle against
the savages outside. This great but cruel and short-reigning king
built many military roads to link the huge empire he had unified,
then fixed the wheel span of chariots and wagons so that all wheeled
vehicles would run in the same ruts, simplifying the maintenance
of these strategic highways. He standardized the monetary system
according to a scale of silver weights, made bonfires all over the land
of dubious philosophical books and commentaries, and isolated
troublesome intellectuals and politicians from their followers, in
all this laying down patterns of activity that have since become
universally familiar and habitual.

The elder of his two sons foolishly conspired against him with

21

cunning and covetous courtiers and was beheaded for his trouble; and though the younger son inherited his father's throne soon afterward, he was inadequate in every way and soon disposed of by rebellious generals.

So dynasty followed dynasty through a thousand years, making no great changes in the daily life of China's millions, who year after year struggled to live on the meager returns of a reluctant earth, fought floods, died by tens of thousands in times of drought, were coerced into the services of kings, princes, feudal lords, rebel leaders, upstart generals, and an assortment of fanatics great and small, who swept back and forth across the land; while side by side with this mass of misery monks, poets, scholars, and artists of all kinds created a soul, a mind, an image of China that is and has remained unique for longer than that of any currently surviving civilization.

By the seventh century this image was already well in focus, laid down on paper in fluid lines of classical calligraphy by poets and philosophers. An image of sad grandeur, of lonely and nostalgic loveliness, of dignified and intimate misery, of poverty repeated century after century. The wandering scholar poet of this time, Tu Fu, limned this everlasting lament of China with his writing brush:

> All our land is mad with war;
> beacon fires smoke,
> corpses lie stinking in the grass
> and blood stains the whole countryside.
>
> Rich meats going bad reek in palace kitchens
> while the bodies of the poor rot in ditches.

He weeps with a young wife whose husband has been taken from her side to swell some petty king's conscripted army:

> We had scarcely warmed our bed together,
> When in the morning after our marriage
> He went away.
> To think how I, a daughter of poor people,
> worked so very hard to get the wedding gown
> now laid aside:
> and he and I, in separation
> allowed only our longing for each other.

Then the young man, returning at last from the war, hears as he stands outside his own door:

> the sound of my wife weeping:
> and going in, find that our little child
> has died of hunger.
> O the shame of being father to a child
> who dies of hunger.
> Grief rises higher
> than the mountains all about me,
> and I see no end to it.

After the brief, catalytic dynasty of Chin came the Han monarchs, and the Tang and the Sung, who were great creators and the first to use gunpowder in battle, but nevertheless were overrun by barbarians from beyond the Wall: Then in the year 1210, Genghis, Great Khan of all the Mongol tribes, ruled in Peking and his men took their pleasure of Chinese women.

For the next seventy years his barbaric cavalry, and that of his successors, pressed southward, though not without difficulty, for they were habituated horsemen accustomed to engagement in swift issues fought on empty deserts and across huge stretches of steppe; troops unused either to mountain warfare or to fighting on domesticated ground, and hindered more in every major move by China's wide, divisive rivers.

At the end of these seventy years the Khans owned all of China, Tibet, and most of Southeast Asia, but only for a hundred years, by which time they, too, had gone soft and rotten and lost everything to the first Ming king, who was first a beggar, then a bandit, then a leader of rebels, and as a general chased the decadent Mongols out of Peking, back through the Great Wall and into Siberia.

So life in China went in similar cycles for as far back as man remembers, only the outlines changing, the pattern remaining always much the same.

These Ming monarchs quickly rebuilt Peking more to their Chinese liking, creating within five years a new city, much of which still stands. Then they extended their authority into Malaya and Indonesia, and sent big ships on voyages of discovery as far as the Persian Gulf and Africa, under the eunuch admiral Cheng Ho, who sailed these eastern seas long before the Spanish and Portuguese and brought back a giraffe for his emperor.

In the seventeenth century the wheel went round again. The Ming dynasty degenerated and another bandit, turned rebel general, led an army of half-starved peasantry against them and occupied Peking. The last Ming monarch, a sickly lad, glad to have done with it all, went into the palace garden and killed himself, so ending the dynasty begun by a beggar three centuries before.

Now another beggar-emperor sat upon the peacock throne—though not for long.

In Manchuria, just beyond the Wall, in the northeastern corner of the continent, a tribal chief with eyes on China wondered how best he might gain entry through the gates without battle and take possession of its riches, even though the way was barred by a clever general whose troops kept the entrances.

This general, Wu by name, had a concubine in Peking whose beauty had so captivated the uncouth new ruler that he took her into his own household and refused to let her go when Wu sent for her to keep him company in his camp.

Then the general, angry that a man so impudent and ill-mannered should occupy the imperial throne, sent a message out to the Manchu leader saying that he could bring his army in through the gateways of the Wall, and that Wu would help him overthrow the upstart in Peking without any payment other than the return of his favorite.

They agreed upon this and, a war ensuing, Wu caught and killed the illiterate king himself. But his lovely lady, having been obscenely treated by the palace troops, was already dead. So leaving the Manchu leader in Peking to found a new dynasty, Wu crossed the Yangtze with his men and coming to Yunnan, in the southwest, became Prince of those parts.

CHAPTER

3

WE WERE a garrulous group of tourists going back to Peking, satisfied and happy after our excursion and this first activating contact with the history of China—impressed with what we had seen and already rehearsing how we would tell it all back home to our friends and neighbors, planning nights with slides and home movies with some nice supper afterward, and everyone envious, admiring our audacity and enterprise in going to China. Red China no less, with all those Communists, and the Cultural Revolution and the Red Guards.

I could hear our happy capitalist in the seat behind me telling Feng, "Honestly, my friend, they won't believe me when I tell them that I walked along the top of the Great Wall of China with a bunch of Communists, but they'll have to when they see my pictures." He patted the camera resting on the ledge of his belly. "I got some good shots, though the light wasn't right. But it's amazing what you can do today with these new Japanese lenses and a bit of fast film." As an afterthought, he added innocently, "It's a pity you can't make color film here in China, though I suppose you'll catch up soon."

"We do not want anything from the West," said Feng without expression. "We are self-reliant in every respect, but have priorities that are decided according to the true needs of the people. Color film is not high on this list at the moment. Our government has a target for food and industrial production that will raise the standard of living equally all over China in the next few years. We are too busy with these basic things to think about unnecessary luxuries such as color film. When the time comes we will show you what we can do in that direction."

The capitalist flipped a hand derisively. "Why wait for the government to do it? Governments should stay out of these things and leave them to private enterprise. That's the way a country and its people make real progress."

"That's capitalism," said Feng flatly. "The exploitation of the masses of the world by a few criminals who get rich on the work of others and call this progress. That is what we had in China before liberation and we will never go back to it. The Moscow revisionists have betrayed the people and China now leads the great socialist revolution."

Miss Ping, sitting across from them, nodded happily, like a young missionary hearing the faith preached openly for the first time to unbelievers, and watched bright-eyed, no longer a shy, uncertain trainee guide, but a true revolutionary, though neophyte, admiring Mr. Feng's assurance, his control, and the smooth flow of his English.

She leaned forward as if anxious to identify more closely with so clever and complete a comrade and seemed excited to see the enemy go red about the neck, affronted and stumbling on the edge of indignation for words adequate to rebut, without overmuch bluntness, the injustice of the insinuation that he was a criminal.

"Fair go, now. That's taking things a bit far, isn't it? A man isn't a criminal just because he makes his own way in life, battles along by himself to make a bit of money and get on in the world by his own efforts. Look at me. I made my money the hard way. Nobody gave me any free gifts, and the government certainly did nothing to help me get a living."

His voice was rising, and we others in the bus listened, smiling quietly at each other, a shade unkindly, having heard the story before, first in Sydney while waiting for the plane to leave, then at dinner in Hong Kong when making closer acquaintance with one another, and again on the way to Peking, with much decorative detail and embellishment, so that already we knew him for what he was, a rich and innocent simpleton.

26

We heard his story still more often before parting from each other in the end, though by then his speech had been whittled down, eroded and encroached upon by doubts, so that toward the last days of our stay it was hesitant, defensive and fragmentary, had lost the sharp edge of resentment, and had become almost apologetic.

Even now, writing at this distance, it is still not difficult to reconstruct in sense and essence what he said to Feng that evening on the way back from the Wall, uncovering with his clumsy speech the genuine dilemma that besets so many of us of the West, men and women of good heart and intent who have been educated to fit and coexist only within the framework of a civilization that no longer has any moral validity; that has run out of inspiration; is unable to meet deep-down needs, yet binds us tightly, circumscribes our minds with doubts and fears so that we dare not venture from the circle of acceptable belief lest someone point the finger and cry "Communist" and so shoot us down in flight.

"Look at me," he said. "I'm about the richest man in this bus and the least educated. I had to leave school at the age of twelve, hardly able to read or write, because there were ten of us at home and not enough money coming in to feed us all decently. I went to work for a carrier who had four wagons and two dozen horses in his stables—this was more than fifty years ago when there were no motor trucks in the Outback and not many in the cities. Just like here in Peking. I looked after the horses for this feller. Kept the stables clean and slept in the hayloft, and had half a day to myself each week. I didn't get much pay but saved almost every penny and in two years was able to buy a horse, an old one, and go into business for myself.

"I had only one ambition. I wanted to be rich because being rich was the opposite of being poor, and I knew that there was no future in that. So I never wasted a cent on booze or women or things of that kind, not me. I put my money into land on the outskirts of the town. Useless land that nobody else wanted because it wouldn't feed a rabbit. Now it's covered with houses and I own the lot. I did it by myself. Nobody helped me, and now I've got more money than I want.

"But I'm a socialist and have been all my life, and I still believe that Jack's as good as his master any day, and if you can't do a man a good turn don't do him a bad one. Don't lend money to friends or do business with women or get mixed up in religion. I've got no kids of my own as far as I know, but I help to educate a few orphans, and when I die my eyes will go to the hospital for some person to make use of.

"We might all be equal in the end, but I believe that some people are savages by nature and will never be civilized no matter how much they get educated. Like the Negroes and some of the Eastern people. I've been everywhere and I've seen them. There's nothing you can do about them and it's no good trying. They'll never be civilized."

It was little Miss Ping who put an end to it, staring at him with horror and astonishment, her thin voice hissing across at him. "What are you saying? The Negroes of America and the other oppressed people of the world are our brothers. You must not insult them. Why do you come to China to talk like this?"

Feng spoke briefly to her and she blushed and was quiet, and reaching into her bag, took out the textbook which she had been reading earlier, and retired into it until in an hour or so we came back to Peking.

I had a drink with the professor and his wife in their room, and among the books lying on the bed was one similar to that which Miss Ping read so diligently.

When I picked it up the professor said, "It is what you might call a Guide's Primer. A handbook for young guides and interpreters to tide them over early difficulties when dealing with curious tourists like your friend."

He gave me Chinese brandy and took the book, and standing by the window, opened it and read from the introduction:

"It says that guides and interpreters should not expect foreign guests, especially those from the capitalist countries, to behave according to the customs of China. Nor will many of them observe in a natural way the polite customs and conventions that are usual in Eastern nations which have had a long history of civilized refinement.

"There will be many occasions, especially at the beginning of a visit, when even the most friendly and well-intentioned foreign guests will behave in a way that would embarrass a poor, unedu-

28

cated peasant, but the true revolutionary guide, by studying the primer along with the works of Chairman Mao, will soon resolve any seeming contradictions and will learn to take these indignities with tranquillity, knowing them to be more often the result of ignorance and not of malice.

"The duty of all officials who meet and mix with foreigners is to show them with patience, and by the correctness of their own behavior, the true and inspiring facts of China's great revolution, keeping always in mind that Western people firmly believe themselves superior to all other races and their way of life to be more enlightened and progressive than any other in history."

He skipped through the pages, stopping here and there to paraphrase.

"Guides should not directly remind foreign guests that China was civilized for more than a thousand years before any European country could claim to be in any way cultured. Such information should be conveyed through visits to national monuments, museums, and factories which produce traditional arts and crafts.

"Nor should guides be guilty of boastful and chauvinistic attitudes, but should remember their own shortcomings, keeping in mind that their revolutionary role is to open the eyes and minds of foreign guests to the unshakable truths of Marxism-Leninism, and so bring closer the world-wide triumph of communism through wide-spreading friendship and understanding, guided by the words of Chairman Mao who has said, 'Once the correct ideas characteristic of the politically advanced classes are grasped by all the masses, these ideas will turn into a material force which will change society and the whole world.'

"Sometimes, as a discipline, and to keep her resolute, Ping will say each morning, 'Long live Chairman Mao,' repeating this ejaculation once for every member of your party and perhaps twice for the capitalist." He smiled.

"Brainwashing," said his wife without looking up, and continued to scribble notes on picture postcards of Peking, the Great Wall, and the tombs of the Ming emperors, which she would send to members of their family, each covered with as many different stamps as she could fit on them.

I began to see, then, that for Miss Ping we were not simply a group of tourists to be shepherded, kept content, smiled at if pleasant, and tolerated if not, but that we were each of us part of her personal way of salvation. Through educating us she would gain in political grace as a nun gains mystical grace through good works and acts of charity—one sustained by prayer and the other by patience and faith in the wisdom of Mao Tse-tung. To Ping we were each a bead in her rosary, a stepping stone along her road to the heaven of Party Membership toward which she aspired. And in this light her brush with our capitalist seemed something deeply moving—the struggle of a young and uncertain novice to relate public function with private faith, to balance charity with personal salvation.

"Tonight," said the professor, "before any of them go to bed, Feng and Wang will analyze the incident with her in dialectical terms. They will try to analyze your friend's social background and explain to little Ping the historical and sociological basis of his statements. Then they will show her how she should have dealt with them, how she should have gently refuted and then corrected his false thinking, and in this way set him safely on the road to redemption.

"They will perhaps spend hours at this, and when it is thrashed out, will choose a suitable passage from the works of Chairman Mao to illustrate and clarify the situation. Then Feng and Wang and Tai will also go through the process of self-examination and will invite criticism of their actions throughout the day, from each other and from Ping."

But it was time for dinner, and finishing the drink, I thanked them and turned to leave. The professor's wife, watching over her glasses, said "Come again, you're good for Henry. He needs an audience and knows that I don't listen." Then, as I left, she called after me, "And don't forget that they talk about you every night too."

We were taken, all of us, to see a film in the evening and settled in our seats, ready for it to begin, each of us with a précis typewritten in our own language and headed *The East Is Red*. Around our own party, in the balcony, the chatter of other foreign guests and their interpreters dwindled to whispers.

We were, perhaps, two hundred visitors in a sea of Chinese: men and women of many nations, many tongues and races—black Africans, Europeans, Japanese and other Asians, people from the Pacific and Australasia, from Canada and Latin America.

But nobody from the U.S.A.

It seems odd and unreal, this consciousness, beginning the minute one leaves Hong Kong, and continuing without diminishment day after day. This strange realization (though one has been prepared for it) that one does not meet Americans in China. That there is a place on this earth where the U.S.A. is only negatively represented by hearsay and false images. That the major part of a hemisphere exists in this century without reference to the United States of America, and that in this huge area the most telling evidence of America's existence is the awareness of an absence of Americans. That in place of any tangible image there is only a kind of Chinese legend or myth that "out there" is a malicious and belligerent spirit which seeks to destroy all that is primarily simple and decent; an ominous presence against which China alone is protected by its size and isolation.

Then more strangely, and with even more difficulty, one tries to grasp that this separated area, developing in an age dominated by the U.S.A., yet without any U.S. ties, contains a quarter of all the human race. The thought becomes obsessive, a mighty contradiction, a paradox of tremendous significance that cannot be explained by simple facts of history or excused by past errors of political judgment.

Pride is as great a force as love, perhaps greater, with power to send people to the moon as well as to hell. And I cannot put aside the fear that pride lies at the bottom of this unnatural rift, this abysmal schism which will some day, and soon, bring untold suffering to the human race. And I think that surely there must be some explanation, some deeper reason for this situation than mere chance or surface stupidity.

Yet nobody in this audience at the cinema seems overtly concerned that there are no Americans among us, though to me it is persistently strange and I wonder, waiting for the film to begin, if I am particularly naïve.

The title music to *The East Is Red* is familiar and I sing to it softly, with Miss Ping beaming because I have already memorized the tune and know the words as well, an achievement to be noted when she and Feng, and the young man Tai, and Wang get together later in the evening, though there is no particular merit in it since the music is played at dawn each day and several times thereafter over loudspeakers in every city, town, commune, factory, school, railway station, and train.

> The Communist Party is like the sun.
> Wherever it rises there is light.
> Where the Party goes
> The people are liberated.

Substitute the word Democratic for Communist and the song could be sung anywhere in the Western world and would be as dubious; but the picture on the screen is truly beautiful.

The précis caption says, "Sunflowers turn toward the sun." We see a hundred slender long-green-skirted girls, each with a pair of yellow fans, form into a single sunflower swaying on its stem, a soft wind lifting its petals lightly as the corolla slowly twists with sinuous shift of hip and wrist to face the great red rising sun.

Feng, in the row behind, leans forward so that his head is alongside mine and says, "Chairman Mao is the red sun in our hearts." I flinch, irritated by these insistent analogues, and wish he would leave me be, let me loose to lose myself in this spectacle and gain from it what I will. For the Chinese are masters of stagecraft and display, and their art, even when constricted and limited to the service of the Party ideology, is intrinsically creative and has astonishing vitality, for they are a race nurtured on a long tradition of craftsmanship and felicitous artistry.

So I made as restrained a gesture of impatience as I thought would fit the situation without giving offense, and hoped that I might be left in peace to gain both pleasure and understanding from this pageant of song and dance (so our notes described it) which brings to life the epic struggle of the biggest nation on earth to free itself from poverty and oppression, during the twenty-eight years of gestation and labor which separated the beginning of the Chinese Communist Party from the founding of the People's Republic.

32

This pageant is a colossal color melomusical, a mass spectacular with a cast of three thousand, marrying the noisy and exaggerated dramatics of traditional Chinese opera to the mighty wide-screen panoramic extravagances of the modern cinema.

It splits a lively slice of history into six major scenes, each subdivided into episodes and evocations dramatically linked and embellished with song and dance and declamation.

The sunflower face of China turning toward the red sun of Mao's thinking sets the theme, states the basic symbolism, then fades away, leaving blackness from which a disembodied voice speaks:

"In the new and revived China of today
    everyone is happy and all the land is beautiful.
    But in our happiness we cannot forget
    the bitter misery that went before
    and the long march that led at last to
    liberation.
    In that China of the past
    the earth was gloomy and the sky was dark.
    Our people carried brutal burdens of misfortune and misery,
    were weighed down with chains,
    held back by fetters,
    crushed under the triple tyranny
    of foreign exploitation, feudalism, and
    corrupt bureaucracy."

There is a burst of fussy, percussive Chinese music and the first scene fades in.

The waterside at Shanghai, circa 1921.

The dominating object, forming a backdrop to the action, is the arrogant black bulk of a ship of the U.S. merchant navy. Against this overbearing background, in the cold, colorless half-light of before dawn, dancers go through a slow choreography of suffering, to the accompaniment of a petulant recitative from a hidden female singer.

Coolies stagger up gangways under preposterous loads, stumble, go down on their knees, and are brutally lashed back to their feet by gangers who are stooges of the foreign bosses and so traitors to their own people. A weeping woman sells her child, unable to provide for it, knowing that it must now grow up to be a slave laborer or concubine in order to survive (the ultimate of existentialism). Such was the plight of China before liberation.

The scene freezes. Shots are heard. Explosions and the shouting of crowds. A red glow appears on the horizon and the downtrodden workers look to it hopefully. The voice speaks again, this time with a note of anxious though suppressed excitement, carrying overtones of hope:

> "As day follows night there comes, in time,
> an end to darkness.
> The gunfire of revolution echoes across the
> land,
> and angry shouts of students in Peking,
> clamoring against the partnership of foreign
> interests
> and corrupt government,
> herald a new day for the Chinese people.
> Out of this tumult the Communist Party of
> China
> is born."

The waterfront scene fades, gives way to a background parade of huge red banners and behind them, bathed in golden radiance, mystical images of Lenin and Marx. Against this background groups of revolutionary students rally and run through Peking, screaming. Peasants gather in the villages and plan to besiege rich landlords in their houses. Workers in the factories, clasping hammers and spanners, strike attitudes while massed choirs sing:

> "Workers arise!
> Unite with the peasants and attack!
> Raise the red flag, let its light shine afar;
> Raise the iron hammer.
> Then mountains and rivers will shake.
> In China the Communist Party is born.
> A spark has set the prairie afire
> and the whole sky is red."

I note that for scenes which show the suffering and degradation of preliberation days, traditional music is used, shrill and indignant, with querulous recitatives, whereas the new revolutionary themes are written in the conventionally Western jingoistic idiom called "heroic." I sniff at some possibly metaphysical significance, but bugles now fling long piercing spears of shining sound which send the idea quickly to a pigeonhole at the back of my mind for later examination.

The screen darkens again, and dancers twirling torches flicker before our eyes like fireflies. Sparks spilling into the grass catch fire, and high tongues of red flame make a backdrop to the dance. Our capitalist, beside me, shakes his head and mutters, "Bloody marvelous!"

The Communist Party is born. The masses sing and dance. Workers' and peasants' movements begin to sweep the whole vast territory of China while anxious imperialists watch, seeing investments diminish, their grip on China weaken, and its wealth slip through their fingers.

They search for a man who can be paid to betray the Chinese people and choose Chiang Kai-shek. They buy him, supply him with all that is necessary to crush the revolution. The blood of good Communists flows in the gutters of the bund along the Whangpoo and Yangtze rivers. Thousands of revolutionary martyrs, betrayed by this Chinese cupboard-Christian, meet death bravely. A worker in chains faces us in full close-up, one hand upraised, singing bravely, though strained and in pain:

> "Paraded through streets in fetters,
> I say farewell to kith and kin.
> To be beheaded by the enemy is nothing
> So long as we cling to the truth.
> I will be killed;
> But the people's revolution still goes
> forward."

So I follow the program notes for almost three hours as we sit through this astonishing and spectacular synthesis of history, having a layer of ignorance stripped from us, being emotionally and mentally buffeted into some sketchy understanding of events that led to the creation of Red China: the China of which we are afraid.

So unremitting is this emotional pressure that chronological continuity is fogged and the significance of incidents in relation to each other is lost in a welter of repetitive emphasis upon the bitterness of the past, the wickedness of foreigners and their running dogs, and the redemptive effect of the revolution. Inevitably it degenerates into a monumental bore, though one is so stunned by the sheer volume of it all, fascinated by the acroballetics and the apparent inexhaustibility of orchestra, singers, and performers, that a state of anesthesia intervenes.

We scarcely notice, then, that the Red flood is temporarily stemmed by the foolishness and chicanery of political opportunists, until the Tsunyi conference in 1935 establishes Mao Tse-tung as supreme leader of the Party and the helmsman of the ship of revolution.

> Now spring thunder crashes,
> The red sun rises to shine over all the land.
> Now Mao Tse-tung leads us onward,
> Mao Tse-tung is at our side.

From now on the epic of the revolution is dominated by this one man. His face is imposed on every flag, shines through each sun. His name, linked with that of the Party and the nation, becomes part of a recurring doxology.

Under his leadership the Red forces regroup and begin the historic long march of six thousand miles to a place of safety in the far northwest. The Japanese invade China. Instead of fighting them, the head of the nominal government, Chiang Kai-shek, spends his energies and U.S. money in harassing the Red patriots.

Years pass and the Japanese are defeated at Hiroshima. Mao now turns his attention to ridding China of Chiang and his foreign backers. A million men of the Red Army cross the Yangtze River. The tyrant is overthrown and retires to Taiwan with his U.S. advisers.

Joyfully the Chinese people celebrate their liberation, and on October 1, 1949, Chairman Mao Tse-tung, standing in the great square of Tien An Men, proclaims the foundation of the People's Republic of China.

> Reactionaries are overthrown,
> Imperialism runs away, its tail between its legs.
> United as one the people throw themselves
> Into the high tide of socialist construction.

36

The lights go up and we look at each other. We are limp, exhausted. Even Feng and Wang have tired smiles. Miss Ping is half asleep. Only Tai is bright and alive.

We don't know what to say to each other. It is no good saying that this film is all lies and propaganda. To do so would be foolish, for we have seen a dramatic presentation of certain facts, however stubbornly we may insist that the emphasis has been twisted. We have been exposed, most of us for the first time, to a new and graphic view of a historical reality, and in spite of its unpalatability and our own ingrained prejudice we are affected, shaken, stunned, and partially disarmed. From now on it is going to be difficult to convince any of us that Communist China does not legitimately exist.

I sat up for a while writing in my room. Then, wanting hot water with which to make tea, I went down the long corridor to the bellboys' office, but could see none on duty though there was light in the room behind the desk and a murmur of voices.

When I tapped at the counter one of the boys came out, buttoning his jacket. Looking past him, I could see three others. Two were lying on their bunks listening, while the other sat in singlet and underpants in the middle of the room, under the light, reading to them from a booklet covered with red plastic, marked with the five-pointed star of China and titled *Quotations from Chairman Mao Tse-tung.*

When I said "Good night" they turned and smiled.

CHAPTER

4

ON MAY the first our captivation by the Chinese people was completed. My own surrender was made to a boy aged eight who took the triangular red scarf of the Young Pioneers from around his neck and gave it to me. His name was Great Leap Forward and he was one of the many among tens of thousands of groups of children dancing and singing in the parks of Peking that morning, beneath the trees, by lakesides, and in the gardens and courtyards of old temples and palaces, to celebrate International Labor Day and the solidarity of the whole world's working classes.

We walked among them until lunchtime, lost in a labyrinth of joy, going from group to group through living laneways of happy, clapping children. When we stopped to watch benches were brought for us so that we could rest, though so caught up were all but the most elderly among us that whenever a new dance started we came to our feet quickly to take part in it, joining hands with the children, imitating their actions awkwardly, and trying to follow their shrill songs.

The capitulation was unanimous: the lawyer, the physician and his wife, the two farmers, the group of schoolteachers, all of us gave way without serious reservation.

Watching all this, one of us, a woman retired from a lifetime of teaching children, said sentimentally that May Day in medieval

England must have had something of this character, with children dressed in their new spring best dancing the Maypole on village greens while their parents and elders walked among them, watching with satisfaction and quiet pride.

"Now May Day is celebrated in most places with political demonstrations and military parades and great displays of weapons that can blow us all to pieces. So instead of our feeling satisfaction and pride in our children, and a wave of new life rising inside us, May Day now makes us feel afraid, wondering what new hate and danger the year will bring us."

Then she said simply, "That's why I like it here today, seeing all these children dance so happily, and no talk of war, and all of us mixing together, whatever our nationality. Just look at him!"

Looking, we could see our innocent capitalist tangled hand and foot in suddenly discovered happiness, lumbering around with infants singing in a ring, crouched clumsily among them, then springing up quickly as they did and with them pointing at the sky, crying, *"Feichi, tchatachatcha,"* afterward fumbling for the words of a short refrain which the children shouted while their teacher beamed.

Tai, our second guide, explained.

"They pretend to be guerrilla peasants in Vietnam working in the rice fields, but they have rifles hidden, and when the U.S. airplanes come by they shoot them down. *Feichi* means airplane, and the *tchatachatcha* is the sound of the rifles all firing together, and the song says:

> "The boys and girls of Vietnam
> Help their parents in the fields.
> When U.S. bandits come
> They shoot them out of the sky like sparrows.
> Long live the heroic children of Vietnam."

"It seems a pity," said the physician to the teacher, "that they must fill the heads of children with this stuff, however bitterly they feel about the Americans. It twists their minds before they've learned to think and keeps this vicious circle of international stupidity intact for at least another generation."

And she, seeming suddenly discouraged, said, "Yes, it is a pity."

39

Then, before anyone else could make much of this discussion, Tai went hurrying with little Ping and Feng to where our happy capitalist now stood scattering pennies all around, calling on the children to scramble for them. But the youngsters, not understanding the gesture or what was wanted of them, watched dumbly while their teacher and our guides quickly gathered up the money.

Wang, waiting to one side, then took and put it back into our friend's hand and gently closed his fingers on it, saying, "Please, not good, not good." Then looking into his face, Wang smiled kindly.

Our friend came back to us, puzzled. "They're funny people, these Communist Chinese. They don't seem to realize the value of money. Perhaps it's because the rich men have all gone from the country and these who are left are poor people who have never had much experience with it."

Nobody answered him and we moved away, leaving the children to their games.

We came, then, to a place in the park where a stage was set up in a grotto of stone, with a hill rising sharply behind it and, on top of the hill, a white pagoda ringed with plum and peach trees. Here we were given seats so that we could hear and see students from the Middle School of Music and groups from the dance and drama schools of Peking.

First there were three vociferous songs of the revolution done in Western style by a choir of two hundred young singers wearing white tunics and red scarves, together with a teen-age symphony orchestra of a hundred pieces, the whole conducted with an assured and forthright beat by a boy of thirteen.

Then, a group of simple folk dances from Tibet and Sinkiang, the performers colorfully costumed and the music traditional, played on a variety of Asian instruments: stringed pipas shaped elegantly like pears, and tombras which have the graceful shapes of amphorae, together with a clutch of the strident horse-headed fiddles of Mongolia, with finger drums, and the ancient blowsuck sheng, which is the forerunner of all mouth organs and has a history going back to an age beyond our knowledge. All of these together made a strangely brittle and stridulant sound except for the sheng, which made anxious animal noises.

40

After that a fat young African woman got up from among the foreign guests and went onto the stage to sing a rousing song which said, "China's today is our tomorrow," trying it in Chinese learned for the occasion and thus earning for herself so much applause that she sang it again with even greater fervor, but forgot the words this second time so that even Wang smiled, though the clapping and the calls of approval were louder than before.

Then six middle-aged Chinese ladies with rouged faces, who were short-course students from the countryside, gave us a jolly action song, strutting back and forth across the front of the stage exchanging doggerel dialogue which said that the women of new China, being freed from the drudgery of the past, now not only reap and spin and raise babies but plow the land with tractors, maintain farm machinery, and take their places in the people's armed militia.

For this they were cheered and clapped loudly by the foreign visitors sitting near the stage, especially the Africans.

The director of the music school, a simple, cheerful woman, sat with us. She was no musician but a Party cadre; and when six of her students came onto the stage to play a suite of their own composing, she explained that they had written this piece after spending eight weeks working in a locomotive factory and had given it the title, "Mao's thought is the locomotive leading the advance of the world's workers." It represented their impressions and measured the depth of their ideological identification with the life and aspirations of the industrial workers with whom they had lived and worked for that period.

These young students, playing their piece, surprised us not only with the technical excellence of their music but by their virtuosity, each of them being able to play at least two instruments; so that the lad who led with the pianoforte in the first movement switched with the fiddler for the second, while the girl who played piccolo took to percussion, and the percussionist sang a recitative in which she described their experiences from the time they had left Peking until they came riding back again on the train, pulled by the new locomotive they had helped to build.

The piece began with the piccolo whistling a simple pastorale as they passed through the countryside, while underneath the melody the piano and percussion beat out a running rhythm. Then came the friendly welcome at the factory expressed in a dialogue for violin and cello with rhetorical interruptions from the drum, and after this a resolute movement full of labored accents and twisted dissonance depicting labor and industrial creativity. And then a gay, light-hearted but triumphant finale flying along with the newly built locomotive on its maiden run, the piccolo flinging uninhibited flourishes above the thumping of the drums and the driving wild cadenzas of the other instruments. It was exciting, and good music of its kind.

Afterward I said to the director that, although music students in my own country were as democratic as most others, they would think twice before spending so much time living and working among industrial people if for no other reason than that they would worry about damaging their fingers, as well as losing that much time from study.

She smiled, as one who sees clearly what others have missed through ignorance, and said that in a people's republic the function of all art and artists is to serve the peasants, workers, and soldiers, to reflect their thoughts and aspirations and to speak for them, and that this can only be done if class and ideological distinctions between artists and the masses of people are abolished.

Then she spoke to us collectively through Feng, who embellished everything she said with textbook and editorial phrases which already we could recognize; and she said that in this question of class relationships lay one of the main differences between the opposite philosophies of socialism and capitalism.

In the West, she said, we have developed a society in which all people become specialists and live separated lives based on vocational and class differences, so that no common culture can be created. In a society of that kind, where the masses have no contact with the most gifted people in the community, the highest forms of art and thought are monopolized by the privileged few, and the gap between these and the rest of the people becomes so wide that artists speak only to each other and have no proper contact with the masses, give them nothing and get nothing from them in return, so that artists become spiritually starved and sterile, and the people lack cultural leadership.

But in a revolutionary society the artists must live freely among

42

the people as fish live in the sea and should never forget that their function is to serve the masses. They must go to the peasants and workers and learn from them, find out the real truth about life, work on it and give it back to the masses in finer and more dramatic form, but clearly understandable so that it gives them encouragement as well as pleasure, and helps them to see the way ahead more clearly.

This attitude, she said through Feng, with Miss Ping nodding agreement, is essential to revolution. Culture must never again be monopolized by bourgeois scholars, specialists, and so-called authorities, because in this way evil class distinctions come into being. Once this is understood the artist can see himself for what he should be—a fighter in the vanguard of social progress; and grasping this, one can have no doubt that it is more fruitful for a musician, or any other kind of artist, to enter wholeheartedly into the labor of peasants and workers, even at the risk of hurting his hands, than to live in selfish, intellectual isolation.

A musician who has truly learned to live with the workers in this way will play more from the heart than from the intellect and will speak more objectively through his music than any delicate hothouse musician who has never held a shovel in his hand, or beaten hot metal on an anvil, or flexed his fingers lifting heavy machinery. And how will a musician play, a dancer dance, or an artist depict the real life and the deepest feelings of peasants if they have never slept on the floor, helped with the harvest, or carried manure to the fields?

The question was rhetorical, and in any case May Day in Peking is no occasion for dialectical wrangling, however interesting the thesis. Later, when I had heard it all many times, day after day, I found it tedious and one-sided and would have argued if there had been any gain in it one way or the other. On each occasion the case was put forward by a Party cadre and not by an artist, writer, or musician, so that dogma bested sense or any artistic reality in these arguments.

Meanwhile tens of thousands of people came and went continuously all around us, stopping to watch awhile, then moving on, not wanting to miss anything; and when there came a break in the concert we, too, moved on and made our way among the dancing

43

groups, the puppet shows and cockshies, the bands and choirs and acrobats, along avenues of trees festooned with lanterns and flags, drifting slowly with the flow, our guides outriding, striving to keep us together, though we, feeling no longer foreign but one with those around us, old and young, had no anxiety.

Photographers operate in the square of Tien An Men to take snaps of holidaymakers, placing them in front of the Heavenly Gate, or on a pediment of the monument to the People's Heroes, or, if preferred, at the bottom of the steps of the Great Hall of the People, or among the columns at the entrance to the museum of China's history.

I had my picture taken with Ping and was placed precisely on a spot which centered us beneath the arched entrance to the Imperial City, under a huge portrait of Chairman Mao, though Ping was bashful and kept her face averted and partly hidden with her hand because people stopped to watch and whisper together. Had Feng not said that this was part of her duties as a guide to foreign guests, she would have refused in spite of my wishing to have this simple souvenir of May Day in Peking.

This city, planned without stint, has been built and rebuilt by generations of emperors and artists; and in this great square, more than in any other place in China, one has the feeling of standing in the middle of a nation's history, though other lovely cities have also been the seat of dynasties, centers of learning, and of much breath-taking richness and magnificence.

Also, from time to time in other parts of China, rebel movements and armed uprisings of significance have begun and spread across huge areas, changing for a while the patterns of internal power. Yet in spite of several periods of political oblivion Peking has long been the generative center of China's unique ethos and formidable civilization, as well as a symbol of resistance to all outside influences. Consequently it is not difficult to agree when affectionate Westerners call it the Paris of East Asia, for like Paris it is a fructifying city, a germinal pool of learning, culture, politics, and history.

Here, where I stand with little Ping in her baggy blue pants to have my picture taken, events have taken place within this generation which are now changing the structure of civilization as surely as the great revolutions of the French, the Americans, and the Russians brought change and gave fresh impetus to the progression of man in his evolutionary journey from protoplasm (if such was his beginning) to a personal identification with the original life force, which some of us call God.

Since Chinese intellectuals learned from Europe and America, early in this present century, that progress and true justice for the oppressed can be achieved only through revolutionary procedures, the Tien An Men square has been the scene of many acts in the drama of a people overthrowing a decadent system of kingship and replacing it with some current form of democracy.

In these few decades students have gathered here to protest, to complain, to march on legations, to demonstrate against governments, and to be shot down for their pains, but eventually, on October 1, 1949, to see their approved leader, Mao Tse-tung, raise the five-starred banner of the Chinese People's Republic and declare, "This nation will no longer be insulted by foreigners. We have stood up."

So these tens of thousands who now swarm over the square in festival dress, who roam through the salons of the Great Hall of the People, the museums and old imperial palaces, understand, even if vaguely, that they are walking around in their own history, just as surely as any American visiting the public buildings and memorials of Washington knows that what he feels there is the heartbeat of his own great nation; as a Frenchman visiting Paris knows without telling that the love, the lust, the blood, the sins, the nobility, and the wisdom which have drenched and cleansed that city for centuries is the fabric and fiber of the France in which he now lives and to which Western civilization still turns for inspiration.

The professor was saying as he helped his wife step up into the bus, "Unless we admit to these equivalents and see each man's history as part of our own, there is no hope for any of us." He pulled himself up after her and added, "Meanwhile I shall be glad to get back to the hotel and have a drink."

The teacher, following him, said, "Yes, it's awfully interesting but exceedingly hard on the feet."

45

It was a cold night.

Searchlights laid a lattice of steely stripes over the sky while we stood in the reviewing stands overlooking Tien An Men, pulling our coat collars and scarves tighter while waiting for the fireworks, and watching a million people dance. Not children this time, but young adults from all over China, from factories, communes, and army units, dancing against the backdrop of huge public buildings floodlit and outlined with strings of white lights. All around, stretching far away along the avenues, colored lanterns hung in the trees like clusters of luminous fruit.

To our right was the huge blockhouse of the Heavenly Gate and above it, under the golden-tiled roof, the balcony from which dignitaries and special guests watched what was happening in the square. Tonight the Albanians were there with the Chairman of the People's Republic, Liu Shao-chi, and Premier Chou En-lai, and the old General Chu Teh, who had been Mao's comrade on the Long March of 1935.

In our stand, kept for lesser guests, people were looking up at this balcony, trying to identify the important personalities. An Englishman using night glasses said, "No sign of the old chap. He must be as sick as the newspapers say, or he wouldn't miss this." Then lowering his glasses, "A man was telling me last week that he's practically blind and has to be led about. Some say he has Parkinson's disease and won't last long. You can bet there'll be trouble when he goes."

The professor, standing beside me, spoke quietly. "It's sad to hear adult and presumably intelligent men talk such utter rubbish, not having the slightest understanding or knowledge of Chinese customs and tradition, or the way in which matters of state are arranged.

"There is no real reason at all why Mao should be here tonight. Shehu, the chief guest, is Chairman of his country's Council of Ministers and is entertained by Liu, who is at present Chairman of the Chinese Republic. This accords strictly with tradition and protocol, and Mao is no doubt sitting comfortably at home seeing all this on television. Any thought that he is very sick is unrealistic and wishful thinking."

His wife said, "Never mind, dear. Most people are stupid and

46

nothing can be done about it. You're always saying this yourself, but you still get upset whenever anybody says something foolish."

Feng said abruptly, "Watch, please, the fireworks begin."

The sea of people in the square surged back toward the edges, then settled, leaving circles of space from which, without more warning, sprang fountains and sprays of golden rain out of the ground. Then, from some unseen firing place, salvos of multistage rockets rose to explode with drum rolls of thunder, ten at a time, and bursting, let down a sky-wide curtain of colors, one overrunning the other: blue wisteria shot through with plumes of gold, then smoothly overlaid with draperies of green and red, cascades of lilac, and scintillating showers of silver spinning down through the night sky like fireflies; then yellow, pink, and orange blobs like luminescent fish drifting in a black pond; and all the time a thunder and rumble and growl as of gunfire, and the chatter of crackers.

A million people watched the sky. Together they gasped, cried out with pleasure and surprise, were delighted, smiled at each other without inquiring, "Who are you? Do you believe in God, witchcraft, politicians, economists, love, or nothing?" They did not ask each other how it felt to be black, white, yellow, red, brown, or gray. They did not feel frightened or angry with each other. They did not hate nor were they ashamed. They watched the fireworks and said to the stranger standing beside them, "My friend, this is so lovely, so clever, so gay."

Yet I, in the middle of all this, could only sigh.

CHAPTER

5

TEN years after Mao Tse-tung had raised the red banner of the Republic over the ancient Gate of Heavenly Peace he officially opened the Great Hall of the People, which faces it across the square.

The National People's Congress meets there in the main auditorium, which is built without pillars and has seating for ten thousand people. The five thousand ground-floor seats are fitted with multilingual translation equipment.

This huge auditorium occupies roughly a fiftieth of the total ground space of the building, the rest containing administrative offices, radio, television, film, and theater facilities, kitchens and banquet hall for five thousand diners, and twenty-two reception and conference halls, each superbly furnished and decorated with examples of the special arts and crafts of each of China's provinces. The wide stairways are marble. The high ceilings, embellished with the work of master artists, are hung with stupendous crystal and gilt chandeliers.

Although most of the building materials on the site were moved about and put into place by hand, the entire construction took only ten months to complete, with much of the labor being donated by people of the city on a part-time basis.

Feng, smiling at young Tai, said that he and other student guides had given three hours of their own time each night for many months as members of one of the dozens of volunteer gangs which worked around the clock in shifts, so that the job never stopped. They worked alongside doctors and shopkeepers, students and housewives, doing most of the unskilled labor, thus leaving the professional craftsmen and artisans free to concentrate on construction.

This achievement and others equally impressive, including the building of bridges, highways, dams, and manufacturing plants in all parts of China, were part of the Great Leap Forward. They underline what is without doubt the major element in China's potential greatness—the incredibly productive and creative capacity of her multiple millions. Theoretically there is nothing they cannot do.

Standing in the center of the great stage in the main auditorium, I told Feng, who was spilling facts and statistics into my ear, that these did not overimpress me because yesterday I had read that in the fifteenth century, during the reign of the Ming king, Yung-lo, the whole of Peking was rebuilt in a matter of five years, using millions of workmen and women.

Then seeing him put off by this discovery of my unsuspected familiarity with snippets of Chinese history, and wishing to consolidate some reputation in this area, I ventured the additional information that when the Mings were driven from the empire some three hundred years ago, an admiral of the dynasty withdrew to Formosa and ruled there independently until he died, and his grandsons, quarreling over the inheritance, lost it. This item, and others of curious likeness, strengthen my untutored suspicion that Chinese history follows a pattern which is constantly repetitive in many of its basic aspects, and that almost any event in China today can be to some degree explained, and even understood, if laid alongside happenings of a previous age.

With polite gestures Feng then moved away from me, saying that he found history very interesting but that many of our party were wandering off and would go astray if he did not quickly gather them together for a visit to the Forbidden City, which was next on our list. We might continue our discussion some other time, but meanwhile, we must keep moving, as we were already behind schedule.

The Forbidden City, first built by Kublai Khan, then recreated on an adjacent site by the early Ming kings, was home to China's subsequent rulers until the abdication of the Manchus in 1912. It covers an area of roughly 170 acres and is today a national museum into which anybody with ten cents may gain entrance to spend the day gaping at the most astonishing jumble of luxury ever to be collected and displayed within a single space—though to study the total content and its historical significance in any detail would require the absolute attention of half a lifetime.

Marco Polo noted that the great Khan kept four wives there and that each of them had a household of ten thousand officials, eunuchs, servants, and slaves. The number of concubines with lesser attendants is not mentioned in his records, presumably because the number was fluctuant, but each, being from an influential clan or family, would have been accommodated decently and provided with adequate staff. Additionally, ten thousand members of the imperial guard were kept in this city, to say nothing of the Khan's own retinue of courtiers, companions, clerks, and advisers. The fact that his dining room held six thousand people suggests that the total population of the Great Within—the Purple Forbidden City, as it was then called—was considerable.

It is a city of palaces, of golden- and green-tiled pavilions with horned corners and eaves. A city of consecutive courtyards, stone-paved and approached over marble bridges or by long and sloping stone ramps, or through great, elaborate gates, and set about with bronzes: lions with dragon hands, turtles signifying fertility, enormous urns and incense burners, alabaster cranes, an ancient armillary sphere, fountains, fishponds, and gardens. A city with architecturally splendid reception halls and throne rooms, where forests of crimson and gilt pillars spring up from a jet-black marble floor, creating strange, breath-taking perspectives.

Elderly peasants, having paid their ten cents, seem stunned as they shuffle from room to room, wondering. One sees them come and stand dumb, in each doorway, expressionless, not comprehending the reality of such riches.

An old man, recognizable instantly as a boxwood figurine, leans on a long stick with his fingers twisted like a knotted string. He has a thin wisp of white beard and a shaven skull, and he wears baggy black pantaloons and straw shoes. His son beside him wears the khaki cotton of the army, a red star in his cap. And the lad's young wife, with their son, stares into a glass case that displays hundreds of ingots of silver recovered from the tomb of a Ming king.

Rivers of history meet here. Pictures pour into the mind like water falling into a cup too small to take it. They come from so far in the past, from behind walls of enclosed time that have even yet been scarcely breached, that they mix and spill over and slip away before one is able to take hold of any complete and tangible impression—except the clear recognition that for thousands of years a comparative few lived prodigiously and waxed willfully rich on the misery of China's millions.

In a small courtyard, only a few yards square and almost hidden between two pavilions, a fragile lilac tree leans over a well in which, it is said, a little concubine, brought to court from some far-off province, drowned herself. Alongside the wall, by the well, is a garden of peonies; and inside the adjoining pavilion there is a display of royal robes inlaid with gold and silver thread and silken embroideries worked by female slaves, golden helmets set profusely with jewels, crowns, and pagodas of gold given to emperors by avaricious, sycophantic, ingratiating, cunning, courtiers. One such, a eunuch, falling out of favor, had his estates confiscated; and in addition to bars of gold, jewels, jade and ivory ornaments of all kinds, his silver, when weighed, was found to tally at something more than 250 million ounces.

To catalogue the valuable bric-a-brac contained within these palaces would be tedious. Thirteen thousand chests of treasure were packed, ready for transhipment to Formosa, when the Communists took Peking. Most of them were recovered. Since then other collections have been unearthed in newly discovered tombs, temples, and hiding places. Wall after wall of the palace rooms are hung with pictures put together from precious metals and gems: golden trees leaved with enamel, jade birds and animals on the branches and jeweled flowers in the grass; dozens of monumental blocks of jade shaped into fabulous and intricate landscapes; tusks of ivory chiseled into miniature seascapes and villages. There are scores of cabinets full of rings, lacquered fans, hairpins and combs, necklets, headbands, earrings, finger stalls, jeweled slippers, girdles of gold and silver, and all the bewitching frippery of women.

In the principal throne room, called the Hall of Supreme

Harmony, the imperial divan is on a platform approached by five stairways intricately carved and balustraded. Stately, larger-than-life cranes with cocked heads and inquiring eyes stand at the head of the stairs. Bronze incense burners, porcelain vats, and golden birdcages embellish this chamber where ambassadors from every part of Asia and the coasts of the Mediterranean came century after century with presents from their rulers. Later they came from Europe, with gifts in their hands but deceit and money hunger in their hearts; and afterward from America, though by this time the sickness of dynastic China had been diagnosed by every Western power. Dignified ghouls, representing their respective governments, gathered to snatch the riches from this vast country which decadent emperors could no longer govern or protect.

China's isolation was over, and soon there were Western legations in Peking manipulating the nation's politics and carving the country into spheres of economic influence, as had already been done in Africa and the Pacific Islands.

But in Shantung province, south of Peking, peasants, sensing some new form of oppression, rose in protest and, following long established historical tradition, marched upon the capital. The Court, not yet understanding Western strength, tentatively blessed the peasants, hoping that their efforts, discreetly assisted by the government militia, would rid the country of foreigners and restore imperial authority.

Inevitably the movement attracted fanatics, and encouraged by implied license, Peking became a playground for these and all light-minded and adventurous elements seeking uninhibited excitement. The wearing of a red ribbon or armband was thought sufficient sanction for acts of vandalism and brutality, including the destruction of any property belonging to foreigners, the burning of shops displaying foreign goods, attacks on people wearing Western fashions or following Western habits, with special attention given to Christian missionaries and their converts—all this anticipating the Red Guard of 1966 by a good half-century.

In the euphemistic idiom of the time they called themselves the Society of the Harmonious Fists, entering into the lists of Western history as the Boxers.

They besieged the legations and seemed likely to achieve their aim of doing away with everything alien, including the foreign diplomats and their families, until the Western powers assembled an international rescue force to raise the siege and, incidentally, to counterattack and capture the Forbidden City.

The French had four little mountain guns with which, from the top of the city wall, they played ratatatat on the golden tiles of the Imperial City while ladies of the legations watched in a state of high excitement. At the same time U.S. infantrymen stormed the walls, crashing through one gate after another with cannon fire, battering rams, and great gallantry until only the crimson enclosure of the Forbidden City itself stood between them and the throne of China.

An American soldier then clambered up and sat astride the wall of the inner city, waving the Stars and Stripes, while gunners moved their pieces into place for a last blast. But the diplomats, always devious, foresaw later dangers in so brash an attack on Chinese sensitivity and counseled caution, having in mind that it would be more profitable to have a chastened monarchy in its collective ambassadorial pocket than to deal for years with a huge nation in a state of anarchy. Diplomacy prevailed. The rotten monarchy was tamed and reinstated, so paving the way for final revolution. Today the pattern of East-West relations remains distastefully familiar.

Less than a half-century later Red Army artillery waited outside the walls of Peking, ready to blow a breach in them with guns made in the U.S.A. and captured from Chiang Kai-shek.

The Communist commander, Lin Piao, who today stands beside Mao Tse-tung, gave thought to which portion of the wall might most expediently be sacrificed to the cause of the people's revolution and, to ease his mind of the matter, discussed it with the city's leading archeologist. After balancing military with aesthetic considerations agreement was reached, and an architecturally inferior portion of the wall was marked down for the breaching.

At this stage I am ready to admit that this skimping and simplification of history may not please scholars, though to do such is not the task I have set myself; but in a work of this kind many edges must be trimmed so that incidents may be fitted sensibly into a bigger picture, and for these liberties I hope to be forgiven. For that matter, it is difficult in the course of a single visit to a country so vast, and with so long and complex a history, to gather more than a rag bag of partial facts, fragmentary information, and intuitive impressions.

Take, for example, our visit to "The Rent Collection Court," a display of life-size clay sculptures made by artists, students, and village people in the province of Szechwan and exhibited at the National Gallery in Peking.

The spectacle purports to represent in an exact and factual way the common yearly scene in the rent-collecting courtyard of a landlord's house in preliberation days, when it was obligatory for peasants to pay their annual ground rents with grain immediately after the harvest.

The lifelike peasant figures in this exhibition reek of poverty, oppression, despair, unlimited misery, and suffocating hate, while the landlord's henchmen are all coarse, brutal, sadistic, and villainous cheats.

The peasants, in tattered rags, bring their grain to be weighed. They bring it in baskets or bundled up in old bits of cloth or canvas. All of them are gaunt, some little more than skin and bone. An old woman with the total suffering of the human race etched on her face leans miserably on a stick, awaiting her turn to pay. She has brought along a skinny chicken to offset the short measure of millet she has been able to glean from the tiny patch of land from which she must eke out a living.

A blind man, almost naked, is led in by his grandchild, and because he cannot pay his tally she is taken to be a housemaid in the landlord's house, leaving the old man helpless and solitary. Next to him an angry young man has raised his shoulder pole to strike at the landlord's lackey while his frightened, pregnant wife puts out her hands to restrain him.

A Westerner, having had no firsthand contact with this kind of life, might rightly ask, "Is this art, a representation of historical fact, melodramatic propaganda, or a little of each?" If the question is addressed to me, the only answer I can give, since I was never in Szechuan, which is on the edge of Tibet, is that when I saw this exhibition, some among the visitors were weeping and others (though only one or two) made struggling, inarticulate sounds of suppressed pain or the deep-down rage of remembered, unjust suffering.

54

One bent old lady in black, glaring at a group of statues, pounded the floor noisily with her stick and shouted imprecations until Wang, usually aloof, and a young woman attendant led her away. Most other people, including me, walked around the exhibition silently, grim-faced, as if viewing actual tragedy.

This display in the Peking gallery, though effective and dramatic, is not complete. The original set of 114 figures, grouped into twenty-four tableaux along the four sides of the courtyard, remain in the small Szechwan town of Anjen, where they were made and set up in a compound of farm buildings and yards belonging to what was once a landlord's manor house.

These figures, large as life, are modeled with a mixture of clay and straw on a skeletal framework of wood, and afterward coated with a layer of clay combined with sand and cotton from which the features and draperies are fashioned. The mixture is cheap and so easy to work that a complete figure can be shaped in a single day at a cost of something like two dollars. This means that sculptors working for the Department of Culture can move into almost any district and quickly produce, on the spot, an exhibition of local relevance and interest.

The basic modeling technique is ancient and was used by the makers of temple images, though these have been displaced by a new generation of sculptors who have learned their craft in the provincial institutes of fine arts and whose work aims straight at reality, with a tendency to rhetoric.

The purpose of this particular exhibition is explicit.

Young Tai, interpreting in place of Feng and little Ping, who were away elsewhere with others of our party, said that the figures bring to life the reality of the class struggle. They show clearly the brutal crimes committed by the despots and the landlord class, the humiliation of the peasants, and the spirit of revolt rising among them in the face of this sustained oppression and injustice.

I was already aware of this, having looked it up in Miss Ping's primer before leaving the hotel. Even so, I thought that Tai seemed strangely vehement for one so young and usually ebullient.

"What you see here is a true picture of the wicked past which has been done away with by the Party and smashed to fragments, though in Africa, Latin America, and other parts of Asia, especially in India, our brothers and sisters still suffer in this way. This exhibition reminds everyone who sees it that we must never forget the past and never give the reactionary capitalists and imperialists the chance to bring it back again."

Then Wang returned and for the first time in our visit seemed actively interested in what we were seeing. Even in the Great Hall of the People he had stayed in the background, showing no concern, nodding and smiling kindly enough if any one of us approached him with signs of approval or pleasure, but otherwise seeming almost bored with us, as well he might have been; but now he stood beside Tai and talked forcefully, pointing to individual figures in the exhibition, explaining details and the significance of their attitudes and postures, though these were plain enough even to us, and explanation seemed unnecessary.

Tai, listening to him, turned to us. "Mr. Wang says that the peasants called this rent collection court 'The Gateway to Hell' because when they came here each year they were always afraid and anxious about what would happen to them. If they had not enough grain to pay the rent, or the money they owed for interest or previous debt, the landlord could take the children in payment, or make the women come and live with him, or conscript the men into the army of the local war lord. If the harvest was sparse, nobody knew what would happen to them on rent-collection day. Any one of the family could be taken."

He turned to Wang again, and for several minutes they talked excitedly, with Wang animated and insistent as if anxious that Tai should have everything exact. We waited, watching the flow of local visitors moving from one tableau to another in groups guided by girls who lectured them emphatically.

One group stood close by us, the girl standing on a box to address them. Her eyes flashed and her voice was clamorous with contempt and indignation as she pointed with a long white stick to the dominating figure in a group, the landlord's overseer, standing foresquare with legs apart, hand on hip, a panama hat on the back of his head, a mastiff squatting beside him. She indicated his fine clothes, the pistol in his waistband, the fan in one hand, a long cigarette holder in the other. How heartless he looks, how arrogant, and how well-fed!

And look at his lackeys! She swung her white stick at another figure, and with one synchronous movement of their heads her group looked.

"See how roughly that despicable class traitor empties the poor widow's grain into a wooden bucket to check whether or not it will meet the amount of her debt. See how he lets some of it spill onto the ground while she watches anxiously. And remember that the measuring bucket is a false one made especially big to cheat the peasants."

Again she swung her stick, and her anger went with it.

"Then see how viciously this other man strikes with his whip at her hungry little son, because he tries to pick up the grain that was spilled."

I remembered the children dancing in the park, the youth orchestra and the choir; and now these sculptures. All part of what is called the Cultural Revolution, the conscription of art and artists to serve in the front rank of the continuing world-wide struggle of the masses (how quickly and well one learned the words).

It is hard to take, yet nothing is gained by saying that all this is spurious and a prostitution of art and artists; that these clay figures are caricatures, and the story they purport to tell a fraudulent distortion of history. One could as well call *Uncle Tom's Cabin* a piece of sentimental misrepresentation or *Oliver Twist* a contrived piece of propaganda. The figures in this gallery are every bit as real as Tom and Oliver, historically as valid and accurate, politically as legitimate and as potent.

Our group moved on, and catching up with Tai, I asked why Wang should show so much more interest in this exhibition than in anything else we had so far seen. He hesitated, seeming reluctant to answer, then said that Wang was a native of the province of Szechwan and remembered the time when such things happened.

Wang, hearing his name spoken, asked what had been said, and my question now being brought out openly, he took me by the arm and led me closer to a single figure; a miserable man sitting on the ground beside a basket of grain, the only tangible result of his year's labor and the skimpy stay of his old age, letting a handful slowly trickle through his fingers before parting with it.

Wang pointed to the figure, then looked at me and spoke into my face. I turned to Tai for translation.

"That is how Mr. Wang remembers his father."

Wang turned back to the statues and stabbed with his finger again—this time to a tableau which showed two women being pulled apart by the landlord's men. One of the women was old and the other young. The old one was holding out a baby which the younger woman could not reach, though she struggled and pleaded hysterically while being dragged back, screaming, into a prison pen. It was clear that the young woman could not pay her rent and was being separated from her baby. The implication was that she would become a slave laborer for the landlord until somebody paid her debts. Meanwhile her old mother and her baby would have no one to keep them. In retrospect I find it a shade overplayed and grotesque, but can hear Tai speaking:

"Mr. Wang says that this happened also, to his sister."

Looking round, I could see my sentimental capitalist friend wiping his eyes and, beside him, our own Australian Communist blowing his nose.

We moved on, and Wang, now more communicative, told how sculptors and peasants had worked together to create this exhibition. The sculptors, mostly students and young instructors from the Fine Arts Institute of Szechwan, went together to this township of Anjen, which is beyond Chungking, to see the infamous rich man's manor house, which, like the Imperial City, is now a museum.

They saw the empty rent collection court and set themselves a work-study project which would re-create within it a living picture of the old days, complete in every detail. To achieve this they first studied the work of local folk artists and learned to handle local tools and materials. They lived with the people, collected stories from them, interviewed hundreds who had suffered the landlord's cruelty, and brought many of them back to the courtyard to relive their own past dramas.

They set up their studio in the courtyard and lived there while they worked, leaving the gates always open so that people could come and go as they pleased to watch, to make suggestions or criticize if they felt inclined. Many peasants offered to be models and stayed to help with the work, and in six months it was done.

Talking quietly in the bus, Tai said that when Wang was still a boy he had left his home to follow the Red Army on its Long

March and had become a Party member as soon as he was able, long before liberation. He said that sometimes Wang spoke about the old days to young men like himself who were aspiring to Party membership, and told stories of his own childhood to help them understand the sufferings of the old days. Two of Wang's sisters were drowned at birth like kittens because there was nothing for them to eat, and a brother was given to a childless uncle and aunt in another village so that he might survive.

Then Tai seemed suddenly shy and uncertain and spoke still more quietly.

"For me it is more difficult. Before liberation my father was a middle-class capitalist in Shanghai. He did bad business with the Japanese aggressors and then with the Americans, and after the Liberation he went to Hong Kong. But my mother was on the side of the people and stayed here, and kept me and one sister with her while the others went with our father.

"I love the Party and our great leader"—his earnestness embarrassed me—"and I will always work hard for the solidarity of the workers everywhere in the world. But because of my father it is not so easy for me to make progress."

I was sorry to see him discouraged, for he was normally a cheerful young fellow, so I said, "Let us sing."

At this he immediately laughed aloud and, putting his arm around me, said, "I will sing one good English song for you. It is called 'Silent Night.' "

So we sang, with the rest of our party joining in and Wang smiling.

AT six-thirty next morning when I went to the sitting room to listen to the news, the professor was already there, standing on one leg, though shakily, with his right arm extended like the curve of a swan's neck and the left looped back behind his head. This posture, seen fleetingly, suggested an elderly teapot in the act of tilting.

When he saw me he teetered, relinquishing the position with apparent relief, sighed, and said, "I always try to finish with that one. It's called the sleeping flamingo, and to do it properly one should come to rest in an attitude of complete and symmetrical relaxation. I find it a fair test of the degree to which one is still able to coordinate the physical, mental, and spiritual mechanisms of the id. When, eventually, one is no longer able to maintain balance on one leg while thinking of completeness, even for a few seconds, it must be regrettably assumed that one is on the way to imminent senility."

I said that I sometimes found difficulty in contemplating completeness while standing on two legs, or even when sitting down, but the remark seemed frivolous, and to cover my confusion I asked if he practiced these exercises each morning.

He sat and lit a cigarette and said, "One should, though at home I rarely do. But while in China I feel that one must try to identify with the national philosophy and general outlook in order to come closer to the Chinese way of thinking. As you have no doubt seen, every living soul in the country engages in some form of early morning calisthenics."

This I knew to be true, for every casual traveler speaks of it, and already in my morning walks I had stopped to watch people in the streets doing these exercises or playing games (already the hotel waiters and bellboys were at their basketball down in the courtyard).

Most of those who do their calisthenics in the street and other public places begin the day with some variation of the ancient game of Chinese boxing called *Wu shu,* in which, even when two or more people are opposed, no blows are struck though the devotees, depending upon age and agility, may go through ferocious and dramatically acrobatic motions of attack and defense reminiscent of the antics of characters in traditional Chinese opera.

But for most people it is enough to stand quietly in one spot and go through a series of slow, rhythmic movements which, far from being vigorous, seem dreamily ritualistic. This is the newly simplified form of *Wu shu,* called *Tai-chi-chuan,* which, roughly interpreted, means the total life force or the completeness of being.

Like many other aspects of Chinese life which seem at first sight strange and inexplicable to the stranger, these intriguing exercises are not merely physical and disciplinary but are a unique expression of the Chinese character and system of thinking, flowering out of thousands of years of introspective history and development.

The actual movements of the body are related to the ancient Taoist concept of the unity and harmony of all things through the equalization of opposites: light and dark, high and low, right and left, and so on. There is no beginning or ending to a circle, only completeness; and total existence is circular.

In its classical form there are a hundred separate movements, but experts of the government department of physical culture have worked out, and taught, a short version of twenty-four fairly simple movements which, when done by even quite old people, flow naturally into each other and together make a combined physical and philosophical exercise as complete as prayer or an affirmation of faith.

For the idea is not simply to stand in the street and go through a series of eurythmics for the health's sake, but to bring oneself completely together in one piece physically, mentally, and spiritually, and so to achieve a personal unity within oneself and with all creation. Thus, to go through the slow movements of a flower bud opening, its petals unfolding into fullness and final drooping, is to identify with the life force by consciously following with the hands, arms, and shoulders and feeling, at the same time, the rising of the sap while mentally contemplating the material, yet mystical miracle of life continuously and everlastingly happening.

The clerk on his way to the office in blue cotton tunic puts down his little bag of bread or rice and dried fish, and the works of Mao Tse-tung, and standing at the bus stop, starts his exercises. Smoothly his arms rise, his fingers extend, and his hands begin to weave slow circles before his face. His eyes close, his hands rise higher. He lifts one foot and turns aside, bends, stretches, still slowly working circles with his hands. What curious tourist, taking snapshots, is to know that this insignificant little man (who earns three dollars a week figuring on an abacus in a hat store) is identifying himself with the solar system, the planets, the stars, the Communist Party, and the entirety of being—while waiting for his bus?

I said to the professor, "How blindly we walk through life, seeing nothing in it more significant than our own antics and anxieties. We tourists come to China and gape at people doing their morning exercises and think, How strange, and how strong a grip must the government have on these simple people to be able to regiment them into this kind of thing, a mass campaign of physical fitness. Not seeing that it is a form of worship. An unself-conscious affirmation that each man is part of a completeness. A daily manifestation of faith that makes the Sunday service in an average Christian church seem a sad and anxious search for something that doesn't exist."

He replied, looking at me quizzically, "You should watch yourself or China will do damage to your mind. It's much too big for most people, especially for those who think. Being here is something like looking through a microscope at the mystery of mankind. What is life-sized in most countries is magnified a hundred times in this giant unity of more than seven hundred million

62

people with a single way of life and mind. Learn what you can from it, but don't throw yourself into the stream or you will be carried away and lost to the place you came from."

I shook my head and said that, like most other visitors, I much admired the practical achievements of the revolutionary regime but had some fundamental reservations which would keep any extravagant enthusiasms in check. But it was difficult not to be impressed and even optimistic when one considered the desolate condition of the Chinese people of even a generation ago and their comparative well-being and confidence today.

I had the Szechwan sculptures still in mind and spoke of them, asking him to explain why these people should have been in such an oppressed and poverty-stricken state. To this he answered that an economy based mainly upon the agricultural production of backward peasants has always been precarious, and China's more so that most because it could never produce enough food by primitive methods of cultivation to feed so great a population.

In seven years out of ten, according to records going back centuries, areas as big as many European countries suffered either drought or flood, while local wars of one kind or another continuously disrupted or broke down the productive cycle of rural life even before foreign intrusions added to China's woes.

Most peasant farmers, being solely dependent from year to year on what they could grow on a small patch of land averaging, perhaps, half an acre for each family, sooner or later fell into debt with moneylenders, merchants, or wealthy landlords who advanced money or goods against future crops and took back payment in flesh and blood and the peasants' few possessions when cash and grain were not forthcoming.

Add to this the fact that justice and taxation were in the hands of the Emperor's officials, often corrupt and in league with local warlords, and it is not surprising that the peasants, as a class, were raw material for exploitation, friendless and expendable.

When the Westerners came they made things worse by flooding China with cheap, machine-made goods from the factories of Europe and America, thus putting middle-class artisans and manufacturers out of business, and taking what little liquid cash there was from local circulation.

63

Then the professor looked at me again. "If, to such history, you add twenty continuous years of international and civil war, your clay figures in the courtyard at Szechwan assume the shapes of reality, and it should be easy to accept as a fact that most Chinese were hungry for the greater part of their lives and ready to follow any leader who would feed them."

He looked at his watch, then got up quickly and went to the radio to switch it on, then fiddled and found what we wanted. A voice, anonymous and unknown, a little affected, yet blessedly comforting because it asked nothing of us. It made no demands upon our sympathies, our judgment or understanding. It looked for neither approval nor dispute. It carefully refrained from awakening the instincts but just stated facts as candidly as a statistician:

"Australian sources report that agreements were signed in Hong Kong yesterday for the sale of new season's wheat to mainland China. Contracts to an estimated value of ninety million dollars were exchanged between representatives of the Peking Government and members of the Australian Wheat Board.

"India's food situation is now more difficult than at the height of last year's food shortage when only a huge flood of grain from the United States and elsewhere saved India from widespread famine. Indian Food Ministry officials said yesterday that large imports were needed for the coming year, but prospects were uncertain because the United States' reserves had dropped to a low level. The Ministry added that India was not able to buy grain because of foreign exchange difficulties. It is estimated that if these difficulties cannot be overcome some sixty million Indians face a lengthy period of starvation.

"World heavyweight champion Cassius Clay . . ."

At the click of the switch I looked up and saw the professor walk away. I followed him out of the sitting room, then went down into the street to watch the people at their exercises.

Later in the morning Miss Ping took me to the Museum of the Revolution. Organizationally this was a nuisance to the Luhsingshe officials because our party had already spent two hours there, this being the time set aside in our schedule. But the Chinese (even the Communist Chinese) are polite, and when I said that I had found it fascinating and would like to make myself still more familiar in detail with the separate phases of China's revolutionary history, there was consultation and it was arranged that while the rest of our party visited the Ming tombs I might go again to the museum, accompanied by Miss Ping, to indulge what was already recognized as an idiosyncratic obsession with informational minutiae.

"This Willimus is an intellectual," said Tai reverently. But Ping pouted, unimpressed until Feng said a trifle impatiently that she ought to be happy to help a foreign guest get closer to the truth about the revolution, for mainly by such means would the filthy lies of the capitalist press be exposed and shown up and the facts of China's bitter history of suffering made known to the peace-loving but misled masses of the West.

So we went together in a taxi, and although she seemed moody and sat as far from me as she comfortably could, studying her Guide's Primer and dubiously consulting with the driver, in Chinese, I felt that her trouble was worry rather than pique or bad manners. For constant striving to be worthy of a place, however humble, within the inner family of the Communist elect can be a strain on postulants who feel handicapped (as Tai does with his capitalist father) or intellectually inadequate, as is apparently the case with little Ping; and it seemed to me that this visit to the museum, without an experienced leader, was causing her anxiety and embarrassment since her detailed knowledge of the political and military history of the revolution might likely be less than mine.

But reaching the museum, we saw among many groups gathered on the steps, below lofty square stone columns, awaiting their turn to go in, a bunch of about one hundred children led by a slim and brisk young man, and with him three women teachers to help keep them together. I made signs that I would like to attach to his party, and when with nods and smiles he seemed to agree, I said to Ping that we should simply follow along with these children and that she should translate for me whatever he said to them.

And this we did.

CHAPTER

7

THEY were small children from a junior school, boys and girls of between ten and twelve wearing the red scarves of Young Pioneers. Together we flocked into the entrance hall, some of the youngsters looking back curiously until the women teachers hissed at them, then frowned at me for being a distraction. We entered the vestibule, past a plaster bust of Mao Tse-tung set in a bower of ferns and flowers; then an annex, high and square, with four red pillars, two banks of red banners, and one red wall upon which is written in letters of gold, and in Mao's calligraphy, his proclamation of the founding of the Republic.

There are eighteen galleries in the revolutionary museum, each containing relics, mementos, declarations, documents, photographs, newspaper clippings, models, maps, sculptures, and paintings of consecutive phases of the revolution, beginning with the early struggles of peasants and workers against the tail end of the Manchu dynasty and the traitorous Kuomintang and concluding with the defeat of Chiang Kai-shek.

This official panorama of liberation begins with the nineteenth-century invasions of China and violations of Chinese rights, first by Britain in the unbelievably hypocritical and callous opium wars, and later by other foreign powers, including the U.S. and Russia, seeking to achieve commercial and missionary advantage from the resultant disruption and degradation of Chinese life.

66

These blatant foreign invasions, opposed with pathetic futility by the Manchus, demonstrated to Chinese intellectuals and peasants alike that the dynasty was no longer able to defend the nation, maintain its dignity, or keep it inviolate or intact.

The discovery triggered off a traditional uprising aimed at displacing the ineffectual dynasty and replacing it with another; but there was a curious and untraditional aspect of this Taiping uprising in that its leader was a self-styled Christian by the name of Hung, who read the Bible, had visions, and although unbaptized, named himself the "Younger Brother of Jesus Christ."

Nothing should have been more exciting to Christendom than the prospect of a Chinese Christian king—an event to be compared only with the conversion of Constantine—and although Hung's lack of baptism was a stumbling block and scandal to rigid Christians, and especially to the Western missionaries, there surely would have been little difficulty, given patience and good intent, in getting this Bible-reading visionary to submit to christening. History provides ample precedent of pagan kings becoming by this means impeccable patrons and even titular leaders of the church.

But in addition to Hung's doubtful orthodoxy, which put the missionaries in a cleft stick, he also showed evidence of secular heretical tendencies in that he believed in the emancipation of women, the common ownership of property, and some form of crop-sharing and land redistribution.

In the light of this vexing combination of sectarian and secular heresies it seemed to Western missionaries, diplomats, and merchants alike that a decadent Manchurian monarch, easily manipulated, was a safer investment than a zealous and probably interfering, unpredictable Christian king.

So reluctantly they gave aid to the dynasty against the prophet Hung and sent troops against him under American and English generals. In a matter of ten years the uprising was put down. Then the Western gentlemen began to divide China and Southeast Asia, thus paving the way for today's confusions in Vietnam and other places.

Whether or not the brisk young man with his white wand, pointing to pictures of Hung, the revolutionary Christian, and Gordon, the gentle English general who defeated him, made all this clear to the children I have no way of knowing, for all that

67

Ping could tell me was that when these poor peasants rose against the wicked Manchu monarchs they were put down ruthlessly by foreign imperialists and missionaries who killed forty million Chinese: the kind of confused simplification which becomes a myth within a decade, history in the course of a generation, and a continuing source of mischief thereafter, until some other prodigal horror supersedes it in immediate significance.

Yet speculatively it seemed to me, as we moved into the next gallery, that in spite of incompleteness and distortion there was still something of a lesson to be learned from this simplified story of an episode in China's history; that what had been a regular national uprising with novel and exotic overtones of Christian teaching was, in fact, the beginning of a critical phase of change in China's evolution out of feudalism into the world of modern technology and politics; that with clearer vision, and less concern with expediency and stiff-necked dogma, the Christian West might have outflanked history a hundred years ago and made friends with China in the name of an accommodating Christ instead of driving it irrevocably, stuffed with bitter enmity, into the arms of Karl Marx.

Meanwhile, Miss Ping, becoming bolder and putting her Guide's Primer under her arm, addressed me directly. "Our children must never forget the long and bitter revolutionary struggle for national liberation and freedom from corrupt rulers which began with these uprisings and continued for a hundred years until the Chinese people, under the leadership of the Party and the guidance of Chairman Mao, achieved final victory and liberation."

I said, "That was very good, but you forgot the foreign despots."

She blushed and, opening the book again, held it closely to her shortsighted eyes and after a few moments said, "Ah, yes, corrupt rulers and foreign despots. Thank you for helping me. Mutual criticism and correction are a necessary part of education."

I suddenly felt proud of her, and warm inside, because I knew now that, given time, we would become friends.

So we went from gallery to gallery with the children, standing behind them when they sat on the floor before some painting or display, and following on as they filed past particular exhibits.

I very much doubt if the dates, names, and statistics that Ping

68

gave me and which I wrote in my notebook that day are accurate, nor do I think it of overmuch account whether they are or not, for I am not writing history but trying to hold my thumb on the pulse of a people of whom I am told by my own leaders to be afraid. I am trying to see their world and my world through their eyes, and to write down what I believe I can see from where they stand. For their view is important to all of us.

And the eyes I try to see through are the eyes of people like little Ping and the children and the brisk young man with the white wand, people who are much like most of us. People who like to hold hands and share good things when they are able and, if it is sometimes necessary, things which are not so good. People who are keen to see each other happy and are prepared to advance halfway toward achieving this; who can also move back at times to let others live whichever way they want, so long as they don't leave too big a stink.

I speak, as I have said, of Ping and the children and the brisk young man and me, and those like us of all creeds, colors, and countries who don't give a damn who runs what so long as it is run decently and with these important things chiefly in mind.

In a gallery which commemorates the beginnings of the Communist Party of China there are, as well as old photographs of the original committee members, pictures which show complementary events: student demonstrations in the Tien An Men, striking coal miners leaving the pits, and railway workers being beaten up by militarized police.

In this gallery the children sat wriggling on the floor, facing five fuzzy old photographs, the middle one of which depicted a lean, lugubrious, long-haired studious figure who bore no evident resemblance to China's present leader; but well before the young man with the stick indicated this picture the answer was fizzing on the children's lips, and discipline tested to the limit awaited with difficulty upon the inevitable question:

"Who is . . ."

"Chairman Mao." The shout drowned out the end of the question (no holy hush in this museum) and its echoes bounced back in overlapping leaps from far parts of the building. The young man beamed, and the three teachers bent their necks sentimentally above the seething children. It was touching but somewhat disconcerting to see children being stuffed with love like Peking ducks.

When the young man delivered a brisk instruction, they swiveled around quickly to face the opposite wall and a framed painting in which the setting was a railway station and the central figure a brave bare-chested man in chains, straining in the grip of two armed guards while his workmates stood aghast and women and children in the background cringed.

Clearly this man in chains was a hero. Of this there could be no doubt. The stamp of simple, selfless nobility marked him as one in the long line which led back to the anonymous man who first stood firm and defiant in the face of injustice. History has a long and indiscriminate list of them—symbols rather than people.

Again the flick of the white wand, the half-asked question, and the answer shouted out loud, "Lin Hsiang-chien."

I looked at Ping and she translated what the young man said:

"After the decay of the corrupt Manchu dynasty the foreign capitalists tightened their grip on China and with the help of gangsters and traitors took control of the mines, workshops, and railways, exploiting and persecuting the workers until they could stand it no longer and went on strike. Then the capitalists called on their friends the warlords, who sent soldiers to ruthlessly suppress the workers.

"They put the people's leaders in chains and tortured them, trying to break their spirit and make them give in and send the men back to work to make more profit for the foreign capitalists. But these heroes understood their duty to the revolution. They defied the imperialists and their jackals. When the warlord's lackey told Lin Hsiang-chien that he would be executed if he refused to send the men back to work, what did he say?"

Hands flew up. The young man pointed dramatically at a little girl who stood up and recited:

"You may cut off my head, but you cannot kill my spirit."

We nodded approvingly, the three lady teachers, Miss Ping, and me. But the brisk young man tapped with his white wand and, scrambling to their feet, the children moved toward the next room. Fifty women from a textile factory came in at the far door to take our places, facing the photograph of Mao and his friends on the original committee. When we entered the next gallery the tail end of a file of young soldiers was just leaving.

Every day in similar museums all over China, seven hundred million people are being consecutively and systematically fed this historical point of view.

Following behind the children, I was aware of this—aware, also, that I was being contaminated. But it did not matter any more. I had been brainwashed since the very first day I went to school. Perhaps even before that. Nothing, now, could change my conviction that every race under the sun (whatever its many merits) was, in total, inferior to my own, that my country was incapable of sin, that there was no god but our god and my leader was his prophet even when he was wrong. I realized, too, that it was very necessary to believe all this in order to survive, to have identity and peace of mind.

We stood around a display case and in question and answer enumerated the contents.

"What are these?"

"Handcuffs."

"Why are they here?"

"To remind us of the suffering of the workers."

Leg irons, heavy chains, straitjackets, cudgels, truncheons, and whips came within this catechism. Then on the other side of the gallery we gathered round a portable gallows "capable of hanging two men at once." Alongside were pictures of workers' and peasants' leaders, all Communists, who had been hanged upon it. It was a cumbersome piece of equipment, made in Birmingham in 1927. A phrase from the Te Deum came into my mind, "The noble army of martyrs praise Thee."

"Who used these things against the workers?"

"The traitor Chiang Kai-shek."

Standing beside the gallows and looking out over us, our young leader said sternly, "Never forget, there is no progress without struggle." The children at the back, near to me, whispered. The women, making clicking noises with their tongues, hissed and herded us on.

Not far from the gallows was a black umbrella, shabby and badly rolled. I was foolish enough to give way to humor and ask Ping, "Did you, too, have a Chamberlain?"

71

She looked blank, then suspicious, and I knew that I had blundered and might easily lose the ground gained today in our relationship, for Miss Ping did not care for jokes about the revolution.

Anxiously I explained, feigning innocence. "We had a Mr. Chamberlain, who was a great statesman and carried an umbrella."

But she was not deceived and said peevishly, "You would not wish me to tease you about Jesus." This confused me. Then, her sense of duty getting the better of resentment, she said, "This umbrella was used by the Red Army."

Fleetingly I could see a million men crouched under this inadequate umbrella, but was aware of Miss Ping watching for the slightest sign of undisciplined wit, so I bent down to peer at the ticketed inscription and, finding it, asked her to translate, which she did grudgingly because her myopia made it difficult and she was still not convinced of my interest.

"A Party member, disguised as a capitalist, carried this umbrella as a badge of bourgeoise respectability to disguise his true activity of distributing revolutionary pamphlets at the Shanghai railway station. He was betrayed and hanged."

I saw him vividly, as in a movie, the crowds hurrying all around him like a river in flood; could hear the hiss and pant and the tooting of impatient railway engines waiting to take people away, the Kuomintang agents watching everybody except the apparently respectable gentleman with the umbrella surreptitiously slipping seditious pamphlets into the hands of shifty-eyed conspirators. And I was sorry that this baggy black umbrella was not adequate to protect him from the bankers in London and Manhattan.

Round about that time, five hundred miles inland and high in the mountains, another revolutionary sat on a gray stone, thinking. Every evening this man went back to his room in the village to write, far into the night. What he wrote can now be read in *The Selected Works of Mao Tse-tung* under such headings as: "Questions of Political Power," "Questions of Party Organization," "The Question of the Character of Revolution."

In the museum there is a picture of him sitting on the stone, and as we entered the gallery (which is dedicated to the Long March of the Red Army) he seemed to be looking down at us from the mountainside. When we were all in the center of this gallery the children squatted down in front of a great glass dia-grammatic map, while the brisk young man took hold of a device which permitted him to illuminate different areas of the map as he spoke.

When he mentioned Mao a red star flickered on the map to mark the spot where he sat on the stone and the village where he wrote at night. Then at a word we all looked up at the painting and saw that Mao was watching us, lonely but full of love—a man born to stand apart, to be a leader of his people.

Miss Ping's eyes glistened behind her thick spectacles.

The Red Army broke out of these mountains to begin the Long March, and all around this gallery are lifelike models of the many incidents which have since become legends of the Liberation and the dramatic matter of epic poems, plays, books, music, operas, and children's games: crossing the Yangtze, climbing the high passes in midwinter, the battles and ambushes, the acts of heroism, and the grim disasters.

Yet for me the next gallery seemed to be more dramatic and more real. This is the gallery which deals with the Japanese inva-sion of 1937.

The central exhibit here is a model village in which the people lived two lives: one above ground and the other in a honeycomb of tunnels. Looking at it, I immediately thought of Vietnam; of invading strangers fighting against a country and its people both.

Each house in this miniature village is linked by tunnels, the entrances to which are hidden under water jars, ovens, beds, and cesspits. Bolt holes and ways of escape begin or end in pigpens, manureheaps, hayricks, or partway down wells and in irrigation ditches. Stone walls are shown to be hideouts for snipers. Hidden pits are man-traps lined with bamboo knives. Children innocently flying kites are primed to trigger off mines.

I felt sorry for today's soldiers in Vietnam, Americans and my own countrymen, having to fight such a combination without quite knowing why.

We moved on, following the white wand until we stopped at the statue of a small boy. The children pressed around possessively.

"Who is this?"

"Wang Po." Miss Ping, beside me, added her different whisper to the children's shout, then said, "Wang Po is their own little hero, a true Young Pioneer. From the beginning of the revolution our children were part of the freedom army. They found food for the soldiers. They were messengers and spies, using their young eyes to find the enemy when even our best soldiers could not see him."

The statue of Wang Po is backed by a pattern of photo enlargements. One shows Chairman Mao leaning down to speak to children who are gathering kindling sticks under a tree.

"Our leader loves the children of China and has always been proud of his Young Pioneers."

In another of these pictures a Red Army soldier is teaching village children to read.

"Before liberation there were no schools for the children of poor people, but the Red Army taught them in the fields, so that they learned to read and write and to love the Party."

In a glass showcase there are a few pieces of flat sandstone, some rock chips, and bits of stick, which Ping said are souvenirs of Wang Po, who was shot by the Japanese when he was thirteen years old.

"That flat piece of sandstone was his slate, and to write his lessons he scratched on it with the rock chips. The crooked stick was his pistol, and the piece of round wood was a make-believe grenade which he threw at the enemy when the children played at defending their village against the Japanese."

"Why did the Japanese shoot him?"

I did not really want to ask the question because I knew the answer, even though I had not heard of Wang Po before this moment. I knew indeed why he had been shot, and why other children, women, old people, invalids, and even heroes will continue to be shot or otherwise disposed of generation after generation, in war after war, in incident after incident. They will be shot or bombed or burned to death because, as we become more and more civilized, our awareness of shame becomes so great that we must in anger and frustration scrape the very bottom of the barrel of fear and hate, scarify our consciences, then face ourselves defiantly and say, "It is not our fault for we are as He made us. Let Him take the blame."

Miss Ping said severely, "They shot him because he would not tell them where the soldiers were hiding. They hurt him first and then, when he wouldn't tell, they shot him to make the other children frightened."

It is simple for Miss Ping. She is not yet aware that we are all insane.

Not far from us, in the same gallery, two Japanese visitors were standing with their guide. As we left them I wondered what he was saying and whether or not they felt any shame.

In the last gallery the central exhibit is a faded red flag with the five stars of the Republic stitched to it. Miss Ping said that it was carried on the Long March and that the stars were sewn on to the banner when the Red Army took Peking. But she was vague and the story did not convince me.

We had now been walking through the museum for two hours and a half, and the children looked tired, but at the tap of the white wand they, the three teachers, and Miss Ping stiffened and fixed their eyes on this tattered flag while the brisk young man stood ramrod straight and spoke into space, over the heads of the children:

"The red scarf of the Young Pioneers which each one of you wears is a corner torn from the flag of the Chinese People's Republic. It is red with the blood of many revolutionary martyrs. You must always wear it proudly and never forget the past, the Party, and our dear Chairman Mao, who saved you."

They sang the "Internationale," then filed out quietly past another red wall bearing this message:

CARRY THE STRUGGLE THROUGH TO THE END

When we came to our taxi the driver was asleep, stretched out on the seat. Mao's little red book of quotations lay on his chest, rising and falling as he breathed.

For dinner there was caviar, eggplant with a wine sauce, pigeon casseroled with chilies, and chicken Kiev on golden-fried bread. The professor's wife read letters from home while we ate.

The professor was saying, "The provision of sanctified heroes for everyone, such as those you have seen in the museum, is part of the Communist technique of political and social cohesion borrowed from the Christians, and for the time being it is the key

75

activity of the Cultural Revolution. Each section of the community is being systematically provided with its own identifiable hero, beatified by the Party."

His wife said, "Marta and Paul both have the measles and Axel has taken the baby away to the farm until they are over them."

"Ah so! The baby will get them just the same." He turned back to the pigeon and, sucking a leg bone, continued to speak. "Nowhere else, at the moment, is this principle of folk-hero orientation being so diligently applied as part of a national policy. The Russians, who began it after their own revolution, have now grown past the kindergarten stage of national re-creation, and although Christian-culture states still have their sentimental calendars of saints, these delightful creatures are functionally out of date and have been replaced by secular stereotypes created by the advertising and entertainment industries."

His wife refolded the first letter and slit open another, then looked at his plate. "My dear, you talk too much. The chili is delicious and you let it get cold. Good food is wasted on you."

He took up a spoon, and when the dish was clean he pushed it to one side and wiped his lips. "After you have been here longer and traveled more widely in China you will have collected the full catalogue of the new revolutionary characters. The worker martyr and guerrilla peasant, the noble young soldier and the iron man of the tractor factory, the heroic schoolboy and the dedicated female teacher. These and dozens of others, inspired to selfless deed of social heroism through grace gained by studying the works of Chairman Mao."

The chicken came and was dealt with in respectful silence; but afterward, in the sitting room, while his wife answered their mail and we sipped brandy, he continued his commentary upon my visit to the Museum of the Revolution. And later, in my own room, I wrote down as much of it as I could remember.

His opinion was that just as the new group of tangible folk figures has become an adequate and acceptable replacement for the banished fairies, household gods, and heavenly spirits of old China, so the Communist system itself, for most of the people, is a satisfactory and understandable replica of the old dynastic structure of society and government.

76

A god-man and his party hierarchy reign in the Forbidden City in place of a divine emperor and his princes. The social philosophy of Marx has supplemented that of Confucius, and Party cadres do the work of the old scholar functionaries. To the mass of the people this broad structure of society and authority is recognizably familiar and traditional. A major variation is that this will continue, which is something quite new in Chinese history.

Equally unusual is the fact that after three thousand years of introspective isolation, China's new-style rulers are now leading their people into an area of international political activity within which they have had minimal experience—an area within which philosophical loquacity, however apt, has no immediately practical value; within which a missionary obsession (Communist or any other) is ineffectual unless backed by overwhelming technical strength.

This present clamorous and uncharacteristic missionary zeal is China's serious weakness (as it was Indonesia's). It is, perhaps, the one new factor, introduced by communism, that is not yet set into sensible perspective. For although China has accomplished wonders in most fields of domestic development, and may honestly believe that to the politically pure in heart all things are possible, it is not yet ready to engage in power games in which both the U.S.A. and Russia play against her.

Not yet!

Peking gossip ascribes two relevant assessments of this situation to Chairman Mao Tse-tung. The first is that the U.S.A. is at present able to destroy within three hours all that China has achieved in the eighteen years since liberation. The second is that within fifteen, given peace, China would be able to retaliate.

We had talked of these things over our brandy (the professor and I) and agreed that, insofar as history can be a guide, the problem for China is to avoid a destructive struggle for power when the present regime passes (as it soon must) between the army and any new and truly fanatical revolutionary group using students as its spearhead and foundation.

"These matters affect China itself more than any other country, but there is danger for everyone in such situations."

The professor had looked dubious. "One can only pray that all who now possess great power will keep in mind that political in-trigues are paid for with lives, and that the future of mankind is of more consequence than the ambitions of great statesmen.

"None of us should want to see Peking's Gate of Heavenly Peace a heap of rubble—remembering that in the past century it is we of the West who have bent history into its present grotesque and dangerous shape."

Part
Two

If by consequence of some internal
upheaval I came to lose successively my faith
in Christ, my faith in a personal God, my
faith in the Spirit, it seems to me that I
should continue to believe in the World.
The World (the value, the infallibility and
the goodness of the World): such in the final
analysis is the first and the only thing in
which I believe. It is by this faith that I
live, and it is to this faith, I feel, that at
the moment of dying I shall, above all doubts,
abandon myself. . . .
To this confused faith in a World, one and
infallible, I abandon myself, wherever it may
lead me.

Pierre Teilhard de Chardin
Comment je crois.

CHAPTER

8

WHEN I said that I wished to visit the city of Chengchow, which is three hundred miles south of Peking on the main railway line, there was a long and doubtful silence. Then Wang asked why, and I explained that I would like to see where the railway workers' strike had been organized in 1923 and perhaps talk to people who had taken part in it. For it seemed to me, after my visit to the museum with little Ping, that this was a key event in the history of the revolution.

Being a writer, I said, some firsthand contact with such people and their environment seemed essential if I hoped to achieve anything more significant than a vague and sentimental sympathy with the Chinese, or to gain any understanding of the reality of the bitter struggle by which the Party had liberated them from the tyranny of corrupt rulers, foreign despots, reactionary capitalists, etc.

I said all this frankly, without smiling, knowing that the use of these familiar and ritual phrases would simplify the processing of my request. I also knew that no official would be fooled into believing that fluent use of the jargon marked me as a genuine revolutionary or an earnest convert to Peking communism, since my application for a visa had stated clearly that I was Catholic and under contract to a U.S. publisher. But it would be clear that I had accepted as fundamental to any discussion of China the validity of this official Chinese point of view.

Wang went dubiously to see his superiors and came back surprised and smiling to say that permission had been given for me to break away from the group itinerary for three days and to make a detour which would take in Chengchow, then link me back with the party at Soochow. He said, also, that as the professor and his wife were going in the same direction to visit the ancient city of Loyang, we would travel by the same train and that Feng could go with us.

When we left next day young Tai came to the station to say good-by and before we parted sang with me the Irish rebel hymn, "Faith of Our Fathers," with which, by diligent repetition, we had doubled his Western repertoire and provided revolutionary balance for his other number, "Silent Night."

Now we came into the huge main marble hall of the railway station, making our way around a fountain and banks of flowers before mounting the wide stairway, letting Feng tell us of escalators and elevators used mainly by old folk, of the seventeen waiting rooms—some set aside, together with nursery and play space, for mothers and their babies. He smiled, delighted to be able to point out that any traveler could use the bathrooms, restaurants, reading rooms, and the cinema. He said that forty thousand passengers passed through the station daily, then showed us how to obtain train information from a central bureau simply by standing before a wall panel and asking questions, the answers coming back directly through small loudspeakers.

As with the Great Hall of the People and other new public buildings, the construction of the railway station was bustled along by tens of thousands of voluntary laborers, many of them coming to Peking as work teams to represent their provinces, so that the whole was completed in less than eight months.

The stationmaster, train guard, and an official from the Cultural Relations office then came to take us to our places on the train. The coach attendant and train chef were presented. We shook hands. Music played as we stood waving at the windows, watching people on the platform slide by.

We had been sitting for less than five minutes when the coach attendant came with a button in the hollow of his hand, saying that it had been picked up in the corridor and probably belonged to one of us. When it was found to have come from the professor's shirtfront his wife clicked her tongue and seemed ashamed, but the coach attendant straightaway took a small tin from the pocket of his blue cotton coat and, picking out needle and thread, sat beside the professor and sewed the button back. Then he went away smiling and came again within a matter of minutes with tea.

"It is," said the professor's wife, "exceedingly difficult to dislike these people."

The trains have three kinds of accommodation: hard, medium, and soft. *Hard* has plain wooden benches. *Medium* is also bare but lined with tiers of bunks so that passengers may stretch out. *Soft* is comfortably upholstered, solidly refined and old-fashioned, with lace antimacassars, curtains, potted plants, and brass ashtrays; but each coach or compartment, soft or hard, is fitted with loudspeakers through which an incessant flow of revolutionary instruction, information, and culture (originating from tapes in the train guard's office) clamors breathlessly. Only in sleeper compartments can it be switched off or the volume controlled, except by the coach attendant. Elsewhere eager insistence is inescapable and, for foreign guests, exasperating.

We were the only Westerners on the train, though Feng said that there were members of a North Korean delegation in our compartment. The rest of the soft-class passengers were Chinese, mostly cadres and other officials holding senior jobs, or private citizens of means.

In a while I went walking, leaving the professor deep in a catalogue of antiquities, his wife nodding, half asleep, with knitting lying slackly on her lap, and Feng playing Chinese chess with a friend he had met. As I passed them he looked up, anxious in case I lacked something, but when I said that I only wanted to wash my hands he seemed satisfied and went back to the game.

Near the end of the coach two men, sitting together and dressed elegantly in Western fashion, looked up and smiled, and seeing me hesitate, one of them patted the seat beside him. So I sat and talked with them, finding that one was a Shanghai businessman who had been sick while visiting in Peking and that his companion was a physician from Hong Kong who had come to see and treat him and was now going back through Canton.

When I looked puzzled and said that to a foreigner this seemed a strange situation, he smiled and explained that he was one of China's officially recognized national capitalists, of whom there were almost a million, and that he was an expert and international dealer in jewelry and precious stones.

He said that the Government, wishing to make use of his special knowledge and foreign trade associations, allowed him to continue in business, though under supervision, so that he earned a great deal more money than any member of the Communist ruling group; so much so that he was easily able to arrange and pay for his Hong Kong doctor friend to visit him.

Then seeing me still dubious, he said that his case was by no means unique. In Shanghai, Canton, and other cities, where foreign business contacts had been centered in the old days, many people of his kind continued to live comfortably and according to their customary standards. They were allowed comparatively high wages, dividends, and rents or profit percentages from enterprises which they formerly owned and were still permitted to operate as individuals, though more or less on behalf of the State, and could invest their excess money in interest-bearing government bonds.

He spoke almost jokingly. "Westerners are sympathetic. It is their nature to be more concerned with the suffering of foreign people, rich and poor, than with the troubles of their own underprivileged. In the old days your missionaries went begging for pennies among Sunday school children to help save us heathen Chinese from sin, while your traders and speculators were stripping us to the skin."

The physician, facing his friend, shook his head and said that this was a grotesque and too simple view of history; and when they had bickered back and forth a little the capitalist admitted that things were not entirely heavenly or very much better, if at all, than they used to be for people of his class and kind.

"Yet when you think back on our history and understand that the whole compelling incentive of the Communist revolution was directed against a ruling partnership of foreign investors and us who were rich, those of us who stayed here are perhaps lucky not to have been liquidated.

"Meanwhile it's true that we cannot leave China, or do business without the supervision of a Party cadre, but neither may anyone else do these things without permission. And on the whole we capitalists still live comfortably and lack for little except complete freedom, which is a scarce commodity in most other countries today."

He flicked open a slim cigarette case and proferred it and, looking up, must have seen that I seemed surprised by his plain speaking, for he smiled and nodded toward the loudspeaker, indicating that its clatter was adequate cover for frankness.

"I confess that I don't particularly like communism and I hope that one day we will outgrow it. But Western hypocrisy, and the ignorance of our old rulers and our wealthy men, made its victory not only inevitable but necessary for China's survival as an independent nation."

He spoke openly, saying that most of the extravagantly rich families and thousands of business people, including many of his friends and relatives, went with Chiang Kai-shek into exile, though these were for the most part people who had been educated in the West, or by missionaries, and represented a small proportion even of the upper classes.

The rest of the moderately rich had carefully considered the uncertain prospects of a decent existence under communism and, weighing these against current corruption and the gangster habits of the Kuomintang, had found in favor of taking a chance with the Red regime, which seemed to offer, on its record in the provinces during twenty years of civil and international war, at least the possibility of honest and objective government.

I was thinking as I listened that this was no new story. In every century people have had to decide whether they would stay in one place or emigrate to escape uncertainty, persecution, or radical change. Within the past two centuries both America and my own country have been largely populated by families who left Europe, wishing to keep their beliefs or their money, or because they saw more chance of living in dignity and security, with better opportunities for themselves and their children in these other countries.

So we agreed that people have been changing places in this way since time began, and that there is nothing historically strange or particularly scandalous in the fact that a few million Chinese did decide that they would feel safer and happier out of Communist range. But he thought that those who stayed behind were, perhaps, happier in their hearts than those who had gone away.

I must have looked unconvinced for he faced me squarely and said, "Perhaps you feel that this song of the bad old days is monotonous and overdone"—the physician nodded—"but it was sung long before liberation, even by foreigners. The American General Stillwell, who came here to help us fight the Japanese, put it in a book. He said that under Chiang Kai-shek we could only expect greed, corruption, favoritism, more taxes, inflation, waste of life, and a disregard for the rights of ordinary men. He told the U.S. Government that the mass of the Chinese people would welcome the Communists as their hope of relief; and he was correct in this.

"In his book he tells what President Roosevelt said about American investors in China; how Roosevelt's grandfather came here in 1829 and made a million dollars, and came back again in 1856 and made another million. So you see, we did have something to complain about long before the Communists took over, and so far none of us has suffered very much under their regime."

We were quiet for a while, watching through the oblong window, seeing the ancient land unroll like a scroll embroidered with traditional Chinese scenes caught briefly: a lad walking endlessly in one spot on a little treadmill, lifting gouts of brown water out of a ditch and into a field of beans; a squat girl with a stick, watching pigs graze on the edge of a river; students cycling in a cavalcade, going along a yellow road toward a commune to help with some project; ducks splashing in a puddle left by last night's rain; then, on the fringe of a village, gravestones almost hidden by ripening wheat.

"You see, there is nothing wasted today. In some places the dead have been collected and buried together, but the people of these villages still have respect for their ancestors and let them lie in what were once their own fields. But they grow grain on their graves, and when the memorial stones fall they will take them home and perhaps build them into a courtyard wall."

I said I thought it strange that people with a legendary respect for ancient ways should submit so eagerly to the disciplines of communism, but he shook his head.

"You must remember that we Chinese have no real tradition of individual freedom in the Western sense, nor of a personal salvation through any form of religious mystical belief. We have always been submissive to the will of the family and clan or community, so that there is no real problem for us in adapting to this new communal system of society and government."

But his friend, still skeptical, said that in general terms he might be right but the fact remained that many people felt hedged about and resentful of the disciplines and restrictions. Nor was there any real assurance of personal security for anyone if the regime should change its tactics later on.

"Neither you nor anyone else on this train would have courage enough to ask the attendant to turn the loudspeakers down, however much they might like to." He shookd his head. "As for the family tradition, your own children feel embarrassed by your capitalist status and uncomfortable about your money. They learn daily to hate all that you stand for and have more respect and affection for Chairman Mao than they have for you. You'll be lonely in your old age unless you give way and completely reject your own personality."

I remembered then young Tai, ashamed of his capitalist father, and felt sorry for this rich man and his predicament, for he seemed a very pleasant fellow; and there was an undertone of resignation when he said that he had no choice but to make the best of his situation, though he still insisted that he had little cause to complain.

"True, I'm not trusted and am regarded officially as a class enemy, and so watched closely. But whereas in the old days my family was cheated by every official, and milked of its money in bribes and commissions, and none of us was safe from thugs and bandits, we no longer have these worries. Whatever the future might have in store, I am not afraid today, either for myself or my children."

When I asked about his children he said that he had three. The eldest, a boy, had gone to work on a pioneer forestation project in a remote part of northwest China and would be away for three years. The second, a girl, was studying medicine and lived in a hostel attached to the provincial hospital and medical school where she did her training. The youngest, also a girl, was still at middle school and lived at home. Her present ambition was to join a traveling cultural team and tour the far western provinces, but first she had to gain admittance to the Conservatory of Music and Drama in Shanghai for a three-year course of study.

I said that there seemed to be no active discrimination against him or his children because of family background, at which he smiled wryly.

"Human nature doesn't change, so there are still officials who make things difficult, but I yet have to deal with a Communist who is clearly dishonest. And although my thinking has been re-molded to the satisfaction of the authorities I will never be a Party member, though I am on several official committees which deal with foreign trade and currency exchange and am still allowed to live in my own house.

"On the other hand, some of my old friends have been a little obstinate and slow to learn and are working out their problems in some commune, or in a factory. A man who was my close friend at school is now a laborer on an irrigation project in Mongolia. Maybe when he learns to cooperate he will be allowed to come back to Shanghai and take his place on the management commit-tee of the textile factory which his family used to own."

Then, as if putting an end to the conversation, he said, "The main thing for all foreigners to understand is that whatever claim Mao and the Party might make on our behalf as devoted followers of Marx, the fact of the matter is that we are nothing of the kind. We older Chinese are Nationalist and patriots, and if some of us still don't altogether like this present way of life, we still prefer it to having our country run by foreigners."

Feng came looking for me and, finding me content to sit awhile with these two men, he introduced himself and took the other vacant seat. So we talked about my trip and what I hoped to see; and when I said that I was looking forward especially to the Shanghai Spring Festival of music the rich man said he hoped that we would meet there.

Then we came to a station, and Feng and I left them.

People on the platform were doing exercises or walking quietly up and down to stretch their legs. Some were washing at stone troughs while others clustered around food vendors, reaching over each other with money to buy balls of steamed bread, pieces of pork or chicken, eggs and fruit. The coach attendants with buckets and long-handled brushes cleaned down the outside of the train, as they do at every major stopping place.

An old man in blue cotton tunic and baggy black pants, standing alone and leaning on a stick, seemed familiar, but when I asked if we had seen him elsewhere, Feng shrugged and asked how this could be, since the old one was clearly a peasant and I had not yet been to the countryside.

Then a young man with a simple, round flat face, wearing white cap and armband, went to him with food, and as the old man took it I remembered and said to Feng that I had seen him in the Forbidden City in Peking.

When we were on our way again we went through the train and found this old man in a hard-class compartment where the people, though crowded and cluttered with packages and bundles, made room for us and seemed amused that I had seen him in Peking and should want to know more about him now.

His name, they said (many speaking at once so that at first we couldn't catch it), was Han Tung-wen, and when Feng had quietened them they watched while I wrote it in my notebook, smiling and nudging at each other, cracking little jokes and wagging their fingers at Han, who sat completely still, as only old people can, all except the young round-faced man with the cap and armband who had brought food for him at the station and now looked nervous and uncertain, plucking the old man's sleeve and whispering at him until Feng, noticing, spoke to them both.

I said, "Is something wrong?"

Feng shook his head. "No, it's all right. The young man is a relative and a policeman in the commune where they live. He has been looking after him in Peking. They are not used to speaking to foreign guests and the young man does not want him to get into trouble. It is nothing. I have explained that you are a friend and that I will be responsible."

They all watched. Only the old man seemed unimpressed and,

when I spoke to him through Feng, answered my questions readily and without embarrassment while the others nodded and prompted, finding his story fitting, bit by bit, into a pattern familiar to all of them.

He was seventy and lived in a commune called Kuo Hsing, which is not far from Chengchow, in the valley of the Yellow River. He had been a peddler from boyhood until six years ago when the commune committee retired him with a small pension.

He lived with his wife in the village house in which his father had lived before him (though it was then owned by a landlord) and shared it with his wife's widowed sister and a son who was married and had two children.

He sat, completely relaxed and self-contained, the center of attention, smoking a thin-stemmed pipe with a tiny metal bowl no bigger than a nut; untroubled, his eyes focused far away as though looking beyond life. Only when I asked about the old days did he look directly at me or show any emotion, and even then, though the others were suddenly animated, he spoke calmly and without resentment.

"In the old days worry was always on our back. Each morning a man got off his bed to begin a new struggle to keep out of debt, yet feed his family. There was never enough to eat. Nothing to spare for feasts.

"Every day, while it was still dark, I used to take up my baskets and shoulder pole and set out to go around the villages or to the market towns. Sometimes I stayed away for many weeks before I could earn enough money to pay the rent. If times were very bad I took my wife and children with me to other provinces to look for work in the countryside. Many times we lived in the fields or in the streets of villages where we had no friends or relations.

"But now we have no worry. We live in our house and pay no rent. The commune gives us food and I look after the children of my son and my neighbors while they work. We eat soup and noodles every day, and sometimes chicken and pig."

Feng said, "We must go now. Maybe you can visit the old man and talk some more with him when we come to Chengchow."

He turned and spoke to Han and to the young man, who nodded and began to make some explanation in which others

90

joined, everyone anxious that Feng should have the correct information as to distance and direction and the name of the commune secretary.

"They say that his son is a cadre and would like you to visit their commune. But it must be arranged with the authorities in Chengchow. Now we must go back to our place on the train."

As we left I turned and called *Tsai-chien* (Good-by), which pleased them, though I was reluctant, and a little impatient with Feng for hurrying me away; and for coming behind me in high spirits as we went back through the coaches, saying, "You can see how the people of the countryside love the Party and dear Chairman Mao."

I SAT with Feng awhile watching the stroboscopic landscape unwind mile after mile of precisely lined fields of seedling cotton. Girls moved between the rows spraying with insecticides. Young men tended irrigation power pumps, each with a little temporary shelter beside it where the attendant might rest when on night shift. Power lines ran gridwise on sticks and saplings and, at intervals, there were clusters of lights rigged for night work, or for insect traps—all improvised. Other young men and girls brought domestic and farmyard manure in buckets or wheeled tubs; and on the horizon men plowed with oxen.

"When I was young," said Feng, "the village people carried images from the temples and walked around the fields, asking these images to kill the insects, or bring rain, or keep the river out of the crops. Now the peasants all study the works of dear Chairman Mao and so learn self-reliance. They take spray pumps and electricity into the fields instead of images, and the crops grow stronger than they did before."

He gave a shy, confiding smile that lit his face, erasing the mask of the cadre; and in place of a prematurely aging government functionary I saw, for a moment, a boy with shining eyes remembering lively days gone by.

"Do you come from these parts?" I asked.

He answered, "I was born over there, beyond where the men are plowing, where you can see a broken brown wall at the foot of the hill, when all this land was mostly owned by landlords.

"I was thirteen when the Japanese invaders came to our village. They said that the people had given food and shelter to Red Army men who had been fighting against them. They took away the young men and women and killed the old people and babies. They knocked them down with their rifles, then put the bayonet through their heads, all of the old people and babies."

He lifted his head and closed his eyes—no longer the ghost of a lively, smiling boy, but again the gray-faced, aging man with long, slim fingers resting on his knees. He raised one hand to his head and made sharp prodding gestures against his temple, screwing up his face in simulated pain. Then he continued with his tale.

"I was taken with other children to carry packs for the Japanese soldiers as they went toward Chengchow. My sister and her young friends were with us. After one day with the Japanese soldiers they took the girls away and we did not see each other until after liberation. My parents and relatives were sent to work in the coal mines and I did not see any of them again.

"It was hard for us small boys to be with the Japanese. They gave us too many things to carry and nothing to eat, and we thought that we would die. Soon I was thin like a stick and became very sick and could not go fast enough to keep up. A soldier beat me with his rifle and I cried.

"In the night I ran away. My friend Liu came with me and when we could go no longer we hid in a ditch. It was very cold, but when anyone came by we stayed under the water. Then I thought of my sister and was angry with the Japanese and forgot to be cold.

"When the enemy soldiers went away I walked for many days with my friend, trying to find the Peasants' and Workers' Red Army. Every village was empty and there was nothing to eat, only grass and bark from the trees, until we came into the hills and found some of our soldiers.

"I joined the Liberation Army and after the victory went to school again. Then to university to learn English so that I could become an interpreter for foreign guests like you."

He looked up suddenly and smiled his boyish smile again. But

93

his eyes, though bright, were wet, and the long, thin fingers resting on his knees were trembling like insects' wings. I would have put out my own hand to rest on his, offering friendship and affection, but held myself in check, afraid that he would be offended, this frail, gray, middle-aged man; this gentle Red with whom I had shared these strange, unsettling days of travel and discovery; this man who represented the dreadful enemy.

Afterward, when we had come to Chengchow, and I was in the hotel resting on my bed, I thought again of Feng and roughly reckoned how many tens of millions of men, women, and children in China have, like him, learned to read and write in the Red Army or since liberation; how many who, having been taught only the limited requisites of basic literacy in a crash campaign designed to teach workers and peasants to read and write a simplified idiom, are not able to read even the classics of their own rich literature, which is written in the scholastic language of preliberation. These several hundred millions (the majority of Chinese) who can read nothing but the new political literature of the revolution can know no other truths than those propounded by Mao Tse-tung and issued under the imprimatur of the Party—these truths which, though partly true, are yet untrue in that they admit of no other view of truth.

Good or bad?

Is it better to be able to read and write something, however one-sided, or not to be able to read and write at all?

Tired after a long day in the train, I found no answers, but understood, in part, why Feng and Wang and little Ping, and the other Chinese who were helping me, seemed to have limited views, simplified attitudes, and a small stock of ready-made answers and opinions derived from the editorials of the *People's Daily,* from the radio and the never-ending flow of "information" coming off tapes in trains, housing estates, factories, and all public places. And, of course, from the writings of Mao Tse-tung, which each of them carries.

Few have had any intellectual or educative experience outside this framework. The Party truth excludes all others and is infallible; and Mao is the benevolent, gentle, all-wise father figure who talks this truth. So when Feng speaks of "Dear Chairman Mao" his

94

sentiment is genuine. He is truly devoted to this idealistic image of his leader, just as a semi-educated Christian is devoted to the image of a benevolent, all-wise, all-loving father figure with white whiskers who lives up in the sky. Or of Jesus, the Good Shepherd, with a lost lamb (which is me) hung across his shoulders.

Indeed Feng, at this level of semi-awareness, reminds me of most of my own friends, except that many if not most of these have stopped believing in anything.

Feng spends an hour each morning reading Mao's works, finding in them answers to his problems. (With less faith, and diminishing hope, I dip each evening into Paul's epistle and go to sleep wondering what has happened to the charity he preaches.)

Each morning Feng greets me with what he calls "A New Truth," discovered in overnight study and discussion. Multiply Feng by an unknown number of Party members, cadres, functionaries, study leaders, teachers, advanced workers and aspirants, and the Mao cult is explicable as a period of intensive spiritual fervor and enthusiasm achieved during the adolescent stage of a nation's metamorphosis.

It is a moralistic stage and therefore dangerous, as are all moralistic fanaticisms whether secular, religious, or strictly political, and the more virulent when opposed from outside and their aggressive potential is consolidated and directed toward an alien enemy who can be identified with the devil. America today is busily (and I believe unnecessarily) building herself into this leading role not only in China but in most of Asia.

Two young bellboys came with tea.

"I'm afraid," said the professor, meeting me in the foyer later, "that we must deny ourselves the pleasure of your company this evening. We are being taken to dinner by the Director of Antiquities from the Honan Provincial Museum. They have been doing remarkable work in this area and I'm sure that it will be interesting"—he smiled at his wife "—though Lise thinks that we shall probably finish in a glass case labeled 'Rare Specimens of Western Imperialists.' "

So I ate alone and afterward Feng and two young men from the Travel Service took me to the movies.

A long and quarrelsome newsreel showed welfare workers in North Vietnam caring for refugee children from the south: some cute, some sad, some sick, some wounded (innocent victims of savage and ruthless U.S. imperialistic aggression). My two young men, in unison, aped the commentator's indignation while Feng gratefully rested.

Then we watched elderly peasants and workers in North Vietnam, assisted by their children, working night and day to offset destruction wrought by the U.S. aerial bandits, while determined young men and women practiced with rifles, bayonets, grenades, and machine guns to prepare themselves to resist further threats of U.S. escalation.

A montage of clips from foreign newsreels showed anti-U.S. demonstrations on five continents, finishing with scenes of armed civil guards in Chicago hunting down "Negro revolutionaries." (Bats flickered about the auditorium, throwing jagged shadows at the screen.)

Similar images (and often exactly these same shots) with almost identical comment will have been seen on television and in cinemas all over the world. Only the phrases are interchangeable. For "U.S. aggression" read "Communist menace." For "members of the liberation forces" use "subversive elements." For "revolutionaries" put "terrorists." The people and the pain are the same in each version. Only the labels change from day to day and from place to place.

At the interval, when I wrote notes, everybody watched, including a group of children who came close and stood looking at the foreigner until Feng, who had been dozing, awoke and sent them away.

I enjoyed the feature film, though the seats in the cinema were hard. The two young men translated the dialogue line by line (except in key parts where they became engrossed and left me fretting), outlined the characters and their motivations, explained the progressions of the plot, annoyingly anticipated dramatic action, and occasionally spat on the floor between their feet.

Afterward I wrote the following synopsis which I give in its completeness because this film is typical, in character and construction, of the twenty entertainment films I saw in Chinese cinemas (not counting newsreels, documentaries, technical and children's films).

Each dramatic film is cast with prototype characters lifted from the catalogue of contemporary Chinese life, ranging downward from Glorious Revolutionary Martyrs to misguided but ultimately redeemable reactionaries (only foreigners are incorrigibly villainous).

The characters are placed in a selected occupational situation and environmental framework, where they expose the essential and relevant conflict between the new and old "thinking" and act out solutions which follow acceptable patterns of Communist behavior. These films have most of the simple characteristics of conventional Western soap opera.

NOTE: Script, construction, general technique, and photography match average Western standards.

THE NEW PEDDLER

A film seen in the People's Municipal Cinema at Chengchow.

Length: One hour and ten minutes.

Theme: The commercial morality of Communists and the ethics of shopkeeping in rural communities.

Location: A small-town general store serving several mountain villages in a fruitgrowing district.

CHARACTERS:

HERO: A young store clerk recently returned from the city, where he has been attending a Study Conference on The Practical Application of the Works of Chairman Mao.

VILLAIN (local and nonmalignant): The store accountant who, though liberated, displays symptoms of lingering capitalistic thinking and chronic profit consciousness.

JUVENILE: A daydreaming junior store clerk who believes that his proper place is in a gunboat gallantly defending the Motherland from foreign aggression.

SEX: Represented by two diligent young female store clerks who use no makeup and study the works of Chairman Mao after

97

hours. They collectively support the hero with no hint of any biological motivation.

THE STORE MANAGER: An honest but confused fellow, age-mate and long-time crony of the accountant. He finds difficulty in resolving contradictions between running the store along lines of traditional profit-making efficiency and of meeting the idealistic requirements of the new society. The predicament is personalized for him in the conflicting attitudes of the accountant (old-think) and the young clerk (new-think), both of whom seek his support.

THE PARTY SECRETARY: An essential character in all Chinese films, plays, novels, stories, etc. Is interchangeable with commune manager, factory secretary, or any supervisory cadre. His function is to symbolize the patient benevolence of the Party and its monopoly of the immutable and irresistible truth. This character equates to the Parish priest in Catholic magazine literature. He keeps a shrewd and compassionate eye on the situation but does not openly interfere.

THE OLD PEASANT: Also an essential character in any dramatic presentation. He remembers the bitter past. Usually male, but occasionally the part is written for an aged widow whose late husband was a Glorious Revolutionary Martyr.

Conclusions and/or Messages

(1) The Party and all officials, functionaries, and cadres exist only to serve the people.

(2) When in doubt consult the works of Chairman Mao.

(3) Never forget the past.

PART 1

Scene 1: Peasants from the mountain villages come to the township and pour into the store. Buy work clothes, tools, domestic items, and minor luxuries (especially for the children). Exchange news, gossip, and opinions about the merchandise. Manager affable and anxious to please. Hero and the two girls follow the Party dictum, "Be cheerful and helpful at all times and in all ways and remember that all customers are your comrades." The young man daydreams of being in the navy. The accountant pushes inferior goods, raises prices on

98

popular lines, and foists high-profit items onto any submissive or meekly compliant customer (classical symptoms of capitalist thinking) but fails to make a sale with a new line of hoes which the men peasants unanimously reject as being unsuitable for their kind of farming.

Scene 2: Harvest time approaches. The peasants are too busy to come to town. There are no customers in the store. The manager and accountant frown over the books, but the Hero suggests that if the peasants are too busy to come to the store the store should go to the peasants. He volunteers to pack baskets and become a New Peddler (Title). The accountant hastens to load him with goods which are hard to shift, including the previously rejected hoes. The Hero agrees to take them in addition to the popular and necessary commodities he has already selected, thus demonstrating his willingness to recognize the accountant's authority while disapproving his attitude (Morality for Beginners).

Climbing the mountain under this abnormally heavy load, he passes an abandoned coal mine where, in the days before liberation, he worked as a child slave laborer because his impoverished family could not pay their rent.

FLASHBACK TO THE BAD OLD DAYS

We see him being cruelly beaten by a brutal foreman (capitalist lackey) because he cannot carry a heavy bag of coal. Now, under the Party, he willingly carries the big basket of store goods on his back and bears it cheerfully up the steep mountain track, knowing that he is now serving the masses. The villagers meet him with shouts of pleasure and praise and buy everything he has, except the hoes.

Scene 3: Back at the store. Approval with overtones of reproach. He is commended for his enterprise and for making good sales, but there is a suggestion that he might have tried harder to get rid of the hoes. Faced with a basic ideological contradiction, the Hero retires to his room and takes a dog-eared copy of *Quotations from Chairman Mao Tse-tung* from under his pillow.

Mao looks down at him from a lithograph on the wall.

99

MUSIC: "Two Suns Shine on China—One in Peking and the Other in the Sky."

By the light of a lantern he reads far into the night while Junior, tossing on his cot, dreams of repelling waterborne invaders from Taiwan.

The Hero finds an appropriate quote and there is a CLOSE-UP of it.

"If you want the people to help you, you must help the people." He wakes Junior and shows it to him.

Scene 4: Hero and Junior (now thinking "correctly" and oriented toward serving the People "Wherever the Party Needs Me"), and assisted by the two girls, pack two huge peddlers, baskets with commodities which will please the peasants, the girls coyly adding little fripperies. The lads set out before daylight, but are caught in a heavy storm and shelter in the mountain hut of the Old Peasant.

He gives them soup and noodles (impossible in the hungry days before liberation) and talks about the bitter past, when he and his wife were poor peddlers and carried their packs all over the mountains.

In those days the peasants had little money to spend, and a peddler's days were long and hard (at this point I remembered the old man we had talked to in the train and turned to Feng to remind him, but he was asleep).

The Old Peasant points to a basket which hangs on the wall of his hut, above a picture of Chairman Mao. He tells the lads a sad story.

FLASHBACK NO. 2   THE BAD OLD DAYS

Scene 5: The Old Peasant and his wife, carrying their baskets along mountain tracks, are intercepted by Kuomintang security police and accused of carrying secret messages for the Communists. The old lady takes fright and runs. The Kuomintang men shoot her dead, then empty her basket into a ravine.

The old man stands on the edge of the ravine mourning his murdered wife. He sees a bright light spreading over the horizon.

REPRISE OF THE SONG: "Two Suns Shine on China."
Return to the old lady's basket hanging on the wall and the Old Man telling the two New Peddlers that they must never forget the past!

Scene 6: A bumper fruit crop in the mountain villages. A celebration. The young men sell the goods, then share in the fun. The Party Secretary, present for the harvest, embraces them affectionately.

PART 2

(This part of the film introduces a secondary plot.)

Scene 7: News comes to the township that there is gloom in the village. Insects are attacking the fruit trees.

The Hero suggests to the Store Manager and Accountant that they buy insecticides and spraying equipment from the State wholesale emporium and introduce these to the villagers.

The Accountant resists this, saying that the peasants have no experience of modern methods of agriculture and will not buy newfangled things which, like the rejected hoes, will stay on the store shelves and gather dust. This, says the Accountant, is bad business in any kind of society.

Scene 8: The Hero, Junior, and the two girls get together over *Quotations from Chairman Mao* (REPRISE OF THEME MUSIC). I am reminded of pre-twentieth-century Christians turning to the Bible for answers to their problems. They study Mao's essay, "On the Correct Handling of Contradictions among the People," and come up with the appropriate quotes. "Put politics in command. Place things in perspective. Study problems on the basis of unity of interest. Dare to think, then dare to act. Use Marxism-Leninism as a guide and there is no difficulty which cannot be overcome." The Hero takes his bicycle and rides by night to the Country Agricultural Research Institute. Arriving at daylight, he discusses the problem with the experts. They show him how to mix the spray and operate a knapsack pump. He goes to the village and demonstrates. (INSERT shot of dead insects.)

Scene 9: Orders pour into the store for insecticides and equipment. The Manager and Accountant are convinced. They send for stocks and distribute them among the villages. Then the store is closed for the day and the total staff climbs the mountain, taking baskets of "consumer goods at fair prices."

Even the Accountant has a basket on his back, including a hoe which he intends to demonstrate.

There is a meeting in the community hall which serves the villages (formerly a landlord's house). The Party Secretary, with a photograph of Mao behind him, makes a speech on the theme "Unity is Strength."

The Old Peddler comes to the meeting, bringing the basket which belonged to his dead wife, and presents it to the New Peddler (the Hero). "She would have wanted you to have it, son."

A picture of Mao appears on the screen.

MUSIC: "Two Suns Shine on China."

The two young men from the Travel Service wakened Feng and together we went back to the hotel.

CHAPTER

10

THE young men from the Travel Service brought me a brochure for my files and a souvenir pin of the Yellow River bridge to wear in my coat. When it was fixed we boarded a minibus and toured Chengchow: the professor, his wife, Feng, the two lads, a driver, and I.

The brochure says that before liberation the population of the city was no more than 150,000 but now it is 700,000, of which number some 600,000 live in new housing. In the old days the city was backward and had narrow, ragged streets. There were no industries apart from locomotive maintenance and repair shops (the city is a junction for two main railways) and some inefficient textile mills owned by capitalists. The people were poor and constituted a substandard consumer community.

Today Chengchow is the capital of Honan Province, which has fifty million people. The whole population of the city lives comfortably and is usefully employed within a balanced producer-consumer economy based upon an integrated modern textile industry using local commune cotton. Secondary industries include the manufacture of spinning, weaving, and general farm machinery, dye and fabric printing works, clothing factories, and a chain of allied and contributory industries including a bicycle factory, plus flour, fruit, tobacco, and edible oil processing. Local coal and ore are distributed by rail from Chengchow to steel and iron foundry towns. (So says the brochure.)

One of the young men spoke to Feng, who then turned to us

and said, "In the old days a poet wrote that 'In summer Cheng-chow is hidden in dust and in winter it is covered with mud.' Now they say that the flowers of Chengchow can be smelled from ten miles away."

The traveler will hear a similar litany with appropriate quotes in every city visited, and allowing for the new high level of national pride plus a tinge of district jingoism, the general evidence gained in a few days spent in and about these places seems to justify the substance if not always the explicit detail of most claims. In this respect Chinese publicists share with their Western brethren a childlike tendency to stretch facts as far as the resilience of statistics and a listener's credulity will permit.

Yet one thing is certain. On the tourist track there is an impressive amount of new construction, new industry and housing, to be seen. Visitors with more widely ranging privileges, including politically disinterested academicians and specialists in various fields whose purposes take them into restricted areas, confirm that this is true of even the most remote provinces. They say that new industries and cities are springing up all over China, situated in relation to newfound mineral deposits, hydroelectric projects, and vast areas of reclaimed or improved pasture, farming, and forest land.

There is no need to argue for or against the detailed truth of these revelations. As Feng says, "U.S. spy planes and satellites watch us day by day. They have mapped and photographed every inch of our country from the sea to the borders of India. That is why the criminals in Washington are afraid and plot with Soviet revisionists to destroy us before we get too big and strong for both of them." He speaks these things more in sorrow than in anger, and certainly not in fear.

One of the young men said, "We are not afraid of anybody. China will crush all aggressors." Feng and the other lad nodded approvingly. I was not impressed, thinking that Miss Ping would have made more of it—realizing, too, that I missed having her around, realizing still more that I was getting bored by these conversational limitations.

Chengchow, nearly new, is clean and neat. Its buildings, built of yellow-gold bricks, sit tidily along streets that are wide, straight, and lined with shade trees. The verges on either side, and the center strip which divides the traffic lanes, grow wheat. As we passed it was being harvested and carried away in handcarts.

The professor's wife, watching this, pointed with her fan. "As a child, if I left anything on my plate uneaten, my parents would say that such a waste was sinful and that I should think of the starving Chinese and feel ashamed. So I continued diligently to eat until the last morsel was crammed into my stomach, though I could never see the logic of stuffing myself uncomfortably as a sign of my family's sympathy for the hungry Chinese."

Feng smiled his gentle, friendly smile and said, "We do not need such sympathy now. You can see that the people are not hungry any more. We do not really need to grow wheat in the streets, but the people like to do this. Every mouthful of food makes our country stronger to resist aggression, so they use every inch of ground to grow things."

The lads said that this growing of wheat in the city was organized by street committees, that the work was voluntary and most people took some part. Once the heavy work was done the old people and the smallest children did the weeding, irrigation, and gleaning. The wheat is sold to the State and the money used by the street committees to provide community amenities and to help people in difficulties.

This city, now fifteen times bigger than it was before liberation, has four sections. (I think such things worth mentioning since they are typical of general trends and happenings in new China. One has only to remember to multiply each reference by some fabulous figure, proportionate to the size and population of the country, to sense the ultimate implications of this development.)

The four areas of Chengchow are these:

(1) Governmental, administrative, and public offices and assembly rooms, at country and provincial level.

(2) Social, educational, and cultural components including all specialized higher education centers, provincial sporting areas, and gymnasiums.

(3) Industrial complexes, each of which has its own basic social and cultural facilities.

(4) The old city, in process of renovation.

We passed through the city quickly, aiming at a place on the riverbank some few miles from town where a ferryboat was waiting to take us on a trip.

The professor had arranged it with his friend the Director of Antiquities, having in mind to photograph the remnants of an ancient dike, now being overbuilt as part of a new plan of land reclamation.

He had said, at breakfast, that to understand a people one must know something of their history, and to understand the history of China one must have some knowledge of its big rivers: the Pearl, the Yangtze, and the Yellow, which is second in length but in every other respect the most important of the three.

"It might interest you to know that for all practical purposes the long history of Chinese civilization began on the Yellow River plains sometime between three and four thousand years ago; and if you had the time to spend in this area, and patience, and the knowledge to read old and new Chinese, you could make a step-by-step study of its development.

"Then, if you extended your study to take in the whole course of the river from its rising in the Himalayas, its northward course into Mongolia, then down again through these central provinces and eastward to the sea, your view of the whole history of mankind would be considerably widened, for some would have it that here was the cradle of the human race."

His wife, licking litchi syrup from her fingertips, had looked at me. "Please do not be offended by his poor manners and lack of tact. It is possible that you know as much of history as he does, but he would find this difficult to believe of anyone. It is the result of a lifetime of bullying students. Please do not let him be belligerent."

Silent and smiling, he watched her decapitate an egg and seemed pleased when it was done without damage. Then he told me of the river trip, which, he said, would occupy an hour. "If you would care to come . . ."

But his wife broke in. "You will be lectured all the way and only have yourself to blame."

We left the minibus under a tree a little way out of town and walked through cotton fields to the riverside to board the ferry, settling ourselves on the afterdeck with Feng singing to himself:

106

> "Sailing safely on the seas of the revolution
> depends upon the helmsman.
> The growth of all things in the fields
> depends upon the sun and dew.
> Making successful revolution
> depends on the thought of Mao Tse-tung."

The crewmen cast off and the steersman, waiting until Feng had done singing, blew two sharp blasts on the whistle.

The Yellow River runs fast, even here in the flat country, where its banks are miles apart and hold not one stream but many running side by side in the same wide bed, swift and gritty (a higher specific gravity than any other river in the world, said Feng, proud even of this dubious distinction). It flows in shining strips like long, smooth furrows of wet earth turning from a plowshare, swirling around islands of collected sediment, flowering under and over, colliding, dividing and again intertwining, plaiting liquid arabesques.

"The first thing to note," said the professor, "is that these great plains, composed of layers and layers of Yellow River silt, lying between the central mountains and the sea, represent more than half of China's arable land.

"Secondly you must remember that this three thousand miles of river is a real Chinese devil and has been the cause of more grief to the people than any other natural source of trouble and suffering. There is, in fact, an old saying in these middle provinces that of every ten seasons nine were calamitous, sometimes because of flood and other times of dryness."

He leaned on the rail and recited:

> "They starve through seasons of drought and flood,
> And good years are too few to feed them all."

Then turning to me, he said, "That complaint was made almost a thousand years ago by a Chinese statesman lamenting that he could not prevent or ease the suffering of the Yellow River peasants. And the fact of the matter is that the main political and practical issues in the whole course of Chinese history have turned largely upon the capacity or the neglect of rulers to protect their people from the destructive power of these big rivers. Almost every major upheaval and change of dynasty, from the beginning up to the present, has been precipitated or aggravated by the misery and dissatisfaction of millions of hungry people made homeless by floods, or populations decimated in dry times for lack of grain."

He talked on, letting me take notes while Feng listened, shaking his head with wonder to hear such knowledge in a foreigner. (Feng later came to me and asked if he might copy some of these things so that he could tell them to other visitors.)

The gist of what the professor said is this:

Go back almost four thousand years to the beginning of China's civilization and you find that the first man to make himself king of a great part of the country was a local leader who lived on these plains and imposed his will upon other regional chieftains in matters of flood control and irrigation.

This man saw that earthworks and ditches, built to protect a single town or small group of villages, merely diverted floodwaters into other areas or held water back from them in time of drought. Only by grouping the river-basin communities together in a food-producing union, consolidating and directing their collective manpower to build continuous dikes and a planned network of canals, could the river be controlled along the whole of its length and the great central plains be brought under orderly and regular cultivation.

The scheme was, of course, disputed by regional leaders who could see a diminution of their own authority in any such collective enterprise, and the result then was, as it would be today, one war after another, self-interest opposing ideas until the strongest prevailed and stayed in power awhile.

And again, technology advanced hand in hand with warfare, as it has done since an ape-man discovered that an enemy could be stabbed with a slither of bone or beaten to death with a stick. More deaths by better methods—such is the progressive record of educated humanity.

Leaders of the peasantry, fighting on these plains for control of the waters, so many centuries ago, rode into battle ahead of their men in armor-clad chariots, carrying weapons and shields of bronze, one servant driving and another riding alongside to hand his leader arrows as they went—all this when Joseph was making his way down to Egypt, and tribesmen in northern Europe were fighting with slings and carried shields of bark or animal skin.

There was peace awhile, then more war. Dikes were damaged, broken down, let crumble. Canals were allowed to fill with silt and become useless until the unruly river ruled the whole land again. Time and again people starved, were drowned, made miserable to a point of desperation and revolt, while the wheel of time spun round and round. And nothing changed.

It is difficult for people living in housebroken lands to imagine the damage that a raging major river can do when let loose in a defenseless peasant community; yet it is not necessary to go very far back in history for illustration.

In 1938 the Generalissimo Chiang Kai-shek, anxious to the edge of desperation to check the Japanese advance from northern China to the south, ordered that the Yellow River dike be opened near the city of Chengchow. It was done; and an estimated 880,000 peasants perished within a year, either drowned or starved to death in the subsequent famine. Twelve million were made homeless.

The Communists have changed all that. Since liberation (with the help of the U.S.S.R., no longer mentioned) they have built forty-six dams and reservoirs which hold in store more water than normally flowed down this river in a single year. They have lengthened and strengthened the dikes and tamed the river from end to end for the first time in history, and thus can claim, quite reasonably, that they are the first rulers of China to control the three big rivers. Consequently it is difficult for these peasants to understand or appreciate the sympathy of foreigners who show fretful concern that communism has taken away their freedom.

We watched the river slip swiftly past our boat; measured the depth of the thick, rich silt that overhangs its edge, and guessed at the crops that girls were weeding; saw in the distance the new bridge, one of the world's longest, a slender, shining thread of steel overriding the river. Then, with a toot, we drew close inshore toward a high embankment where a hundred men were working, moving blocks of white stone, shaping and laying them against its face as trucks and trains came and went with more stone, and cranes lifted them into place.

Feng, the ferrymaster, and the professor stood together talking in Chinese (I envied him) and we went closer, probing for a place which would suit his purposes. They called to the workmen, who stopped what they were doing, listened, and then directed us upstream a little way where we found a small section of an old wall made of packed mud and faced with a plaster of some kind, with a faded inscription or symbol on it.

We watched while the professor took his pictures and made notes and were quiet until he nodded with some satisfaction and thanked the ferrymaster and Feng. We turned and went back downstream again, waving to the workers.

As we slid with the stream, one of our young men pointed across the water to far hills partly hidden in a dusty haze, and when he had spoken Feng said that he was telling us that commune members and students from Chengchow were camped there, making terraces and planting half a million trees.

It was good, he said, that the Government had made dams to hold water back when the snow melted in the mountains and spring rains fell on the plains. And good that there should be big ditches to lead the river wherever it was needed. But the commune people also worked hard to keep the river free from the silt which made it overflow.

He took my brochure from me and opened it to show what had been done by the peasants in this district to overcome erosion. Commune members, with student help, had terraced 50,000 acres of hill country (formerly as bare as a monk's skull) and planted it, along with other doubtful ground amounting to 165,000 acres, with trees and grasses; they planned to do better next season.

"Write down, then," said the professor, "and put in your book that the Communists have achieved what the first kings of China tried to do thirty-five hundred years ago. They have organized the Chinese people into a huge and flexible labor force that can be deployed and used systematically for the benefit of the country as a whole. Conditioned critics in the West will call this forced labor, though in their own countries they approve the conscription of men for military purposes with little enough compunction."

He put his notebook away and came to sit with his wife.

"The next historical step, unless the nature of man suddenly changes, is another war which will destroy all this, and such Yellow River peasants as survive the bomb will again be reduced to misery and forced to make once more the long march back to civilized dignity."

We separated in Chengchow, the professor going by train a few hours westward to Loyang, ancient capital of nine early dynasties and now an industrial city busy with the manufacture of tractors.

While waiting for his train we had tea and talked a little more. He told me that he hoped to be allowed to go for a few days with the Provincial Archaeological Survey team, of which his friend was head, but that there was a standing prohibition against foreigners taking part in any excavations.

"They resent the fact that much of China's historical treasure was taken away in the old days to stock museums in other countries, and they hold this very much against us, so I shall be lucky if I get permission to spend more than a day or two in the area." He made a gesture of resignation. "Pride is a delicate plant. One must see their point of view and accept it with good grace, though for me it will be disappointing not to spend at least a week in this area which, from a historical and archaeological point of view, is enormously interesting and important.

"They have unearthed treasures here in the past ten years that fill great gaps in our knowledge of the evolution of society, and what they have found is no doubt only a fraction of what remains buried under thousands of years of sediment left by floods. Now, for the first time, it is being uncovered by engineers, builders, and prospectors, layer after layer of history preserved in buried villages, temples, palaces, and rich men's tombs."

But his wife said, "I hope that you've packed a change of shoes, for you'll get your feet wet if they let you loose in any new diggings and next thing you'll be in bed with a cold that will make you miserable and sorry for yourself, and bad-tempered with everyone else."

He answered, smiling, "I watched you this morning, my love, put them in my bag." Then to me, "A foolish woman is clamorous, but the worth of a woman of virtue is far above rubies."

He stood up and shook hands.

"I hope that we catch up with you in a day or two. When we do I will tell you what I have found out about old China, and you can tell me what you think of the new. And of the two tasks yours is the harder."

111

CHAPTER

11

FENG took me to one of the six new textile mills which, placed contiguously, form a self-contained complex employing, housing, and providing social, political, and welfare services for 35,000 workers and their families. These mills, planned in 1954, were built and in partial operation a year later and continue to improve and expand as the communes produce more cotton.

A thin and nondescript young man, whom Feng introduced as secretary of the factory management committee (though in sloppy blue tunic and cotton shoes he could have passed for a street sweeper), met us at the gate and led us through an avenue of trees and flower beds into a walled courtyard where study groups of mill girls sat in the shade, listening to one of their number read from the works of Mao Tse-tung and then discussing them. These tableaux may have been staged for my sake, though I think not, for it all seemed natural enough, with none of them self-conscious or acting awkwardly.

Other girls, work shifts finished, were coming from a bathhouse to dry their hair in the sun. Lads on a ladder tacked posters to a billboard. Feng read the biggest, which said: "Mobilizing the enthusiastic spirit of the workers, this mill has fulfilled its production target once again by more than ten percent."

The study groups, seeing me make notes while Feng translated, began to clap and laugh and show their pride and pleasure, and thus encouraged, the secretary spoke up, though morosely and without expression:

"With the guidance of Chairman Mao's thinking our workers are holding high the red banner of the revolution and surging forward under the glorious leadership of the Party in a new production drive.

"This year we reached top rating in the scale of Approved National Quality Specifications, and at the same time dropped production costs by applying approved political consciousness which develops the skills and techniques of the workers. Since studying Chairman Mao's essay, 'Mankind Makes Constant Progress and Nature Undergoes Constant Change,' some of our operators can now manage up to sixteen hundred spindles instead of the basic twelve hundred.

"Our revolutionary progress has been the direct result of higher efficiency achieved through a concentrated study of the works of our dear leader and the application of principles of self-reliance."

Recognizing Feng's personal interpolations, I knew that there was no real need to listen to these speeches. He would let the secretary have his say, then render back to me a routine patter decorated with such statistics as he understood. I thus felt free to look about and let my mind wander, for I would hear nothing much from these two worth remembering.

Not that I underestimate in any way these evident achievements of the regime which, themselves astonishing, become no more impressive when overlaid with declamatory fantasies that serve only to strain patience and make many of these routine visits wearisome.

Refusing, then, to be sidetracked or trapped in a tangle of juvenile dialectics, the visitor must stay with the main facts, which are themselves sufficient to frame the over-all pattern into which these mills fit: the grand design of modern China which cannot be irritably dismissed, or denigrated by bigoted criticism, however much one might feel opposed to the philosophical approach upon which the material achievements of communism are founded.

For example, it is true that peasants have been growing cotton on the Yellow River plains since men first began to plant crops of any kind. It is equally true that for the better part of several thousand years the mass of these people were serfs, slaves, or at best

113

poor peasants who gained no more than a minimum existence from their labor.

When the industrial revolution brought Europeans into Asia in search of raw materials for their factories and mills, profits from the cotton crop were drained from the local economy via railways built by Europeans for this purpose. The cotton went to Canton, Shanghai, or Peking for processing, manufacture, or immediate export and was paid for with cheap factory goods imported by the foreigners. Chengchow and hundreds of similar towns degenerated into little more than impoverished rural railheads handling a one-way traffic.

The cost in human suffering has been hugely documented and dramatized and has no place in this narrative. It is enough to say, at this stage, that if the West had balanced business acumen and efficiency with equal proportions of Christian benevolence, China could have become a liberal democracy.

But the West left it to the Communists to modernize China: to tame the huge rivers, marshal labor, rationalize the use of land, and canalize human energy and enthusiasm through the commune system. It is they, then, who have made it possible to change a primitive and practically slave-based economy (in this district, as elsewhere in China) into a modern complex of interrelated primary and secondary industries within a decade, an accomplishment which cannot simply be dismissed with ridicule.

We had tea and statistics in the conference room, and picking figures at random, I noted that the mills have a total of 45,000 spindles and 15,000 looms together with the necessary number of precision combers and high-speed rolling, wefting, and twisting machines "all made in China." Whether or not the machinery is first-class I have no way of telling, but I have heard it said by visiting specialists that for the most part China's industrial output is good, at its best is excellent, and in several fields, including textiles, is worrying competitors in international markets. A Danish engineer to whom I put the question later shrugged and said, "Any country that can make an effective nuclear device can make pretty good machinery."

The mills themselves are bigger than any I remember from visits in other countries, with banks of machinery reaching as far as I could see (Feng said that one section through which we walked was a thousand meters in length) and everything clean, neat, and busy.

I have no feeling or instinct for mechanical things and so venture no opinion as to the efficiency in terms of cost or operation of these mills or others that I saw in China, though the obvious combination of fervor, eager zeal, and sheer size staggers the imaginative faculties when one contemplates the potential of 700 million people kept keyed to an almost fanatical pitch of dedicated productivity.

In a section where some of the machines were decorated with paper flowers, girls were gathered for a demonstration, grouped around a woman who, with swift manipulative movements, showed them a trick of mending a broken thread in three seconds, without leaving ugly ends that later would need to be trimmed.

We watched awhile, and seeing me interested, she showed me, slowly, how it was done, the girls all smiling and eager for me to try, though I would not, knowing my lack of facility in such things; but they clapped happily when I shook hands with her and went my way.

The secretary said that she was an advanced worker from Shanghai, touring provincial mills to teach techniques and detailed skills, developed by time-and-motion and political studies at research and experiment centers. She was a well-known textile-worker heroine, whose story had been much told in newspapers, popular songs, and displays set up in factories and workers' cultural palaces.

Then Feng, putting on his cadre's mask, said that a picture book about her life had been written for children. It showed her, a child of six, crouched beside her father with her mother alongside, leaning over him and weeping. "Because he was dead," said Feng. "Dead from having nothing to eat. Lying there on a heap of dirty straw gathered from the streets because he had sold his bed to buy food for his wife and child."

When her father was buried she and her mother went begging, but after four more years, when she was ten, her mother also died, hungry—"In Shanghai, among rich people."

Then she went to work in a cotton mill, giving labor in exchange for food and shelter, but after a year took sick with typhoid fever. Her workmates hid her under the straw, where they all slept together like kittens, but the foreman found her and, thinking her dead, took her body in a wheelbarrow and sold it for a few cents to a medical school conducted by missionaries.

A professor, having her on the bench ready for dissection, saw that she was not yet dead, so put her to bed until she was well enough to go back to the factory. But in hospital she had learned how the Communists were working for the poor and through a nurse made contact with them. She helped in the revolutionary underground and at the time of the civil war became a Party member, surviving the Kuomintang massacres which accounted for most of the city Communists.

After the Liberation she went back to the mill, now owned by the people (the owner had gone to Taiwan). She learned to read and write at night school and now leads girls in study groups, reading the essays of Chairman Mao and teaching "advanced techniques" to young operatives. This simple, squat, round-faced amiable, middle-aged lady: this People's Heroine of the textile industry.

Factory space in this Chengchow complex covers half a million square meters (according to Feng) and an equivalent area is taken up with housing and amenities for workers and their families. Accommodation is allocated at the rate of one room for a family of three, or two rooms for a family with dependent elders or more than one child. A small kitchen is additional. Bathroom facilities are shared by two or three families.

Electric lighting, steam heat, and running water cost nothing. Cooking fires burn coal bricks, which are made locally and are cheap. Rent is calculated at the approximate equivalent of something above a dollar a month for each room, which means that unmarried people, sharing three to a room, pay no more than thirty or forty cents each month in room rent.

Take-home pay for millworkers ranges between $17 and $35 a month—a figure that can be bettered in Shanghai and some other places. A man and wife, both working, claimed to save ten dollars a month between them and owned a transistor radio, a sewing machine, and a bicycle to show for this thrift—as well as four children.

Ancillary to accommodation basics are the usual socialist amenities: a medical center, nurseries, kindergartens, schools up to top primary, cooperative food stores, meeting halls, a playhouse and cinema, a gymnasium, playing fields, and facilities for adult education and part-time study. Garden allotments are free for all, though mostly used by elderly and retired folk with time to spare for supplementing family food and supplies in this fashion, or by youth groups with "project" enthusiasms. Canteens operate around the clock, providing meals for shift workers.

By middle-class Western standards accommodations are cramped and domestic amenities no more than adequate. Searching around for some Western parallel with which to equate the general home-life look, I could think only of the postwar barrack camps for displaced persons in Western Germany; but if one measures against the mud-and-straw-hut level of yesterday's generation, these people live comfortably and well. At least that is what a group of elderly folk gave me to believe, through Feng, when we walked in the residential area among them and the children and chickens and looked into a few of the rooms.

I paid five cents for a canteen meal of a measure of rice (more than I could eat) with a bowl of vegetables and meat, chosen from a range of forty hot dishes. Cake, fruit, and ice cream or some other follow-up would have cost two cents more. Three chubby girls with whom I shared a table said that they eat this way three times daily and giggled when I said that they certainly seemed well-fed.

The secretary, with a gloomy look, hoped that the workers in my country would soon overthrow their capitalist oppressors and achieve similar conditions, adding uncertainly, "The Chinese masses are happy, and do their best, because they see clearly that they are fighting in the forefront of the revolution which will free all of the world's workers from capitalist oppression."

CHAPTER

12

THERE was a stranger waiting in the foyer with Feng when I came downstairs from my midday rest, and the two young men from the Travel Service stood a little apart with the driver of our car, ready to set out as soon as our program was settled.

Feng said, "You are invited to visit the commune where your friend the old peddler is living. This is his son, who is a cadre there and has come to take us if you agree."

The way lay through fields of ripe wheat and long stretches of seedling cotton, past walled villages set back from the road among trees, with duck ponds and little streams, geese, people carrying sheaves on shoulder poles, a man washing an ox.

A kingfisher flashed in front of us as if challenging our passage, displaying for a split second such colors as one could only guess at. A white crane, stately, unafraid, standing at the edge of a ditch, as if listening, stabbed suddenly into a clump of reeds with his long beak, then flicked his head from side to side.

An hour from town our guide, looking around, said, "This is our land," and I sensed the pride that underlay the statement. Leaning forward and looking through the windows, first left, then right, I asked how much they had, and was it good or bad or average land? When Feng had put my question to him and teased out detailed answers, he told me that they cultivated 12,000 acres and had almost as much more which still needed treating in one way or another before it could be made productive.

Some such land, he said, lay below floodwater level and must have deep drains all around, as well as dikes. Other parts, too rough and broken about for leveling with the plow, would be terraced in time and sown with sweet potato and other root or vine crops. Then they had a big patch of alkaline marsh and sand-dune land that would take time and effort to reclaim, and the help of neighbors.

We stopped at such a spot to watch two hundred men at work scraping the white crust from a long stretch of this alkaline land, piling it in heaps to be carted away to where others were raising minor dikes to divert marsh drainage. The cadre said that when they had stripped the salt away they would turn the earth to a depth of three feet and mix in with it tons of green stuff grown in another part of the commune.

Groups of men from three brigades were busy with this work, reclaiming eighty acres. Others, helped by strong young girls, were carting river silt to lay over patches of shifting sand, spreading it two feet thick, then planting trees to bind sand and silt together. In a year or two, when it was set and stabilized, crops could be sown there.

Feng said that there was much country of this kind along the edges of the Yellow River, and now that the new ways made an adequate food crop certain each season they could turn their attention to regenerating this bad land that had lain waste for decades. In two or three years they would double the amount of cultivation. Meanwhile the output of each arable acre had been increased by three and four times above the preliberation figure. This was typical, he said, of the situation in most parts of China.

One-fifth of the total world population lives in these communes. Because many of these people were formerly landlords or rich peasants employing the labor of their neighbors, it is certain that some of them would prefer the old way of life; but by and large, on the evidence available to visitors, the majority of peasants at present seem better than contented. And if the material condition of China's self-reliant rural population is measured (for example) against that of India's rustic communities, dependant to a large extent on the arbitrary charity of foreigners, there can be no doubt as to where the most hope and happiness lies.

It is foolish, in the face of facts as big as boulders, for sinophobes to rail against the commune system, on either ideological or practical grounds, when it so manifestly offers a proven, if partial, solution to the world-wide problem of bridging the economic gap between rural and industrialized societies.

No peasant working only with a hoe, anywhere, can give his family the amenities and opportunities of twentieth-century life on the proceeds of an acre of land. The best that he can do is to stay alive and provide his dependents with the bare necessities of a dignified existence.

Only by utilizing all the land within a community to its best total advantage—pooling labor, tools, machinery and working animals, the intangibles of collective incentive, acumen and knowledge, and farming on a large scale with collective facilities—can backward peasant populations begin to raise their status either as individuals or as communities.

This is no outrageous revolutionary theory. In many territories which were recently, or still are, under colonial government collective peasant enterprises are encouraged and made much of as a sign of progress. Why, then, do so many critics of China persistently and bitterly assail the commune system? In dissipating so much anger and indignation against a phenomenon demonstrably productive of infinite good they misspend their breath and discredit themselves as objective commentators.

In spite of the stubborn insistence of sinophobes the commune system cannot be equated in any way with forced labor (though this is not to deny that there are considerable numbers of Chinese working out their social or political rehabilitation, under supervision, in a few communes selected for this purpose).

Few uncommitted visitors will flatly reject the evident impression that the commune system generally has developed in a natural and spontaneous way out of the vision, initiative, and wishes of the mass of the peasant people, stimulated by the Communist regime and led by local Party committees and cadres.

It has reached its present organizational shape and level of achievement through stages of trial and error, sustained by the stimulating effects of incentive and opportunities of creative responsibility. The commune system is, in fact, an astonishing and historic example of collective free enterprise in which thousands of rural community groups, each of about thirty thousand people, and in large measure self-contained, are able at present to plan and carry out their own rate and scale of development, at the same time adding strength and stature to the nation as an entity.

Similar systems, if developed in Africa and South America, could bring into existence huge new power blocks which would change the balance, the course and nature of civilization within two generations.

We drove around the commune wherever there were roads. We passed through villages and in one of them stopped to see a Production Brigade committee in discussion and were given tea and peanuts. The Brigade leader said that they were sorting out suggestions for winter projects and that these would be presented to all members of the Brigade (2,200 people, including old folk and children) at an evening meeting. Then, when their ideas were clarified and accepted, the Brigade leaders would put them to a meeting of the commune management committee at a session of over-all planning.

They had in mind, he said, to build a new housing block to replace some decrepit cottages, to buy a new lathe and other equipment for the farm-machinery workshop, and to turn some of their very poor land into fishponds and stock them with Yellow River carp, which were good food and would breed easily.

The cadre said as we left, "You see, we can now plan new progress every year, and it has been like this since 1960 when we first controlled the river. In 1961 we had a terrible drought, but for the first time in history nobody went hungry, nobody was short of clothes, no families left our villages to go begging in the towns, none hired themselves to work for others in exchange for one bowl of soup a day. We grew enough in that year, with almost no rain, to feed everybody in the commune and had grain left over to sell to the State, as well as a good crop of cotton for the mills in Chengchow—all because we had our two big dams and three hundred and eighty-seven wells.

"This year we are having a good season and wages will rise a little; but most of our profit will be used to buy tractors and to extend electrification to every field that needs a power pump. The new flour mill will be driven by electricity so that the women will not need to grind their own grain every day. And every house in this brigade will have electric light."

They took me to visit the old peddler Han Tung-wen and his wife, a neat little woman with smiling eyes and miniature feet, who live in a boxlike mud-brick cottage, thatched and white-washed and divided inside into three small rooms of equal size: a sitting room in the center and a bedroom on either side. One of these, with a curtained and canopied bed, was used by the cadre son and his wife. The children and the wife's young sister used the other room, sleeping on a *kang* (which is an oven built of brick). The sitting room, with a door opening onto a courtyard, was almost filled by a table with a heavy, high-backed chair on either side, one for the old man and the other for his wife, who sat like a king and queen to receive us.

They served warm water in lidded cups and talked for a little while about the old days; how in the worst years of drought hundreds of families left the village to go begging in areas less affected. Some sold their children. Others simply huddled together and quietly died of hunger, while many men, unable to feed their families, hanged themselves for shame.

"But there were Communists in the village even then, who robbed the rich landlords' barns by night and gave grain to the poorest peasants, which many ate uncooked because they were afraid to light fires and give themselves away."

The cadre, sitting on a stool at his father's feet, looked at me without expression.

"The West will never understand these things. There is some blindness in you which does not see the reality of suffering, some bluntness that does not feel other people's pain. You are all too busy being rich and separate individuals."

We were silent awhile, watching the cadre's large wife moving unhurriedly about the courtyard with a fat, padded baby straddled on her hip, sweeping leaves into a heap and scolding chickens as they cheeped about her feet.

The old man put his hand upon a book that lay on the table and

122

spoke to Feng, who took it and turned the pages, then looked up; they talked together, all of them, about the book until Feng said:

"This book tells the story of Chiao Yu-lu, the good Party secretary who came to this county and taught the people how to organize themselves and change the face of the land, and not to be afraid of flood and drought but to overcome all difficulties, and to fight to build a new life for themselves and their children."

I took it and leafed through, looking at pictures which showed a brisk, compact, medium man with no spare flesh. Wide shoulders and narrow waist. Broad forehead, high cheekbones, rounded chin with lines of humor running round his mouth. A friendly, intelligent, amiable face. Thick, black swept-back hair. He seemed always to wear a high-necked sweater, and a jacket hung on his shoulders, as some sailors do. A man to get things done. A man one might trust.

As I turned the pages Feng was saying, "He worked hard among the people of this district, day and night all year round, in snow and flood and drought, saying to the Party committees and cadres that leaders must lead, that men could move mountains if they believed in their own strength and were encouraged.

"Many times he came here to this village to learn from the old people, to encourage the cadres, to teach young men and women to study the works of Chairman Mao. He is dead now, but the people remember him and tell their children his story from this book."

Chiao Yu-lu is buried in the sand dunes of a nearby commune. His staff, his shoes, the little canvas bag in which he carried his few books, are displayed in the Art Gallery in Chengchow. The room in the Provincial Hospital where he spent his last days is kept empty, with the curtains drawn. Speak of Chiao Yu-lu in this district and the people are silent and still; tears come to their eyes.

That night I read his story and in the morning went to the gallery where the graphic narrative of his life is set out in photographs, sketches, models, and mementos, and pilgrims tour in groups led by dedicated and passionately declamatory girls.

He was born of poor peasants in 1922 and died of cancer of the liver in 1962. He never owned a complete change of clothing and left nothing to his children but a copy of *The Selected Works of*

Mao Tse-tung. The mourners at his funeral were said to number fifty thousand, and every day three thousand people file through the gallery at Chengchow to view the few souvenirs of his career and to listen to the pigtailed maidens tell his story.

It begins traditionally, in Communist custom, with pictures of his parents, miserable, hungry and suffering. Then the child, Chiao, six years old, scrambling up a mountainside through snow to gather faggots and carry them on his back from house to house to sell to the comfortable rich. Dickens would have made much of him.

He grew, working in the fields in season, seeking odd jobs in between; and when he was eighteen he became a seller of coal, which he carried in baskets hung from a shoulder pole: the traditional Chinese figure made familiar on willow-pattern pottery.

When invading Japanese occupied this district they put him to work in a coal mine, but he escaped and, as was the way with other young men, joined the guerrillas. Once among them he learned to make and throw grenades, to lay mines and bamboo dagger traps, to use a bayonet (a blown-up snapshot shows a pockmarked tree upon which he and his friends practiced). He learned to read and write the ideology, to recognize the idealistic objective of the Party, discovered the logic of Communist doctrine, saw the light, the goal, and the way. The formula thus far is standard.

Along with this progress in political understanding came greater activist responsibility. Soon he was leading forays against police and troops of the Kuomintang, and having in these exercises proved himself practical as well as ardent, he was received into the Party. Such was the syllabus of preparation. Then came a period of active apostolate among the country people. (One must understand that there is nothing haphazard about the making of a Communist cadre.)

He was among many who served their novitiate as activists by stirring up peasants and leading them against local autocrats. They forced landlords to burn rent books and return deeds of ownership held against debt. They split up big farms, sharing them and the livestock among the landless—freed slaves and concubines who had been sold into service in order that their families might survive.

There were, inevitably, times when excitement led to license, tripped up discipline, and let impatience for revenge overrun justice. Landlords were hanged, their lackeys thrashed and turned adrift, wrong judgments given, correction overlaid with hate. But in the main these early essays in revolution were carried through with surprising restraint by such dedicated novices of communism as Chiao Yu-lu.

After the Liberation, when he had served his political apprenticeship as a cadre among peasants, the Party sent him to take charge of a workshop in a mining-machine factory at Loyang, where he was a leading activist: one who would hold high the red banner and gather the workers together under it; would teach them, as he had been taught, to love the Party, to aspire to be worthy, to work continuously for the revolution, to prepare China to withstand imperialist aggression, to preach the word of Mao Tse-tung and, by unceasing example, to show that no sacrifice made for the masses would be too great.

So in the Art Gallery in Chengchow there are photographs and sketches of Chiao working in the factory; and beneath them is the wooden bench where he slept when, exhausted after daylong pace-making in the workshop and nights of preaching and teaching, he fell asleep for a few hours beside the equipment which he tended.

In 1962 the Provincial Committee of the Party sent for Chiao and told him of the troubles of the 360,000 peasants of Lankao County, which lies in a bend of the Yellow River. They said that after four consecutive years of calamity the people were dispirited and leaving the district.

The passsing year had been disastrous, beginning badly when spring sandstorms smothered the young wheat. A second sowing struggled through summer drought to a harvest pitifully skimpy, with stalks too sparse and spindly to reap in sheaves. Late autumn floods then laid waste 150,000 acres of arable land and brought alkaline salt to the surface, spoiling it all for the next spring planting. Now, in November, snow was already falling and a bitter winter was predicted.

"There is no point in socialism," said the chairman of the Provincial Committee of the Party, "no truth in the words of our great leader Chairman Mao if people suffer as much under us as

125

they did under the corrupt rulers and foreign despots of former times. These Yellow River peasants need someone to teach them how to overcome their difficulties."

Chiao Yu-lu took the train to Lankao County, and at every station on the way he saw scores of families waiting to be taken to other places where they might at least have hope of survival. Coming to Lankao, he called the county committee together and said:

"As members of the Party we have only one function: to serve the people; and to serve them we must help them liberate themselves from negative thinking.

"But first we ourselves must learn from the masses of the people. Must study their problems with them. Must go out into the fields when it rains and see which way the water runs to wash out gulleys. Watch how the winds make sand dunes drift. Measure the depth and strength of floods when they overrun the country. Map the land inch by inch, mark each trouble spot, every configuration which contributes to disaster. Each one of us must share the suffering of the people, show them that we are their brothers. Bread chewed by others has no taste."

He got together a work team of 120 members—cadres, farmers, and technicians—and kept them busy all winter studying problems and working out plans to manage them. When the weather was at its worst and snow piled against the door of the hut which was his office he told the cadres, "This is not the time to put more wood on the fire. This is the time to go visiting poor people who have no firewood—the sick, the old, the lonely, and those in trouble. Let them know that the Party is thinking of them."

He went to an old couple who were childless. The old man was sick in bed and the wife blind. They said, "Why have you come?"

He answered, "Chairman Mao has sent me. You are his children, and I am your son."

They wept and comforted each other.

All around the walls of this gallery in Chengchow there are pictures. As works of art they are of little consequence, but they illustrate episodes in the life of the Good Party Secretary Chiao Yu-lu and to this end they serve their purpose.

They show him standing thigh-deep in floodwaters, trudging through snowstorms, sharing his food with poor people, talking to village groups, coming home on his bicycle after a long day of visiting in the communes.

His children cling to him. In the evening he tells them revolutionary stories, sings revolutionary songs. He shows them the photographs of their grandfather's grave, saying, "The landlord took away every bit of his grain to pay his debts, so he hanged himself. Never forget."

The little hut which was his office is in this gallery at Chengchow, with one wall removed so that the inside can be seen. I sat on a bench beside it while one of the vestal virgins, on a box, gave a passionate commentary to a group of high-school students crowding all about me. She said, "You are all successors to the proletarian revolution." (She was a pretty girl, herself not long out of school.)

The County office is spare and economical—wooden walls, a brick floor, one table, and an office chair. An upright hatstand in the corner has a patched jacket hanging on it, a mangy cap, and a woolen scarf with unraveled edges. A canvas rain cape on a nail. Ears of dried sorghum. A feather duster. A worn straw broom. A shovel to clear away the snow.

The chair has a plaited bucket seat. A hole, big enough to take a man's hand, has been cut in the left side. It allowed Chiao Yu-lu to press his hand against the pain caused by the carcinoma in his liver. And the day came when the pain was so great that he could not write down what his committeemen were saying. When the pencil fell from his fingers, everyone was silent, watching while he slowly picked it up.

Until someone spoke and said, "Chiao Yu-lu, there is a time when the willing ox must rest; when the body tells the heart that no man is beyond the reach of sickness."

There is a gray fascination in this surfeit of sorrow which overhangs the landscape of China's grim history; and an innocent simplicity marks the worker and peasant martyrs who people this monotonous and melancholy panorama of suffering, putting each of them beyond the reach of common mockery.

Perhaps it is an absence of self-consciousness, of hypocrisy or hysteria of any kind that saves them from being suspect, for few latter-day Franciscan monks, nuns, or brothers can match their modesty or genuine attachment to poverty. One cannot rob a man who has nothing, cannot take away the dignity of one whose humility protects him from derision.

Chiao Yu-lu was a Communist; an anathema to all Christians good and bad and yet a better man, by all reports, than almost any I know of in my own society. Certainly better than I, a true believer.

I am tempted, then, to suggest that there is more of true compassion in the charity of a Chiao Yu-lu, who followed his irreligious faith to its conclusion and gave his life for his fellows with no hope of heaven or belief in God's commendation, than there is in the devotion of many religious who are consciously anxious instruments of God's grace.

On the following day I had occasion to visit the hospital in Chengchow for some minor matter of my own and, having been received and treated with much courtesy, was taken to the sickroom where Chiao had spent his last weeks.

The U.S.-educated senior physician, and others of the staff, came with me and stood by the empty bed quietly talking about him, saying that when he was in pain he remained continuously anxious about the people of Lankao, worried when the rains were heavy in case the new drains were unable to carry the floodwater away; feeling ashamed that he was lying in bed while others worked; being overjoyed when a young man and his wife came to show him the first ears of wheat to be grown on a patch of alkaline land.

His only possessions when he died were two books: a volume of the *Selected Works of Mao Tse-tung,* and *How to Be a Good Communist.* They were there by his bedside, as he had left them.

The physician said, "He helped us to understand each other and to feel as one. Doctors and nurses worked in the fields alongside village people and students and government functionaries. We all helped dig the ditches and plant trees and drag loads of river silt onto the fields. Now we feel that we are all equally part of the revolution in this district. There is no separation between us and our patients. We are one people."

A woman surgeon standing alongside me spoke softly. "He was a good man. When he died the city was silent. When we buried him in the sand dunes at Lankao an old man stepped out of the crowd and spoke over his grave:

" 'Good Secretary Chiao, you worked so hard for us that you died. When times were bad you worried about us. When we were sick you came to see us. If we were hungry you found something for us to eat. Now, when we begin to live well, and have food enough for a funeral feast, you lie here by yourself.' "

There was silence, and when I looked at those around me they were crying.

I COULD sense that Feng had kept something from me and so was ready for surprise of some kind when we came by train to the triple city of Wuhan on the river Yangtze; but I had not expected to find Miss Ping at the station, smiling.

She could see that I was pleased and, blushing, tried to take my travel bag as we went to the reception room to drink tea while officials dealt with my passport and travel permit. Waiting, she said that two of our Peking party had flown in that day (she with them) to see the heavy industries set up around and about Wuhan since liberation.

It was, said Feng, cutting in, one of the most impressive achievements of the revolution and the Party's program of self-sufficiency, and he thought that I also should see something of these things instead of spending so much time speaking to people vaguely of minor matters. To this I answered, not wishing to seem disinterested, that this would certainly please me though I had no understanding of machinery or any knowledge with which to measure the worth of an industry, and first I would like to send a cable to my aunt in Australia, who was about to be eighty.

They were immediately interested (how much more easily do people meet on such common ground as appreciation of an aged lady's birthday than in the assessment of the technical merit of some stupendous steelworks!) and as soon as my papers were cleared we went to the Posts and Telegraph Office on the bund beside the river, by the customs house, where the head clerk searched for overseas cable forms among papers that had been put aside a long time ago.

When he found them I wrote my message, then waited while he slowly typed it onto a new form with one finger, the other clerks gathering around him to watch, a dozen of them, mostly girls except an elderly man who sold me stamps and pasted them onto my letters.

Feng said, "This man was working here when almost every building on the waterfront was owned by foreign merchants, and the clerks in this office were busy all day long sending and receiving cables in English, French, German, Russian, and Japanese. The river was full of foreign ships taking away our iron and coal, our wheat, cotton, silk, pottery, wooden chests, and other things. Their own policemen walked up and down the bund, and their gunboats patrolled six hundred miles of river between here and Shanghai to protect their ships from pirates.

"A British company owned the passenger boats which go inland for a thousand miles, but no Chinese could travel in the first-class part: only white people. For many years this city was a foreign base like Shanghai, Canton, and many other places—an opening in China's side through which they drained her rich blood away." (Ping's eyes opened wide and she took out her notebook, and I, impressed by this flow of poetic resentment, looked at Feng, surprised, but he seemed quite calm. Later, looking through a local travel brochure, I found most of this written in the official description of the city.)

The staff around the cable clerk moved back to let him come to the counter, then gathered again; and the customers on my side crowded around while he checked the message with me and swiftly clicked out the cost on an abacus. Then we all watched while he went to a desk and, setting his spectacles straight, tapped on a Morse transmitter key affectionate greetings to my aunt. When he was done we bobbed and bowed to each other all around, smiling, while the customers watched, clapping happily as I left with Feng and Ping.

131

Two rivers meet here, the Yangtze and the Han, splitting this city of two million into three parts: one part on the Yangtze bank and the others on each side of the Han. They are both big rivers, draining a large part of middle China so that the commerce of tens of thousands of square miles of country converges here, making the triple city a place of major consequence both economically and politically.

It was here, in 1911, that the Republic of China was first proclaimed when army officers rebelled against the last of the Manchu rulers. But this military revolution degenerated quickly (as others have done since) into a cynical struggle among ambitious generals and politicians, with no gain or settlement made that would lead to an easing of the burdens of the people.

Instead of losing their grip the foreigners thrived on this confusion, consolidating control of China's commerce and politics. They rejected the gentle revolutionary Sun Yat-sen and put their money on a succession of military dictators, backing one general against another, playing the ancient game of buying influence with armaments and bribes, keeping the country divided and, incidentally, paving the way for a Japanese invasion a few years later.

But they were never at ease in China. Their presence was never accepted as inevitable. Foreigners, unless useful, friendly, and polite, were parasites, treated as such and constantly reminded by student demonstrations, workers' strikes, and acts of defiance that sooner or later they would be sent packing; that China could and would do without them, as she had done during the long years of her classical civilization, and would regard any subsequent interference with her national dignity by the upstart West (or lesser Orientals) as evidence of its continuing barbarity.

This was the elemental truth that Chiang Kai-shek relinquished when he inherited the leadership of the Nationalist movement from Sun Yat-sen. It was the rock upon which his hopeful coalition with the Communists crashed and came apart, leaving him shipwrecked and castaway on an island, dependent upon America, while Mao Tse-tung survived and, with the help of the common people of China, triumphed.

As we walked along the bund toward the hotel Feng was saying, "In the bad times when our people were starving they came here to beg, bringing their hungry children, but the merchants and bankers complained and their policemen put barricades around the warehouses and banks and let the people die outside. Their bodies were taken away from the town and thrown into the river, hundreds every day."

In spite of much kindness, and their excellence in matters of personal attention, the guides and interpreters of China are not historical authorities; nor should a tourist expect them to be. Listening to Feng, I had to remember that he came from these parts; that the drama of those days had for him been translated by domestic repetition into the one-dimensional language of legend; also, that his official function was chiefly to evoke emotional impressions which had the general verisimilitude of truth.

But I cannot travel happily in blinkers or be completely satisfied with scraps. Places and scenery, though filled with people and the memory of people, are meaningless to me unless quickened with the living spirit of history. A mountain is a mountain, a town is a town, people in the street are pedestrians unless related to the continuing unity of being, having connection with the past and with the future. And in China, which has the longest continuing civilization still in existence, this sense of completeness, of timeless integration, and of the identification of people with the minutiae of their environment and history, is almost palpable.

I was glad then when Feng suggested that later in the evening he would bring a friend who was, he said, a lecturer at one of Wuhan's universities.

"You ask so many questions that I think it better to bring Mr. Cheng to talk to you. Then you will not expect so much from me and little Ping."

I had dinner with my fellow tourists, one of them the simple, rich man and the other a technical college teacher, and was aware of a feeling of relief, of freedom from the need to be discreet, pleased to speak of simple things again, to hear news of the others of our group, to be able to make little jokes without being carefully explicit—above all to be freed from the clutch of instruction.

But they ate quickly, saying that Miss Ping was to take them to some entertainment and that we would join forces in the morning.

So they went; and in a while Feng came with his friend (a fat man) and in the sepia half light of late evening we sat on a little balcony outside my room looking down on the wide, brown river. A few junks drifted with the stream. Some men in fuzzy silhouette were mending tackle at the water's edge, watched by little children. Older boys and girls in groups sat separately on the sloping sides of the dike, singing.

Across the river, in the Workers' Cultural Palace and Pleasure Garden, a concert had begun (Ping would be there with my friends). We could hear the thin jingle of cymbals and strings and the insistent thump of a drum. Feng smiled, beating time, but Mr. Cheng, looking up, was watching wild ducks flying high, in a line.

He said quietly, as though satisfied, "They are going to the East Lake to rest."

Then, away upriver, a long and heavy freight train rumbled over the new Yangtze River bridge. Cheng took a cigarette, and when it was lit he gestured with it.

"That bridge is evidence of the revolution. A sign of the new China. In ancient days it was said that the Yellow River would not stay within its banks nor the Yangtze be crossed by a bridge unless the sun shone every day. Now we have the sun of Chairman Mao's thoughts shining on us all the time, and under the leadership of the Party the Yellow River is tamed and the Yangtze has its bridge."

I had hoped for something better than this and looked at Feng; but he was expressionless. Yet as Cheng went on to sketch the past half-century of China's history with an extravagant mixture of fantasy embellished with revolutionary legend and rhetoric, the picture gained shape and sense and an insistent validity. And it seemed to me that in the complex pattern and interplay of mixed issues and innumerable events which led, in the end, to the transmutation of China into a Communist state, there was a thread of inevitability which Mao Tse-tung discerned from the beginning and followed with unremitting and astonishing confidence to its end.

My own knowledge was not enough to let me follow with certainty every step of Cheng's commentary, or to assess the correctness of each emphasis; but as he spoke a man began to come to life. A man who had so far been for me a white, lackluster bust set somewhat incongruously among potted plants in the foyer of every public building. A benevolent and elderly photo-frontispiece in every weekly magazine. The calligrapher of untranslatable Chinese aphorisms displayed on hundreds of thousands of billboards, posters, bookplates, walls, and obelisks.

Now Cheng was saying, "He knew that the 1911 revolution of intellectuals, businessmen, and generals would never benefit the peasants; could see that China's usual cycle was ready to repeat itself, and that another family dynasty would soon arise out of the revolutionary confusion, leaving the peasants and workers where they were before.

"He knew that the peasants, especially, would need to make their own revolution, take over China and reshape it in such a way that they would never again be pushed back into the mud to work as dumb oxen for other people's profit.

"The Communist revolution in Russia lit a beacon, showed a possible way; and Mao was among the dozen who took hold of the vision and started a Communist Party in China, looking toward Moscow for advice.

"But the new Russian leaders would not believe that any revolution based on peasantry was possible. They said that in China, as in Russia, a start should be made in the major industrial cities and then spread into the countryside; though they did agree that the Chinese Communists, being a small and weak group, should unite for a while with the Sun Yat-sen Republicans to get rid of rival warlords who, with the help of foreign governments, were running private fights all over northern China in a struggle to take control of the creaking government machinery in Peking."

The history of this period is complex, a tangle too intricate for unweaving here. But to understand anything of present-day China one must try at least to follow the story of Mao Tse-tung: his emergence from the obscurity of a minor clerkship in the university library in Peking to become a trade union organizer and political analyst; then a foundation member of the Communist Party of China; eventually its undisputed leader and pilot of the People's Revolution; and finally a kind of demigod, equal or superior in authority to any emperor, divine or otherwise, who had ruled from the Forbidden City.

For a while he went quietly. The Party, with others leading it, grew in numbers and influence. Taking direction from Moscow, it aligned with Sun Yat-sen's Republicans, who were trying to bring some semblance of political order into China, but were getting no help from other foreign powers who found the warlord confusion a boost to their own business interests.

With Russian aid the Republican-Communist coalition made progress. Its army, under Sun Yat-sen's protégé, Chiang Kai-shek (educated in Japan and army-trained in Moscow), captured the southern part of China and made Wuhan its capital.

Meanwhile Mao busied himself among the peasants and working people. He studied their ways, their needs, their strength and revolutionary potential. He set up institutes from which grew a system of political teaching and the training of cadres and activists. (There was one such established here in Wuhan in which Mao was headmaster and Chou En-lai a teacher. Now it is a memorial museum, a place of pilgrimage.)

Wherever the Nationalist armies went the Communists were present as partners. While the army set up some kind of government the Communists set up cells, preached their gospel, taught, gained strength. Chiang Kai-shek saw this, as did the rich Chinese and the foreigners in Wuhan, Shanghai, and elsewhere; and one night in the spring of 1927 Chiang turned against his Communist colleagues and killed as many as he could lay hands on. It is said by some who have had best access to evidence that four of every five Communists were executed. Among those who escaped, though narrowly, were Mao Tse-tung and Chou En-lai.

Because of the size of China, and the poor state of roads and other communications, it was possible for the escapees, and some army units who went with them, to continue a guerrilla existence in the hilly country of the central provinces for the next ten years. The area south and west of Wuhan became the center of the Communist struggle for revenge, a training and recruiting ground for what was to become the Red Army of the revolution.

This period provided a historical pastiche, an extravaganza of incidents, uprisings, carefully organized rebellions within the Nationalist army, strikes, attacks on cities and towns, the setting up of little soviets; above all the perfecting of principles, plans, and strategies that led to the ultimate Communist triumph. It is the stuff of which today's operas, films, books, ballets, and plays are made—the flowers of Mao Tse-tung's thinking, in the hills, in attics, in peasant huts, in caves.

Other Communist leaders carried out attacks on cities which for a while made brave flame and clamor, but fizzled out in a series of disastrous defeats because the Party was not yet big enough or ready for such steps; nor was the time right. It became clear that Russian methods would not work in China for a long time to come; that Mao's system of winning the mass of China's millions, and surrounding the cities with a cohesive sea of peasants, was the way to approach and plan the final revolution.

With hindsight it is easy to say that when Chiang Kai-shek broke with the Communists he broke with the mass of the Chinese people and was consequently doomed to lose control of the country. But it is likely that if he had captured and executed Mao he might have beaten the Communists. For until Mao took charge of the Party its fortunes were declining and it is doubtful if it would have long survived the series of defeats inflicted in the cities.

Today the Chinese speak of Chiang's "betrayal" of the People's Republic, and it is difficult to find any, even among his friends of then or now, who regard him highly. Yet it is likely that he believed that he was doing the right thing by China in trying to save it from communism and in giving the people a chance to work toward some kind of Western-style democracy. It is even conceivable that he might have pulled this off if the Japanese had not attacked China a few years later. When they did they kept Chiang and his Kuomintang armies occupied in and around the cities and chief towns, leaving the vast countryside to be consolidated by Mao's peasant armies and People's militia.

Feng's friend, Mr. Cheng, sitting in the shadows on the little balcony, said, "When the Japanese invaded China, Chiang Kai-shek opened the Yellow River dikes and flooded the countryside. But with Chairman Mao it was the opposite. When the Japanese left China the Red Army flowed in from the countryside and flooded the cities. This was exactly what he had planned from the beginning."

If one can accept the belief that a man foresaw and then directed the destiny of a quarter of the human race within his own lifetime, it is easier to appreciate the mass acceptance by the Chinese people of a mystical image which personalizes, yet defies this man who leads them.

"He is our savior," said Cheng. "He has released China from foreign bandage and made all people equal. For us he is both Moses and Jesus. Perhaps this is why you are afraid of him."

They talked together briefly in Chinese. Then Cheng said, "I was taught by Christian missionaries here in Wuhan, and the rest of my family went away with them after liberation because they were frightened of the Communists. I don't blame them, but I think they made a mistake. They should have stayed and tested their faith. Maybe they would have lost it, but they would have gained a new faith as I have; one that gives the people bread today instead of promises for tomorrow. I have found it more satisfying and exciting to believe in the goodness and the possibilities of man struggling here on earth than to believe in dreams of meaningless peace beyond the skies."

So, as I sat in this old hotel in Wuhan, overlooking the river, seeing the lights and hearing a clash and clang of revolutionary music coming from the Workers' Cultural Palace and Pleasure Garden, Chairman Mao Tse-tung took shape, became (for me) a person in time and place. In this particular place, this city in which he and his friends, now rulers of all China, spent part of their peripatetic and fugitive existence, planning, plotting, triggering off strikes and uprisings against the "traitor" Chiang Kai-shek and his Kuomintang army, against the foreigners, the warlords, and the Chinese rich; at times fleeing for their lives, leaving behind dead friends killed in gun battles on the bund.

Ironically it was in Wuhan that the only armed uprising against the present regime was attempted: and its leaders executed.

This year, on July 16, five thousand swimmers crossed the Yangtze: groups from factories and from the women's armed militia, Party cadres and members of committees, army men with red banners. Some pushed poster boards on floats, dotting the river with slogans bobbing on the wash of riverboats. The biggest of them read:

THE U.S. IMPERIALISTS TRY TO FRIGHTEN US.
SOON WE WILL TURN AND FRIGHTEN THEM.

138

Another, towed by two hundred Young Pioneers from primary schools, quoted from the works of Mao:

STUDY DILIGENTLY. MAKE PROGRESS EVERY DAY.

A launch sped downriver toward the swimmers that day and stopped above the bridge, close to where the tea shops used to be. Thousands on the riverbanks shouted, "Long live our great leader." The two hundred swimming children turned toward the launch singing, "We are successors to the noble cause of communism." Mao entered the water and the crowds on the riverbanks sang "The East Is Red."

The old man swam among them for an hour or more, resting now and then on his back to chat with those close by, alternately swimming and drifting, finishing downstream on the other side.

The Western press is skeptical of this swimming business, thinks it a somewhat ridiculous stunt. There are doubts that Mao is fit enough to swim for more than a few minutes without assistance, though Miss Ping said that the British Lord Montgomery came to Wuhan in 1960 and, watching the Chairman swim the river, wished that he, too, could do it.

She said, "This Englishman is very famous but not strong enough to swim in the Yangtze; but Mao shows us that we must be courageous and surmount every difficulty to win victory."

I do not believe that her hero Mao Tse-tung is simply a benevolent old gentleman who likes to swim a bit and so set example to the masses, nor that he is an ailing and evil deceiver.

He is, I think, a clear-sighted political realist who knows that people in the mass are weak and need to be constantly driven or gently led; that left unprotected, they will drift, go different and individual ways, compete, split into fragmentary divisions, and be vulnerable to their own spiritual fragility and the inept manipulations of unprincipled politicians and pressure groups.

He believes, nonetheless, that the astonishing possibilities of mankind's future on earth reside entirely within man himself; yet he knows as well as any priest that collective material progress is only achieved through individual spiritual disciplines, that in his natural state almost any peasant would as soon be selfishly rich as be a saint.

He also believes (as most of us do) that among mankind's astonishing possibilities is that of self-annihilation, and that in order to survive mankind must unify its thinking; that one-world requires one-mind, and the ultimate elimination of individual ambition.

He believes that his own "thought" supplies the blueprint for China's collective mind; that given time, the red banner of his brilliant thinking will fly out above the masses of mankind; that if the Chinese people can be kept of one mind for long enough, nothing will prevent their ideological triumph over all imperialists, revisionists, capitalists, splittists, and other degenerates and retrogressives whose inferior thinking keeps mankind from achieving a collectively majestic destiny.

This is why every aspect of Red China's propaganda is so insistent and unrelenting. Mao's thinking must first be indelibly imprinted on the mass mind of China and afterward on all the earth. Anything which tends to keep undisciplined individualistic tendencies alive must be wiped out. This, I think, is the significance of the Cultural Revolution and its offshoot, the Red Guard: Mao's philosophical progeny, whose minds must be tightly bound to the tower of his truth, so that their generation, and the generation which they beget, will stand fast, grasping the red banner bravely, until the rest of the world catches up or capitulates.

Crossing the fine, new Yangtze bridge with little Miss Ping beside me, her ragged plaits tied with red ribbon, I had doubts about Mao's vision. Prophets have dreamed this dream from the beginning. The reality still lies beyond our reach and beyond our present comprehension, to be approached step by step until we are ready to face and embrace it. Nor is it possible to bind the minds of future generations to a dream: the business of living is insistent and unpredictable.

An old man in black cotton tunic, skull cap, and old-fashioned pants came slowly toward us with his wife, who was short and fat and hung on to his arm as she hobbled. When they came close enough for shortsighted Ping to see them she turned her face away. She dislikes these signs of old China and the days when they bound women's feet.

CHAPTER

14

OUR capitalist, attacking eggs and bacon, faced me across the breakfast table and pointed forward with his fork.

"You must give your head a rest. Stop filling it with all this fiddle-faddle about the leadership of the masses and the dictatorship of the working class, and look at the practical side of things, which is what counts in the long run." He sucked at his upper lip, ran his tongue over his teeth, and looked at the schoolteacher. "Don't you agree?"

But the teacher only grinned and gave himself more coffee.

I tried to seem untouched but knew that I was about to give in and go with them both to the Wuhan Iron and Steel Combine and, afterward, to the Heavy Machine Tools Plant instead of to the Peasants' Institute as I had planned.

The capitalist mopped his plate with a piece of bread. "My father used to say, 'Sticks and stones can break your bones, but words won't even bruise you,' which is true. It's not what the Chinese say that matters, it's what they can do that counts as far as we're concerned, and you won't find out much about that in these museums and places where you seem to spend so much time filling up notebooks."

He took another slice of bread and covered it with butter and jam, neatly, with the precision of a conscientious laborer spreading cement, and continued speaking.

"From what I've seen and read I reckon that the Chinese are fifteen years behind the times industrially, and the way they are at present the U.S. or the Russians could blow them to glory in a week if they wanted to. But when you look at what they can do, and have done in the past few years, I'd be prepared to bet that they'll catch up with both of them in pretty quick time, say ten or twelve years, if they can keep going the way they are. This is what really matters to the rest of the world, not this windy stuff about holding high the red banner of thingamabob's thinking. That's only for the locals."

I wondered for a moment if I ought to point out that the two things went together, the exhortations and the effort, the faith and the works, then realized that in a way he was right, and in any case in full spate and not to be denied or diverted, talking while he ate.

"When the Commies took over this country the production of steel was round about a hundred and fifty thousand tons a year all told. Not enough to make a decent teakettle for every family. In ten years they had raised production to eighteen million tons and were making a quarter of this in backyard factories, and on the communes so that they could make their own farm machinery. I tell you, the way they've got labor organized, wages held down, and the people keyed up, there's nothing these people can't do if they put their minds to it."

Then he looked up, belligerently, almost as though he were admonishing himself for praising the Chinese too highly.

"But they've got their troubles like the rest of us. This split with the Russians has set them back more than a bit, though the guides and interpreters don't usually admit it. The Russian experts left before they had their big installations completed, and at the same time a lot of the communes gave away steelmaking because they'd overdone it and agriculture was suffering from lack of labor. In 1960 steel production dropped back to ten million tons or thereabouts, mainly because they had to sit down and figure out things about equipment which the Russians hadn't shown them or explained. Then they had to train people to take over the top technical jobs left vacant, and this takes time and mistakes. But it seems that they're picking up and going ahead again, and the only

142

thing that'll stop them this time is a war, which they don't want."

I am impressed but somehow troubled by the facility with which practical people digest, regurgitate, and live by dubious facts and figures, finding in them courage, a substitute for faith, a shield against the mystery and uncertainty of existence; and I was comforted when the schoolteacher answered him:

"Most of the figures you quote are speculative estimates arrived at by foreigners without direct evidence, so they can only be a guide, though they turn up as gospel truth week after week in books and papers and magazines all over the world. The magic of figures seems to have replaced the superstitions of religion in this day and age. Nobody, probably not even the Chinese, has precise knowledge of current industrial production in this enormous country. We don't even know for sure how many big iron and steel plants there are in China, though most expert assessments say twenty and put Wuhan among the top five."

Wiping his lips with his napkin, he looked at me. "You really should come along. Even if you don't like factories you'll learn something, and the Travel Service people will be a bit put out if you don't show some interest in the district's major industry."

Of course, they were right and it was interesting: especially to see young women manipulating the overhead machinery which lifts and smoothly carries huge, incandescent billets of molten metal across the workshops and lays them onto rollers. And other girls employed in various ways—bringing drinks to the men on "hot" jobs, running first-aid stations, operating switchgear in the rolling mills. One, a girl from Chungking, with the refined and expressionless face of an angel, stationed in a big-windowed office facing the open-hearth furnaces, let me question her through Feng while she worked.

Miss Tang, he said, was twenty-five and a final-year student of metallurgy from the University of Szechwan, doing a term of practical work before graduating.

"It's usual for all students in technical schools and faculties," said the schoolteacher. "A basic part of the educational method. So much more practical and productive than our own apprenticeship system. There seems to be more method-and-work-force flexibility

143

in China at the moment than in countries where a profit-motive economy affects the attitude of both workers and management and tends to fix industrial patterns firmly within the framework of government and labor-union regulations, leaving not much room for new attitudes and approaches. The developing countries have an advantage over us in this. They don't yet have to contend with management and labor antagonisms, or to stick to profit-proven systems of operation."

The capitalist said, "That'll come once they catch up with us. The Russians found out that you can't compete with capitalism except by using the same general methods. The only real difference is State ownership of resources and equipment, and the fact that union and management leaders work for the same boss."

They argued while I photographed Miss Tang by the wild light of furnace flame, she leaning over a bench using slide rule and microscope, then sending work signals by microphone to the furnace men. Absentmindedly she felt for loose hair, hanging on her forehead, and tucked it back under her cotton cap, leaving a smudge of dust; and when I thanked her for letting me take pictures she smiled vaguely and went on with her work.

We left, and Feng, glancing at his notebook, said, "Miss Tang is especially trained in micromathematics." Then he put the book into his pocket and went on with fluency. "Women who do the same work as men receive the same pay but also get special leave allowances when they have babies, and afterward their working hours are arranged to allow for feeding times and other needs."

When we had walked around for two hours we rested, took tea and talked with the secretary of the plant management committee. He said that the whole complex of iron and steel and coking plant, covering a little more than six square miles, stands on the land that was formerly occupied by three townships with a combined population of less than 10,000; it presently employs 73,000 people, whose dependents bring the total population to something over 200,000. Of these, some 7000 families engage in food production for the industrial group.

A little less than half the force is occupied with new construction and installation, which should be completed within two or three years, at which time the people will probably be transferred with their families to other industrial construction jobs, perhaps in the outer provinces.

As well as the usual kindergarten, primary, middle, and technical schools, the plant runs its own technical institute at university level, graduating enough students each year to keep pace with expansion and to fill places left when experienced technicians are sent to set up plants in other places.

When the secretary had finished these explanations the schoolteacher and the capitalist asked questions while I made notes. The schoolteacher said that although the plant seemed efficient it was not as modern as it might be. He thought that any steelworks now under construction ought to be fitted with high-pressure oxygen equipment instead of being tied to the open-hearth system of steelmaking.

Feng and the secretary discussed this observation at great length; then Feng, satisfied that he had the answers straight, turned back to us. Shorn of most of the ideological ornament, his explanation seemed simple, though tinged with resentment.

He said that when the plant was planned in 1955, high-pressure oxygen techniques had not been mentioned by the U.S.S.R. experts and the question of including the necessary equipment in the Wuhan complex had not arisen. It was probable that the Russians were at that time using the process in their own new plants, though it was not until "the Khrushchev revisionists betrayed the world revolution" in 1960 that any thoughts of this kind were considered.

Until then, forty-five Russian experts had been supervising at Wuhan, and except for a handful of Chinese specialists from other steelworks (whose main function was technical interpretation and liaison) these were the only men who knew what to do.

Of the total work force engaged in the first stages of preparation, construction, and installation 85 percent was local peasant labor with no previous experience of anything but subsistence farming. Administration and general management was looked after by Party cadres and Red Army veterans, also with little industrial experience. Yet in spite of these basic handicaps, once properly under way, the work had progressed so well that the first steel was poured in 1958. Relations between the Russian experts and their colleagues were excellent and affectionate at this time.

Feng said, "When the split came they were sorry to go. They liked being here, but their leaders betrayed them as well as us. The Russians and Chinese who were working together on this project were like brothers and many wept when they left."

The plans called for nine open-hearth furnaces and a complete complex of rolling and plate mills; but when the Russian technicians left, taking their blueprints with them, only six of the furnaces had been completed and a small part of the processing equipment made and installed. Chinese engineers went on with the work slowly, studying textbooks, discovering proper procedures by methods of trial and error; and the project is not yet completed.

Ping, sitting with me, spoke for the first time. "It is always like this. The people of the world wish to be friends, but their governments do not let them. It is the same everywhere. We know that many Americans would like to come and help us, but their government tells them to hate us instead."

We all looked at Ping and she blushed and fumbled in her plastic bag for a handkerchief. Feng shook his head slowly from side to side, but smiled. The capitalist frowned doubtfully, while the schoolteacher, touched by such innocence, sighed and said, "If only it were as simple as that."

I wanted to say, You are right, little Ping, so right. You have been right since the beginning of the tribal history of mankind and you will be right when, at last, it ends in a final exchange of violent, stubborn, idiot lies that obscure the purpose and the goal of life. You, little Ping, are the private voice of the people of all time. The last man will die with the same "Why?" crying inside his heart and mind as it cries in yours and mine.

But I said nothing.

Then Feng, looking at his watch, suggested that we should now go to the Heavy Machine Tools Plant; and as if at a signal, a girl came straightway into the room carrying three Wuhan steelworks stickpins on a piece of black cloth, which she held out while the secretary took them one by one and handed them to us, Feng standing with his head cocked on one side, beaming. And Ping blowing her nose.

146

The Heavy Machine Tools Plant employs between 7000 and 7500 people and uses most of the steel output of the Wuhan complex. It produces lathes up to 240 tons, metal planers weighing 340 tons, gear-cutting machinery, and vertical and horizontal drilling equipment that can be used on components up to twenty-five feet in diameter.

The capitalist and the schoolteacher, fascinated by the size of everything, said that what they could see was good; but Ping and I drifted aimlessly in their wake, neither of us having criteria with which to make a measure of excellence. She hid for a few minutes behind a big machine and took her Guide's Primer from her plastic bag. Then, catching up to me, she said resentfully, "Betraying the revolutionary message of Marx, the Khrushchev revisionists also interrupted progress in this factory by taking away their technicians, blueprints, and key pieces of equipment." Her delivery was awkward and unconvincing, though to please her I wrote down what she said.

Then, as we were led through huge workshops, conversation became frayed and overlaid with the clatter and clang of mechanical hammers, the roar of furnaces and forges, the swish and hiss of steam-cleaning equipment, and the whining of cranes high overhead; so that we seemed like amiable mutes smiling and nodding at men and girls who watched while we passed among them, making exaggerated gestures of amazement and good-will.

Our guide for this item of the day's itinerary was Office Manager Nu, who, having brought us to the inevitable reception room for tea and discussion, proved more outgoing than most and with a little encouragement spoke freely of his own history, which I took down as Feng translated.

He spoke simply, saying that he was thirty-three, the son of a peasant farmer of these parts, and that he had joined the Liberation Army while still a child at primary school.

"I was for six years a soldier and when not fighting studied politics and revolutionary culture. I learned to be a proper Communist and to understand the social and historical objectives of our struggle.

"I was a child when I joined the army, and still young when we liberated China from the imperialists, traitors, and despots, yet I knew and remembered well the darkness of the old society in which I was born.

"The workers and peasants labored all day, every day, but still could not get enough to eat. They had no political leaders to help them, no chance to speak even if anyone high up would listen. The poor were less important to the rich than their animals. My mother and young brother died of hunger. My father was killed by Japanese imperialists because he picked up grains of rice that had been thrown away by their army cooks.

"When I think of the old society I am full of hate for those who oppress the poor. I understand why Chairman Mao tells us never to forget the past, because all over the world millions of people still live as we lived, still suffer as we suffered when I was a child.

"When our country was liberated I felt as though chains had been taken from my feet, but we who are now free must work and study all the more for the sake of those who still suffer." He spoke quite calmly. "I understand this more clearly every year and know that I have much more to learn from Chairman Mao's works and can never study enough. Communism is my life."

Mrs. Nu is an electrician. She also works in the Machine Tools Plant, and they have four children ranging in age from four to nine years. Her father, who lived in one of the villages demolished to make room for the industrial complex, lives with them and helps look after the children. Mostly they eat in the plant canteen.

"My children will be part of the new generation of revolutionaries. Their task will be to hold high the red banner of Chairman Mao's thinking"—our capitalist flapped his hands and made irritable faces—"to liberate the oppressed masses of Asia and Africa as we have been liberated, and above all to help our comrades in the Soviet Union to rid themselves of their revisionist leaders so that the revolutionary workers of the world may be again united under the leadership of the Party."

I looked at Ping, waiting for her to say "Amen," but she was busy, as I was, writing all this down in her notebook.

I learned nothing about steelmaking or the manufacture of machine tools from these visits, nor did I reach any assessment of my own about China's industrial potential. Such technical information as is contained in these pages, and much more, can be

148

culled from "authoritative sources" by the score, but may prove no more true or useful than the little I have written.

But sitting in the minibus going back to Wuhan, I tried to analyze and understand the implications raised by the unfinished buildings, the incompleted installations, the reluctance of our Chinese friends to discuss the defalcation of the Russians except in limited terms and phrases provided by the Party propaganda department; and it seemed to me that beneath the decent pride in what has already been achieved with and without Soviet assistance, and underlying the solid confidence in their ability to "go it alone," there was, in the attitude of these junior officials, a deep feeling of disappointment, of disenchantment, of having been let down by the Russians in a fundamental way.

This feeling, once separated from general impressions, seems adequate to explain the campaign of vitriolic denunciation unleashed against Soviet revisionists. It is an outraged, religious indignation; a traumatic hate that has more basic substance than China's hatred of the U.S.A., which is the conventional, workaday, political hate for a temporary enemy—hate compounded of equal parts of fear, envy, resentment, and memorized rhetoric—whereas this hate against Russia is a revulsion, a sudden deep distrust; the virulent bitterness of people who have been betrayed by a member of their own family.

The rift is intrinsically decisive, the issues and effects more immediately significant than those which obscure the ultimate outcome of the now familiar East-West contest, with its fantastic extensions into outer space.

This Sino-Soviet split suggests that the Communist vision of an all-embracing, classless brotherhood of man has been drastically diminished, if not tacitly abandoned by the red sects of the West. The argument that world-wide communism can provide a unifying force and ideology for mankind's betterment will no longer convince the uncommitted of Africa and the rest of the Third World. We, the people, are back where we started before Marx.

We begin again, with the knowledge reaffirmed that power alone, spiritual or material, can control the direction of the masses and the destiny of man; that the age-old contest between these two primal powers will continue until they merge, combine, become one, being necessary to each other.

149

International communism is now seen to be a sideshow, a historical diversion, and as much a paper tiger as U.S. imperialism. The smoke from this diverting skirmish has cleared and the major battle can go on again: the battle between mankind's two components, X and Y, Good and Evil, God and Mammon (call them what you will).

The professor and his wife were back with us and already at the table, when we came in for dinner, which pleased me because I wished to test my theory on him.

But his wife said, "We two have been living in the bronze age ever since we left you in Chengchow and if your theory refers to the twentieth century you'll get little sense from him this evening. His head is so full of antique mortuary ornaments it's a wonder it doesn't rattle."

She then excused herself, saying that she had written no letters for two days and must do some at once, otherwise the children would begin to worry. And looking over her shoulder as she left, she said, "Don't stay up late, Henry. Remember that you want to complete your notes on the Tien excavations, and if you sit drinking you'll nod off the minute you begin to write."

We settled in the sitting room, and when I had made my recital, to which he listened politely, he said, "Perhaps, as you suggest, communism has been merely a historical diversion, but I think we could also see it as an inevitable diversion necessary to arrest and correct the lopsided development of Western democracy with its emphasis on freedom for the individual to make progress at the expense of everybody. We could admit, I think, that by developing without check, our material progress has so far outstripped the spiritual that we have forgotten where we are going or what we can offer those who follow.

"In this context communism has by no means lost its potency, and in spite of the rift and its consequences it still offers example and inspiration to more than a half of mankind. It is a system in which, theoretically at least, body and soul grow upward as one—a religion which is practical and valid for hundreds of millions of people.

"The West should recognize now that it has been misled by its own feelings of guilt into adopting an aggressive defense attitude toward communism. It has, in fact, no need to try to batter communism out of existence. All it needs to do is to outbid it both spiritually and materially, an undertaking for which it should have more than adequate resources.

"In any clash between ideology and reality, reality usually wins. The Russians withdrew from Cuba, the Americans tolerate the situation in Berlin, your country sends soldiers to fight Communists in Vietnam and wheat to feed Communists in China. Applying realism of this kind to the point of view of an Asian peasant (who will do for a symbol of half the human race), the Communists continue to offer an austere sort of benevolence plus bread, while the West offers God and bombs. It is clear that we make it difficult for ourselves to win converts.

"The Sino-Soviet split may be a setback to Communist unity, but if we truly believe that the notion of an all-Red world is shown to be poppycock, then we are no longer justified in behaving as if communism is a mortal danger to us. We might admit, instead, that it may be simply a violent manifestation of suppressed nationalism which can provide depressed countries with a new starting point for development. In this case the dubious argument that the "Communist advance" in Asia is a menace to the West and must be stemmed anywhere, and at any price, should be re-examined; it will, I think, be shown to be no longer justified, and any policy based on a fundamentally wrong assumption is doomed to failure in the long run."

Then, as an afterthought, filling his glass:

"The Cultural Revolution, and this Red Guard movement now starting, seem to be well-considered exercises designed to discipline every level of Chinese society, from top to bottom, to cope with the prospect of an extension of war in Vietnam and possibly beyond. What is going on in China at the moment bears the unmistakable imprint of Mao's pragmatic thinking.

"As for the Americans, they could, perhaps, fulfill their own dream of becoming the greatest nation of all time if they were not afraid of being wrong occasionally or losing face. Together with the Russians they could, indeed, create what you might call a 'state of grace' upon this earth, in which neither they nor China nor any other nation need be afraid.

"The principal lack, perhaps, is humility—the one essential attribute of those who would be truly great."

CHAPTER

15

AT BREAKFAST, in reply to a question put by the schoolteacher, I said, "No, I would rather not visit the Wuhan Meat Processing Factory though six thousand pigs enter it each morning squealing, and by midday rest rigidly in cold stores which hold seventeen thousand five hundred tons of frozen pork, while their residue is being converted into some hundreds of by-products ranging from glue to pharmaceuticals."

Taking advantage of a moderately astonished silence, I was able to add that before liberation many Chinese people died because capitalist owners of abattoirs processed diseased meat, whereas socialist food-processing enterprises are run with scrupulous consideration for the health of the workers, and of the 2800 employees of the Wuhan plant 130 are qualified veterinary inspectors.

"Then," I said, "there is this question of revisionism. Many workers at the meat-processing plant were opposed to the export of Chinese pork to Russia, but after studying the works of Chairman Mao a meeting of workers' representatives and management decided that in honesty and brotherly love they could not deprive the people of the U.S.S.R. of pork because of the sins of their leaders. They thought, also, that the continued export of pig meat to Russia would help combat Khrushchev's barbarous slanders that the Chinese people are so poor that five men share one pair of trousers. Accordingly in 1966 a consignment of four thousand tons of pork went from Wuhan to the U.S.S.R."

The professor's wife, buttering her husband's toast, said that I was evidently inventing this information, and then refused to believe me when I said that I had read it, and much more, in a brochure while lying in bed and therefore saw no reason to spend a morning being escorted over a seven-storied mausoleum for pork to chase the same story.

I said that I would rather spend the time at the Railway Workers' Club drinking tea and discussing with Chang Shih-han the events which led to the general strike and demonstration of February, 1923; for it seemed to me that this would be more interesting and relevant to any student or tourist, and considerably less fatiguing.

"And who," said the professor's wife, "is Chang Shih-han?"

Tacitly thanking her for the lead, and trying not to seem smug, I said that he was an elderly person, perhaps approaching eighty, who, as a much younger man, had been a member of the original committee of this club, which was one of several such begun in 1921 with the help of Mao Tse-tung and other activists of the newly formed Communist Party of China.

"Workers' clubs and peasant institutions founded at this time," I said, "were a starting point, a seedbed of Red revolution; and the strikes and uprisings planned by their members were the first battles fought by the Communists to free China from the clutches of a corrupt government, cynical warlords, and foreign despots."

To this she answered that I was beginning to sound more like a Travel Service interpreter each day, and that she could now see how easy it was for the Communists to indoctrinate even an apparently intelligent person with a very short time by continuous exposure to persistent propaganda.

Ping came with me and was, I think, happy to miss the pig-killing, though happier still at the prospect of speaking to someone who had known and studied with Chairman Mao before he became famous, and perhaps had helped plan with him, here in Wuhan, the first active steps of the revolution of the masses; but she was curious, also, to discover how I had come to know about Chang Shi-han, the revolutionary railwayman.

So I explained that I had read about him in an illustrated magazine in which pictures showed him telling the story of the railroad workers' strike to little children, then leading them to the obelisk which stands in the garden of the Workers' Club to commemorate the men who died at that time at the hands of the capitalists and their lackeys.

Chang Shih-han, who from now on I will call Chang for simplicity's sake, was there in the garden, near the obelisk, waiting for us to come. He was a medium-sized, smiling old man in serviceable blue tunic, still healthy and firmly fleshed, with gray hair *en brosse*, spade beard, and bright eyes. With him were two other men: one of them as old as himself but bigger and with much stomach, bald, moon-faced, and inclined to perspire (he used a small black paper fan continuously); the other a much younger man, clearly the Party cadre responsible for running the club and the memorial museum which is part of it.

The younger man gave us the background. He explained that at the time of the general strike of the railwaymen in 1923, some 30,000 of them worked in this district, the majority earning seven yuan a month, which was sufficient, then, to buy two pounds of rice each day. It was, of course, before the bridge was built, when trains from Peking stopped on the north bank of the Yangtze and those from Canton on the south, and thousands of laborers were engaged to load and unload freight which boatmen then ferried across the river.

The railways, built by foreign investors, were run by the government and protected by warlords who "taxed" both the foreign owners and the laborers and worked hand in glove with most of the provincial officials.

Back in Sydney I scanned files of the *London Times* of this period and culled the following quotes from news items and editorials:

15.2.1923: . . . on the railways built by foreign capital but under Chinese control . . . earnings have dwindled so low they are barely self-supporting.

16.2.1923: . . . the Central Government in Peking is powerless and on the point of collapse. Parliament, as was expected, has proved a dismal sham, officials plunder the country, and rich generals devastate and rob it with more than usual energy . . . indifferent to the fact that

154

receipts and rolling stocks are security for British loans. General Chang Tso-lin takes much of the profits of the Peking-Mukden line . . . [while] General Wu Pei-fu is dominant on the Peking-Hangkow [Wuhan] line. Unless interested foreign powers intervene the insolvency of the government will continue indefinitely.

Railwayman Chang worked here in Wuhan as a blacksmith's assistant, while his fat friend Shao was then a coolie in Chengchow, jogging about the railway yards with baskets of coal hung on his shoulder pole.

Now they sat, one on either side of me, on a velveteen settee with Miss Ping and the cadre facing us across a low tea table. Slowly we pieced together, from their recollections, the story of the great railway strike in which both took part, knowing that they were starting a new national revolution; aware that they, a handful of illiterate laborers, were challenging their own government in Peking, the warlords, and the foreign powers who had their offices on the bund and their consulates in the capital.

The young man explained this and what followed to Ping, who jotted down Chinese characters in her notebook, then reconstructed their meaning for me phrase by phrase until we had the story straight, or straight enough at least for me to see clearly one side of a catalytic episode which may be taken as an indication of the way in which each step of the revolution was planned and carried out: not always to immediate advantage but to ultimate gain, the extension of folk involvement in the revolutionary legend, and the early creation of community heroes and martyrs.

Ping was flustered at first and inclined to make desperate guesses at the significance of what was being said, but I asked her to take time to be precise and not to worry if the process of translation seemed slow, for we were trying to understand and not simply to know. So she pressed the old men, checked one against the other, made them remember as accurately as they might these things that happened more than forty years ago; and the old man Shao, scratching his bald head with the black fan, began:

"The comrades who came to us from Shanghai started sixteen workers' clubs, some here in the three parts of Wuhan, others in Chengchow on the Yellow River where the north-south and east-west railroads cross, and some along the line. They told us that if the thirty thousand workers in this area would unite, they could stop most of the rail traffic in China and force the government to give them justice."

Then Chang, thinking back, said, "In the beginning not many would come to the clubs. The married men, especially, were afraid that if we started trouble they would lose their jobs. They didn't understand that the government and the foreign companies needed us even more than we needed them."

So a dialogue developed between the two old men which Ping and I took down: Shao, a little deaf, leaning forward with one hand cupped behind an ear and the other wagging his fan, though sometimes he snapped it shut to slap his leg in emphasis, to point at Chang and shake his head, disagreeing (a fine thread of spittle slipping down his chin); then pausing, each of them, to frown and screw up their faces in an effort of remembering.

Shao said, "I learned to read and write a little at the Workers' Club. Our teacher used to take a character and write it on the blackboard. A word, for example, such as *Worker*. When we men had copied it six times on our slates he would say, 'What is a worker? A worker is a man or woman who makes dead things come to life, who takes earth and metal and wood and makes them useful and productive. A worker creates all that is valuable in the world. So the world belongs to him. He should be able to make it a paradise for himself and for all other men except that he has an enemy. This enemy is the imperialist; and his running dogs are warlords, landlords, and capitalists. They rob the worker of the wealth that his hands create. They make a slave of him. Yet the workers can overcome this enemy if only they will unite with all the other workers of the world. One chopstick is easily broken, but a handful of chopsticks cannot be cut even with a hatchet. You are all workers. Unity is strength.' "

Chang's eyes twinkled as he listened to his vehement friend. "That's right, that's how we learned three lessons at one time. To read, to write, and to think politically. That was Chairman Mao's metnod. That's how he taught the poor people of China that they were strong enough to make a revolution."

The young man, filling in, said that by 1923 the workers' clubs had become a cover for the labor union movement. Each club was the front for a branch of the union, and the central secretariat in

Shanghai doubled as headquarters for the Federation of Labor Unions and the Communist Party.

Ping was thrilled, like a child at a pantomime, eyes wide with the difficulty of believing, her face (usually so empty of expression) now bright with excitement as she wrote quick notes, inspired by this encounter with original revolutionaries, old men so courageous in youth and now so gentle. And in a while she needed no prompting from me to be insistent and meticulous, as much as we were able, in our prying of the old men's minds.

Now Chang was speaking, telling us how he and other club officials worked in secret to spread the labor union message, for they were all suspect and the warlord's secret police watched them continuously.

"I was a Buddhist in those days, and of the others on the committee some were of this religion and others were Taoists. When we became club officials we went to temple ceremonies to mix with the people and pass messages in whispers, pretending that we were praying. And when we kowtowed in front of the images we left behind revolutionary pamphlets and slips of paper with slogans on them. But although I went to the temple I stopped believing in religion and became a member of the Party, because the priests could do nothing to help us workers get justice."

Shao, reluctant to be outdone, told of two cadres who had come to the Chengchow club with instructions from the union leaders in Shanghai.

"We organized a secret meeting in the cellar of our clubroom and I was sent to meet these men and lead them in. I was standing in the side doorway of the cinema, which was alongside our meeting place, watching for them, and could see them coming, as arranged, acting as though they were going to the picture show. But as they crossed a narrow footbridge over an open drain that ran beside the street a bunch of the warlord's thugs sprang out of the shadows and trapped them, and cut their throats while I watched no more than twenty paces away.

"I tell you, my insides turned to hot water and I felt sick, and when the gangsters went I was too much afraid to look at the two dead men, but went, instead, to the meeting room where the committee was waiting and told them what had happened."

Shao, agitated by these recollections, wiped his shiny pate with a red handkerchief and flapped his fan, watching anxiously while Ping wrote down what he had told us.

Then Chang said, "They were bad days. The workmen sometimes waited weeks for their pay while their families, if they had any, went begging on the bund. But the warlord's captains lived in big houses and had the best of everything, with their fancy women, and good food and drink provided by the foreigners."

In 1923 the leaders of the Federation of Labor Unions felt strong enough to ask the government in Peking to recognize them as legal representatives of the railway workers and to authorize a joint meeting of all branch officials of the union to meet and frame a list of grievances. The director of the Railways Bureau agreed and gave permission for the meeting to be held in Chengchow.

"Oh, how simple we were," said Shao, slapping his leg with his fan. "How easily we believed that the director, being Chinese and a government official, would support and help us to unite against the foreigners and warlords. But while we were congratulating our delegates on their success in Peking, the warlord Wu Pei-fu at Loyang was reading a telegram from the director of the Bureau, telling him of our plans.

"It said that our meeting would bring together in one place all the leaders of the railway workers' union from every branch between Wuhan and Chengchow, as well as delegates from other lines and advisers from Shanghai, and that Wu Pei-fu should surround the meeting place with his troops and provoke incidents which would make the workers hit back with violence and thus lay themselves open to arrest and punishment for rioting in the streets."

The young cadre broke in then to say that this fellow in Peking, this traitor, was eventually hanged when the Party came to power; but Shao, impatient to keep the flow of his story going, shook the fan at him and turned again to Ping.

"The soldiers were there, all around our clubroom and outside the cinema where we were to hold our meeting, and in the streets leading to it. Some of them tried to keep us from reaching the meeting place, but the delegates pushed past them. We thought, then, that the soldiers were afraid to use force against us, but afterward we understood that they were only trying to stir us up a bit and that they were really waiting for all of us to walk into the trap before they sprang it."

Then Chang took up the thread dramatically:

"There were three hundred of us at the meeting, most of us sitting in the cinema seats, feeling twice as big and strong as we had ever felt before, wondering why we had not known how easily courage comes with numbers properly organized. And up on the stage were the headmen of the Federation and some of our own local leaders and teachers, with a big red banner behind them.

"All of us were excited. Not afraid of the soldiers outside, only sorry for them and ashamed that these men who were our neighbors should threaten us with foreign rifles—weapons given to their warlord boss by foreign capitalists, to protect their profits. Only this part of it made me feel angry and ill for a few minutes. But I was so happy to be at this meeting and my heart so singing that I soon forgot them."

Shao then began to beat time with his fan and his foot and to sing raucously, like a raven and out of tune, panting for lack of breath, so that the sound he made was unmusical. But we listened, smiling, and suddenly were surprised to hear some English words come through clearly: "Joe Hill is at their side."

"Joe Hill!" I was so astonished that I laughed out loud and the others looked at me confused, and the more so when I began to sing with Shao:

> "From San Diego up to Maine
> In every mine and mill
> Where working men are out on strike
> It's there you'll find Joe Hill."

Then Chang joined in, and Ping shyly, trying to follow us, and the cadre grinning and keeping time too.

> "Joe Hill ain't dead, he says to me,
> Joe Hill ain't never died.
> Where working men are out on strike
> Joe Hill is at their side."

This kind of thing makes me want to cry with a mixture of

anguish and happiness. Sitting here in the middle of Red China with two old revolutionaries and the young nunlike Communist Ping, and a Party cadre, singing an American folk song about a U.S. labor organizer who (say all good unionists) was framed by the bosses on a murder rap back in 1915 and sentenced on behalf of the big-money men to execution. Then eight years later he is a legend, a world-wide folk figure; an example to set before a group of Chinese striving to gain the same justice that working men in the Western World had already achieved for themselves. (One has to remind oneself that these Chinese are not people. They are Communists, and one must not be sentimental about them because they strive to bind us all in metaphorical chains of godlessness and hate.)

While Shao was wiping his head and face, wet with sweat and the running of his old eyes, Chang took charge again:

"Six hours we stayed at the meeting making speeches, singing, shouting slogans and beating drums, and making a list of grievances and things we wanted changed so that we could live as human beings. On the stage was our leader from Shanghai, Lin Hsiang-chien, secretary-general of the Federation of Labor Unions, who gave the main speech and banged on the table as he gave out the slogans, 'Down with the reactionary imperialists and their running dogs; long live the solidarity of the workers and the working class.' And we others in the hall repeated them after him, shouting."

Chang, proud to have been there in the beginning, lifted his head high and saw it all again: the red flag on the platform, the committeemen sitting self-consciously in a row, and Lin Hsiang-chien with fists clenched and eyes flashing, reaching out to the delegates in the hall, calling upon them to make history:

"Our fight is not for wages, not for working hours, but for the right of humanity everywhere to be freed from exploitation by the few. We have no guns, no warships on the river. Our only weapons are courage and the strike, but with them we must carry this struggle for justice through to the end."

They sang more songs, shouted more slogans, not knowing that under cover of the din the warlord's men were wrecking their club, smashing windows, doors, and benches. And when they left their meeting and tried to find lodgings and places to eat they found soldiers barring the way to every hotel and eating place.

Lin Hsiang-chien went to the warlord next morning to demand compensation for the damage done to the club and sent the grievances of the meeting to the Railways Bureau in Peking, asking for just wages and working conditions; and when everything was refused he called the strike as the general meeting had agreed.

Chang said, "As soon as the strike was decided we all went home. Lin, the general-secretary, came here to Wuhan to set up headquarters and organize demonstrations. Those of us who had learned to write at the workers' clubs made posters proclaiming the strike and our aims, and others went around the town putting them up in busy places. Members of the committee talked in the streets to explain our case and get the support of the people and other workers, and although it was cold and snowing, and all the roads were thick with mud and slush, we made banners and marched through those sections of the city where the foreigners had their offices."

The cadre, keeping the Party view in focus, said, "The American and British consuls in Peking sent for the director of the Railways Bureau as if he were their servant instead of an official of the Chinese People's government. Then they called the warlord Wu Pei-fu from Loyang and gave him money and instructions to break the strike and put the workers' leaders into prison, or even to kill them. That's how it was in those days when foreigners could order Chinese soldiers to make war on their own countrymen."

Shao, breaking in, gestured at Ping's notebook with his fan. "Write down that they sent four thousand soldiers against us but we were not afraid. In Chengchow we organized our members into 'Dare to Die' brigades and went out with sticks and stones and a few homemade guns to fight them. Of course they beat us and made prisoners of our leaders." Then he grinned and said, "They put chains on my feet and tied me to a post in the street and whipped me, but the people of Chengchow crowded around and made the soldiers let us go." He sat back and fanned himself, looking smug and satisfied.

It was not like that at Wuhan, which was the center of the strike and where the warlord himself took charge and set out to smash

161

the unions and the clubs completely. When his men clashed with the "Dare to Die" brigades he ordered them to fire, and as the strikers broke and separated into groups he set out to hunt them down and destroy them one by one, without mercy.

Thirty-seven railway workers were shot dead that day, two hundred more wounded, and sixty thrown into prison. The group, led by Secretary-General Lin Hsiang-chien, held out at the railroad station until late in the afternoon, but by sundown they were surrounded and each man taken prisoner and bound.

Chang, who was one of them, took up the tale:

"Many other people left their work to protest against this brutal killing of their friends. The city powerhouse attendants walked out and there were no lights in the streets or at the railroad station; and when we had all been tied up the general came round with two soldiers holding lanterns, looking for Lin and the other union leaders.

"When they found him they put manacles on his wrists and ankles and tied him to a lamppost in the station, and while the soldiers held the lanterns up high to light his face the general threatened Lin with his sword and said that if he didn't send the men back to work at once he would be executed there and then."

Lin would not agree. He said that he was a paid official of the union, a servant of the workers and not their master. Only the elected representatives of the men could make any such decision, and to do this they must have a proper meeting.

The general was angry. He held his sword over Lin's head and threatened to strike him dead if he didn't do as he was told. But Lin looked at the general and again refused.

He said, "Cut off my head if that is what you want to do. My blood will color the snow, but my tongue will not betray the working people."

The general brought his sword down savagely on Lin's shoulder; hacked at him again and again about the neck and head until he was dead and his head hanging. Snowflakes settling gently on his thin clothing mixed with his blood and melted; and the crowd so still, so quiet, so frozen for a moment with horror that everyone could hear the blood dripping into a little puddle be-

162

tween his feet. Then men began to groan and weep and some were sick, even among the soldiers, to see such an evil thing done by one Chinese to another, for foreign money.

The other union leaders of Wuhan, including Chang, were put into prison, and the Party sent a lawyer from Shanghai to help them. His name was Shih Yang and he was a solemn little man, owl-like in looks, with drooping, sparse moustaches that hung over his mouth like an archway. But in pursuing what he understood to be his duty he was strong, and, of course, a Communist.

Then, as now, rich people and those in authority could not understand that a man could be a Communist and at the same time sane and honest. Representatives of the foreign interests which had financed the building of the railroads, and for the most part controlled them, took Shih aside and tried to reason with him, offered him money and well-paid employment in his own profession if he would advise the strikers to return to work.

They said, appealing plaintively to reason, "You are not a laborer but an educated, cultured man. One of us. If you encourage these men to persist in their mischief you are a traitor to your own class and to the civilization which you represent—the civilization which these agitators are trying to destroy."

Shih, with his drooping moustaches, glasses, and black hat, looking like the somber funnyman in a farce, gave his answer:

"I am a lawyer. My clients are these Chinese people of the working class whom you oppress. They trust me to represent them to the best of my ability. To use my education on their behalf, not to be a traitor to them."

The general said, "If you love them all so well, these workingmen you call your friends, I will execute you as I executed their leader, Lin Hsiang-chien."

Shih looked at the ground and spread his hands apart. "As you will. You can kill me as you killed him and the others, but you cannot now put out the fire that you and your foreign friends have lit."

So they took Shih to a hill outside the town and cut his head off.

Ping dropped her eyes as she translated these last lines, and we were all quiet while the cadre poured more tea for us and offered cigarettes all around. Then when we were settled he said, "The men went back to work and it seemed to many that the strike had been a failure and a waste of many lives. But politically the workers' cause had been launched, their forces organized, their aims defined. Their leaders knew that even if the road was long and lined with trouble and much more suffering they must follow it; that perseverance would bring victory.

"They had seen that courageous and careful organization was able to carry the mass of the people forward like a wave. How unity and the will to win can produce a power which is irresistible. And because the Party had shown them this, and given them encouragement, the masses accepted its leadership.

"They had also seen, openly exposed, the natural brutality and ruthlessness of the class enemy. The underlying ugliness of economic imperialism had been clearly shown to them. They had seen, in those few days of the strike, the true face of their enemy and knew, now, what to do."

I turned to Chang and said, "Were you kept in prison for a long time? How did they treat you?" And when Ping had put my questions to him he seemed to shrink a little and look lost, and I was sorry, realizing that I had put my finger on a sore spot inside him.

When he answered he spoke slowly and soberly, without dramatic exaggeration or excitement, while Shao closed his eyes and was silent, smoking a cigarette elegantly with one hand and flapping his fan with the other.

"There were twenty-eight of us in one cell, all officials of the clubs and union branches. Each of us was chained to the wall with our legs in irons. The daily food ration for each was a bowl of thin corn soup and two pieces of salted turnip. Every day we were taken out and tortured and told to give the warlord's men a list of all union officials and Party members. But nobody spoke.

"I was married only a short while when they put me in prison, and my wife was expecting our first child. One day my mother came to say that the baby had been born, a son, but it was dead; that my wife, having no money and nobody to help her, had left Wuhan and gone back to her own village.

"My mother was old, more than sixty. She had no money for

164

food or to pay rent. She lived in the open with no chopsticks and no bowl, and had begged her way day by day to come to tell me about my son who was dead. She left me two small pieces of corn cake which she had begged from a peasant. I told her to leave me in prison and to make her way to the town where she had another son, my older brother, who would give her shelter.

"After that my wife came and took to begging in the town where the prison was, so that she could bring me food. She slept in a temple, but because of hunger and cold she became sick, and leg ulcers made her lame so that she has been a cripple ever since, though still alive. But we had no more children."

He turned and, laying his hand on my knee, said, "This is the legacy that I got from the class enemy. This is why I hate imperialists and foreign exploiters." Then he began to sing again, boldly, a song they had sung in prison:

> "Down with all imperialists
> And their running dogs the warlords.
> Fight your way forward, comrades.
> Work for the revolution.
> Struggle upward, never give in.
> Even if we die our comrades will win!"

The cadre spoke to him and he took off his shirt to show us a slanting scar which, with Ping watching, I measured with my fingers and figured it some fifteen inches long, an inch wide, and deep enough for me to lay two fingers in. He said that the gash had been made with a leather whip soaked in water to make it more flexible, and that when he had still refused to speak they had turned him loose, into the street, with the wound still raw and bleeding.

We went quickly through the small museum in which relics of the February strike are kept and saw Chang's prison clothes in a glass case together with the manacles and leg-irons. Other display cases contained iron rods, rough spears, and homemade guns used as weapons by the workers against the warlord's guns.

We looked at fuzzy old photographs, among them one which showed the death of the director of the Railways Bureau who betrayed the Union men and was himself publicly executed on the spot where Secretary-General Lin Hsiang-chien had been butchered twenty-eight years before.

There were paintings done by students of the Art School: unsophisticated things, almost making a mockery of the drama and disaster of those days. One shows union men, simple, eager, and earnest, meeting in secret to plan their strike, while a complementary picture caricatures the "enemy" in a plush apartment in Peking, with arrogant foreign consuls in fine clothes giving instructions to a cringing Chinese official while the warlord, hung with medals, makes aggressive gestures with his sword.

In another picture a poor worker is comforting his wife as they watch their starved child die; and alongside this we see a police chief sitting in comfort with a fat lady on his knee eating peaches, bottles of wine beside them, and an aproned maid bringing tea and cake.

As we were leaving, old Shao took my hand and, standing as proudly as age and his heavy stomach would allow, said loudly, "Under the leadership of the Party and Chairman Mao we have achieved all we set out to fight for on that day of the meeting at Chengchow. Many died then, and a million have died since, but we have won the battle and the imperialists will never take away our victory."

But Chang, coming with us to the car, said, "We have won our victory in China, but in other countries the workers are still fighting foreign imperialists and we must help them. All men are comrades, but corrupt governments mislead them and face them in the wrong direction. If we understand one another and strive only for justice, there need be no trouble between people."

When we had shaken hands all around little Ping and I drove away, waving to the three men standing in the gateway of the Wuhan Railway Workers' Club.

Looking again at extracts culled from the *London Times*, I note that the story as told by Chang and Shao may be summed up simply, and that it is possible to see the issues in a somewhat different light.

The *Times* says: ". . . workers on the line had recently formed a union and when its offices were raided by troops the employees ceased work as a protest. Although well paid and reasonably treated, they demanded increased privileges, among them the right to approve the selection of a General Manager. Three strikers were promptly executed and in several cases meetings were fired upon with considerable loss of life. After four days the strike ended and full traffic has now resumed.

"The exact cause of the strike remains obscure, but it is attributed to agitators who sought to establish a state of affairs in which the railway workers would control traffic and be able to hamper military movements. There is a suspicion that the originators belong to that section of the southern revolutionary party which is favorable to (General) Chang Tso-lin and opposed to (General) Wu Pei-fu.

"Owing to the turmoil, merchants are hard hit, trade is at a standstill, and it is impossible to make the customary New Year settlements."

We were entertained at dinner by gentlemen from the Travel Service and the Association for Cultural Relations with humor, good food, and local wine, which, to my taste, though palatable, has little character (later I discovered it to be made from sweet potato); and because we had all been busy during the day in different ways there was much talk which kept Feng and Ping busy with translating.

The professor had been browsing through manuscripts at the Buddhist temple of Kuei Yuan Szu, which the monks are paid by the government to maintain as a museum and teahouse, and a place of worship for any who still care to use it as such, though these are not many.

"There were a few women," said the professor's wife, "lighting incense sticks and bowing before images while their children, all of them Young Pioneers, played in the courtyard." She talked for a while about the five hundred wooden images of Buddhist holy men, who, she said, reminded her of Catholic saints, each of them being identified by some personal characteristic, as, for instance, is Francis talking to the birds, Cecilia with her music, Peter and his keys; so, too, do these Buddhist images show each holy man in some special attitude or activity.

The capitalist had been happy all day, first at the meatworks where he had shared a meal with the workers such as he would have dreamed of as a boy and his parents so poor. "Soup with great chunks of pork in it. Three sausages with cabbage and beans, and some sweet pastry to follow. And they can get this three times a day if they wish, for less than ten cents." He dug back into his dinner of chicken Kiev.

The schoolteacher believed that of all he had seen during the day (and he had been to the abattoir, the Yangtze River Navigation School, and boating on East Lake) the most interesting had been the young men and women of the militia making parachute jumps from a tower in one of Wuhan's parks. But he was concerned that there seemed to be more than an ordinary preoccupation with militaristic thinking within the educational system.

Our host, having this translated to him, answered cautiously. "We are ringed about by enemies and threatened with invasion, and we are also still in the midst of our own continuing revolution. We cannot afford to let our children think peacefully because they still have to continue the struggle that their parents began. As Chairman Mao tells us, 'A revolution is not a dinner party, a painting, a picture, or doing embroidery; it cannot be so refined, so leisurely, so gentle, so temperate, kind, courteous, restrained, and magnanimous.' No, we would like to teach our children to believe in peace, to be friends with everybody, but we must never let them forget the past and the fact that the old imperialistic enemies are still trying to climb over our gate."

Then he smiled and asked that our glasses be filled and, rising to his feet, made a courteous speech thanking us for our visit and asking us to drink to friendship, which we did, standing and touching glasses with each other, our capitalist the most vocal among us.

When we were sitting and our glasses were full again, I said to Ping, "May I drink to your health and our own continuing friendship, little Ping?"

At this she hiccuped and blushed and, lifting her glass, said, "Yes, the people of your country and mine must always be friends, but you should not call me little Ping. You may call me Comrade."

168

CHAPTER

16

WE LEFT Wuhan by plane next day and in Nanking rejoined our original traveling companions (and the cadre Wang) and went with them by coach, southward in summer sunshine, through the rich river plains of Kiangsu Province and by midday came to Soochow, an ancient city of half a million people which sits in the middle of a web of canals and waterways not far from Shanghai.

It seemed most gentle and pleasant, placed near the edge of a lake and hedged with hills—a city less feverish, more tranquil and leisurely than most others we had seen, its tempo set by the slow traffic of junks and barges and long rafts of uncut logs, and the steady, deliberate tread of men, women, and children in shoulder harness leaning forward, hauling on long ropes, measuring their span of life step by step along the towpaths of China's seventy thousand miles of inland waterways.

Soochow was the chief city of the prosperous and peaceful kingdom of Wu five centuries before Christ. Then, as now, its people farmed the richly irrigated flatlands of the Yangtze basin and because of the mildness of the climate cropped continuously all year round. Canals were dug to take their surpluses to less favored places, and in time Soochow became one of the great centers of Eastern China's waterborne trade, a wealthy city where the best families, landlords, and rich officials lived in leisurely elegance and splendor.

They built public temples and pagodas to gratify the gods and to excuse their affluence, but for private pleasure and aesthetic satisfaction they employed poets and painters to design and contrive lavish parks and landscaped gardens that remain famous to this day.

Their rich lands in the Yangtze basin and around Soochow are now contained within the people's communes. The temples and pagodas, empty of ceremony, are historical monuments and museums. Their parks and gardens are public pleasure grounds and a principal attraction for tourists.

We spent our first night quietly and in the morning met Mr. Sung, Chairman of the Soochow Committee for Restoring the People's Parks and Gardens and Preserving the Cultural Remains of Their National Heritages (at least that was the title given me by Ping).

In youth he had been a guerrilla fighter with the Red Army, but now, past seventy, he plays guide to foreign guests, smiling all the time widely and showing two rows of metallic teeth while telling endless, empty tales of the long-dead noblemen, mandarins, merchants, and rich officials who owned these gardens, and of their lovely wives and concubines, all seemingly sorrowful and lonely in the midst of splendor and plenty.

I thought it odd, even tedious, of those responsible for fixing our program to list visits to five such gardens in a single day and said as much to the professor as we strolled in the second of them, the Liu Yuan Garden (Garden to Linger In); but when we stopped to rest in a red and gold pavilion by the side of a miniature landscaped lake he sat on a stone balustrade and explained.

One must remember, he said, that the Chinese are traditionally intimidated by, and obsessed with, their landscape—with the hugeness and intractability of it. They spend their lives trying to placate and tame it. They exist explicitly in it, by it, for it; are part of it at all times: when working in the fields, while peddling those endless belts of little buckets in irrigation ditches, flinging fishnets onto ponds, or poling punts and junks against the river's current.

They are part of the earth they plow with slow-plodding oxen. Their feet take hold of it as tree roots reach downward to feed and find sustenance.

170

They give a name and fable to every scenic feature; capture every facet, every detail of it in their painting and poetry, in their jade and ivory carving, in ornaments, on scrolls, pottery, woodwork, weaving, and embroidery.

In making their parks and gardens rich men tried to condense the hugeness of the landscape, to reduce it to a size that the mind could encompass. So, of all the domestic arts of China, that of making gardens was the highest.

Each pathway, each plant, pond, star- or moon-shaped window, wall, or little bridge is set in relative perspective to a pavilion or resting place from which planned vistas extend, each in itself a complete scene.

A gentleman and his friends might spend all day in such a garden going slowly through changing landscapes as they moved from pavilion to pavilion—stopping here and there to feed goldfish, to admire a lotus flower, to marvel at the colorful wonder of kingfishers skimming a lily pond, to sit in the shade and write quatrains, to take tea, to listen to an old friend recite Confucian analects, or concubines make music, to teach talking birds new words, to read, to discuss politics and philosophy.

While we were speaking of these things a small procession came marching through the garden, some twenty people with a large sign which said, "The hearts of the sanitary workers are red. They love the party and are loyal to Chairman Mao."

They waved to us and when Sung smiled and called some greeting, showing his metal teeth in a big grin, they stopped. Then gathering together under a willow tree, they sang for us, "We help to grow good cabbages for our comrades in the tractor factory."

When the song was sung we clapped enthusiastically and called for more (our capitalist calling out the loudest), but after some brief argument between them they went their way, walking briskly and singing, "I love best to read the works of our Chairman."

We rested awhile, then went a little way by bus and came to the Garden of the Humble Administrator, the most lavish and elaborate of them all, with mirrors cleverly set to reflect and extend its long perspectives. As we came through the gate Sung gave a short address, which Feng translated:

"This garden was made by a corrupt official who collected

171

bribes from everyone who came to him for favors. It was very costly and took many years to complete, but when it was finished he lost it in a few minutes one evening, gambling with a friend in the Upper Chamber for Viewing the Mountain, and his favorite concubine with it. That is how the rich lived in those days, wasting the people's money and labor with their bad behavior and selfish pleasures."

But in spite of this stricture we spent a pleasant hour there and later, in the Garden of Heavenly Tranquillity, took tea while a loudspeaker fixed in the eaves shouted, "Down with the old world of corruption. Clean up the muck and slime left behind by the old society. Let all aristocrats and capitalists tremble before the irresistible force of the people's revolution. Oppose all modern revisionists, monsters, ghosts, and demons. Attack the handful of bourgeois rightists who have wormed their way into the Party and are taking the capitalist road. In the midst of our mighty struggle we must all creatively study and apply the highest thought of Mao Tse-tung."

An orchestra played "The East Is Red," and the professor, frowning, turned and talked Chinese with Wang while we others watched a group of girls take pictures of each other with a box camera, going in couples to pose on a large stone beside the lotus pond where, in the end, our capitalist (taking Ping to talk for him) snapped them all together in a giggling group and came back saying, "It's little enough they know or care about these monsters, ghosts, or demons and the irresistible force of the people's revolution. They're as simple and scatterbrained as young girls anywhere."

In the morning I went walking while the air was cool and fresh and the leaves still wet with overnight rain. I saw a man pushing a barrow on which was fixed a kind of iron oven or retort almost as big as a football, though pear-shaped and set upon a spindle, and under it a charcoal fire in a vertical pipe with bellows let into it.

So I followed him across a small but steeply pitched stone bridge, over a narrow canal, disturbing geese going ahead of us so that they ran with ungainly flapping feet and wagging heads, honking their displeasure. But on the other side we and the geese went separate ways, and the man with the barrow turned into an unpaved street lined with tiny houses, where he stopped, sat on a stool and, giving a single sharp cry, soon had a crowd of women and children around him holding bags and dishes.

I saw that they had rice or maize in them, or sliced potatoes, no more than a double handful in each case, which they gave in turn to the man, then waited while he put the grain or potato into his iron retort, closed it tightly with clamps, and set it over the fire. Then he pumped the bellows with one hand and turned the spindle with the other and after a few minutes swiveled the retort away from the fire, wrapped it in a hessian bag, and kicked away the clamps, causing a loud report. Then uncovering what he had done, he disclosed the grain or potato cooked crisply and parched like popcorn.

A woman, watching me, held out her dish and made signs that I should try some rice, and when, having done this, I held up my thumb and nodded compliments to the cook, they all smiled widely and offered me more; and other people looked out from their houses to see why the children were chattering and laughing.

I left them to their breakfasts and followed along the little canal until it met with a wider one, and here I stood awhile and watched barges go past poled by young men wearing wide hats and grass capes, some loaded with vegetables and grain and baskets of other farm produce, and some with bales which I guessed held silk, for this district is famous for its embroideries.

A lad came and stood beside me while I watched and, speaking a little English, said that these barges came from the communes and that it was possible for their produce to go all the way to Peking by canal, which is almost a thousand miles. His knowledge of the English language was scant, but I understood that his father had been a mission-school student in the old days and, though forgetful of much that he had learned so long ago, still tried to teach his own children English, hoping that one of them might be chosen to go to the language institute in Shanghai and so qualify for a job in some government department.

He came with me into another street where many small shops were already doing business although it was not yet seven o'clock—among them a shoemaker squatting on a box, making careful measurements of a girl's foot with a piece of knotted string, jotting them down in the dust with his finger. Then he stood her upon a piece of old motor tire and outlined the size of her sole. Several pairs of shoes were set to one side in the sun—blue cotton canvas tops stitched to rubber soles, then made wet and packed with wooden wedges to stretch and take shape. Each pair would cost a customer roughly forty cents.

Next door the tinsmith was already busy, with much work waiting and as much done and ready to take away: mostly watering cans, kettles, tin pails and dishes, and a rack full of oiled-paper umbrellas with damaged ribs to be fixed. He seemed content, bent over his tiny bench with a soldering iron, mending a bucket, a pair of half-glasses on the end of his nose, and a smoldering stub of cigarette hanging from his lips. I wished then that Ping had come with me so that we might have talked to him, but having watched awhile there was nothing to be done but to nod and smile and make vague gestures of friendship, then leave him to his work.

A night-soil cart went past, a wooden tun hung between high, rubber-tired wheels and pulled by a buffalo with a rope through its nose. A huge, happy man dressed only in tattered jacket and calf-length pants went ahead, and two strong girls followed behind, laughing and chattering. When I made as if to take a picture they pummeled each other in fun and ran to the far side of the cart to hide while the buffalo plodded on; but getting out of range, they came out into the open again and stood in the middle of the street looking back at me, gaily waving. Then, laughing, they turned and ran after the cart.

A gentle apothecary across the way looked up from his scales and smiled, and when I crossed the street he made a gracious gesture suggesting that I might like to look inside his little office. I watched while he filled prescriptions, which he kept in two separate sheaves, each sheaf clipped to a small board, and by signs he showed me that one set of prescriptions called for Western medicines and the other for herbs and such other traditional medicaments as powdered fish, which is used for pulmonary complaints and blown down the throat through a tube; spider casts to reduce fevers; nettles and other irritant weeds which, when applied to the skin, bring out stubborn sicknesses which reject internal remedies;

174

and the ash of water-lily leaves burned in a bronze pit and pulverized, which is said to be an effective contraceptive, as are live tadpoles swallowed whole before their legs are fully formed.

I returned then to the hotel by way of narrow lanes, walking between high walls, glancing through doorways and tall, arched entrances into gray courtyards and cool rooms so that I seemed to be leafing quickly through the pages of a picture book: seeing an old man shelling beans, a woman emptying a chamber pot into a stone trough, a child tugging at a dog, families sitting on stone steps with bowls and chopsticks eating the morning meal, a thin man at a table, with a writing brush poised upright above the paper.

A baby crawling toward me looked up and froze with sudden surprise and fright. Neat women, cleanly clothed, passed by, carrying shopping baskets, and stared at me with straight, expressionless faces. But when I smiled their answering grins were quick.

Coming closer to the hotel, I stopped to admire a child sleeping in a basket, swung under a tree, and in a minute was surrounded by a crowd, curious but friendly, but was adamantly discouraged from taking a photograph.

When, after breakfast, I told Feng where I had been, he said that I could now tell my friends at home I had seen for myself that the people of China were content and busy, living (as he put it) happy and in good condition, whereas before liberation the busiest places in Soochow and neighboring Wusih had been the brothels, pawnshops, and opium dens, all of which paid out much money in bribes to rich city officials while tradesmen sat idly waiting for work.

Cadre Wang asked what we were saying, and after some discussion between them Feng turned back to me and added that in the old days there were more temples and pagodas in these cities than there were workshops or factories to give people employment, but now everybody had a job, and Soochow and Wusih were producer cities.

Then, when I had made a careful note of this, Wang nodded, satisfied.

Part
Three

*If only men loved one another—in
the context of something greater than themselves—
how changed the world would be, how invincible
and armed for every conquest.*

Pierre Teilhard de Chardin
Letters from a Traveller
Tientsin, February 1924

CHAPTER

17

IT SEEMS not unreasonable to say here that all China Travel Service officials did their best, within the limits of whatever authority each of them possessed, to meet requests made by members of our party who wished to pursue individual interests.

At almost each location one or another of us, discussing a pre-selected program, would ask if some substitute visit could be arranged to take the place of an excursion which seemed to offer no special benefit or pleasure. The invariable upshot was that each day we made two groups, the majority following the planned itinerary and a few splitting off to follow some personal or professional line of inquiry.

I was able then, this morning, without giving offense or creating confusion, to excuse myself from going with the rest of my friends to see a figurine factory and the Soochow Embroidery Institute and elected instead to join the physician in our group for whom arrangements had been made to visit a hospital and a workers' sanitorium.

Among those who received us on the steps of the hospital was the medical superintendent, who, having studied in Edinburgh and practiced for some years in London, was fluent in English. Being as well a pleasant fellow, he was, if anything, amused by our combination of curiosity and ignorance, and accommodating to our humor, so that, although the senior official among those who met us was not this doctor, but the Party political cadre in charge of the hospital committee, the visit was for the most part uninhibited by language restrictions and free from ideological divagation.

The doctor seemed artful also in the delicate business of self-effacement and contrived to make it seem that the cadre and Feng (who had come with us) were in control of the occasion, though both were busy keeping each other abreast of the technicalities of the conversation.

We saw all that we asked to see and for my part (having no stomach for blood) more than I wished when we went with a group of students to watch two surgical teams in session and were given the best positions in the observation dome, and binoculars so that we could observe the work of the surgeons more closely, one of them a man and the other a woman.

Of the two cases, one was a male textile worker, aged forty, having his spleen removed and the splenetic vein spliced to the kidney vein. The other, a woman, aged fifty-nine, had been sent in from a commune clinic for a complete removal of the uterus (a carcinoma). Total cost of the operation and hospitalization in each case would be around five U.S. dollars, the equivalent of a laborer's weekly wage, and this paid by the patient's community group.

Then, making a general inspection, we watched a patient being treated for cancer of the esophagus with cobalt 60 equipment from Canada; and in another room saw students studying X-rays projected by television from an inspection center.

But a few minutes later we went through wards where dozens of patients were undergoing acupuncture, moxibustion, cupping, and other traditional treatments, some lying about on benches with long, thin needles stuck into their flesh—in legs, arms, chests, foreheads, faces; others with hot cups stuck onto their backs, thighs, or buttocks; and still others being schooled in particular systems of breathing, together with contemplative exercises.

Physicians of world-wide reputation have divided minds on the matter of China's traditional methods of healing, yet few Western men of medicine, even if skeptical, are ready to reject outright the probable efficacy of acupuncture properly applied in certain kinds of sickness (though many may well suspect as legendary the belief held widely in China that a few needles, judiciously applied, will assist men and women with procreative difficulties).

I asked the superintendent about this and he laughed and said that Western science had overrun itself so often in the present century that only vain or very stupid people would put limits to the possibilities of knowledge, or despise traditional ideas simply because they seem to be not sufficiently proven in relation to so-called rational facts.

"The old absolutes of time, weight, and space by which Western men measured the mysteries of existence have been made obsolete by your own scientists, beginning with Einstein. Your classical theories about the structure and behavior of matter are being revised day by day, and Western ideas about the ties between body and mind now seem to be very elementary and incomplete.

"We Chinese know that general health is mostly a matter of interior harmony in which all parts of the body work smoothly together, guided by a tranquil mind. We know, too, that a disorder in one part of the body can bring pain to another; and we believe that there are hundreds of points along the nervous system which, when something goes wrong, can be stimulated and made to trigger off responses in other parts of the body which will help to bring all of its elements back into balance and so restore the natural order.

"These points connect with mechanisms and circulatory systems which cannot be laid open and exposed by the surgeon's knife or reached directly with medicines. But they can be reached immediately through the skin; and this is the belief underlying acupuncture, which we have been practicing for more than two thousand years."

We stood in the middle of a room with whitewashed walls, beside a low bench where a young woman lay flat on her back with one trouser leg rolled up to the knee. Already there were two threadlike silver pins sticking in her shin, and the doctor, bending low over her, was feeling with his fingertips round about her ankle. Then, having fixed upon a spot, he pressed it with what looked like a ballpoint pen, and when this was lifted there was another pin in place, shot in by a spring. He twisted it very gently until it had entered in about an inch or maybe a little more, then began to explore the hollow of her heel, seeking a place for another pin.

The girl showed no sign of irritation or pain, made no move of any kind, but remained completely still and quiet, as if under sedation. When I asked what her sickness was the superintendent checked and said that she had a headache.

I must have seemed surprised at the idea of pins in the feet being a cure for pains in the head, for he laughed and said, "A headache might mean one of a hundred things, and we've already checked for eye trouble, stomach upsets, blood pressure, and other possible causes of the pain. And she is scheduled for other tests. Meanwhile the acupuncture treatment might relieve tensions that so far she hasn't told us about or figured for herself."

Then as we went along a corridor:

"It is not the Eastern way to search insistently for a single 'why,' or to try to prove conclusively what 'is.' In medicine, as in our relations with one another, and our way of life, we leave room for a variety of feelings and beliefs which together make a completeness.

"In many matters we have been left behind by you Westerners because we have refused to let go of a way of life in order to pursue happiness in a single direction. On the other hand, we Chinese and other Eastern people have long accepted and acted upon truths which you are still reaching for through your step-by-step methods of reasoning.

"In these days we of the East show our willingness to learn from the West many of the things which seem useful and worthwhile if people are to live better lives. But you of the West do not seem to be prepared to learn anything from us, which is a pity, for in some ways we might be wiser than you are."

He was a smiling man of lively mind, and if what he said seems provocative on paper it is because my writing lacks the lightness of his manner. And although I took down the substance of all he said I will not swear that what is written here carries the correct inflection.

He and my friend the physician, discussing differences between the medical systems within which each worked, ranged widely, leaving me free to make the notes from which I now quote:

"Foreign visitors," he said, "when they come to China, must constantly remind themselves that it is necessary to adjust their mental and emotional focus if they wish to understand our reasoning. You need to be able to see that we believe, quite simply, that your Western social and economic systems are now obsolete and an obstacle to mankind's evolutionary progress.

"In other words, we see that it is you who are the backward nations. All your wealth and new machinery and trips to the moon mean nothing because you have stopped thinking about the reasons for existence and have nothing but hobbies to occupy your minds, whereas we are busy pioneering the new and revolutionary frontiers of mankind's progress toward an ideal society.

"In the West you have come to the end of your tether. Have played your part, made your pile, and have retired behind high walls to live with your riches. Your castles and your barns are ringed around with expensive protective weapons and guarded by hired armies, while you sit inside, isolated, alone, afraid, strangers to the mass of mankind which continues to live outside in the villages, winning a living from the fields."

Then speaking of their own profession, the superintendent said, "We consider that Western medical systems are inefficient. The services of the most successful or the best specialists are available only to the rich, while the mass of the people are served inadequately by overworked general practitioners who meet their patients only when these are too sick to go on living without pills or surgical treatment and must have attention so that they can continue to work and meet their bills."

He was smiling as he spoke, and pouring tea for us, but one could see that he was sincere and meant what he said and believed it implicitly. He looked up at my friend.

"Most doctors are good people, whatever their politics, and do their best for their patients, but the Western general practitioner cannot possibly keep up with the latest discoveries in medicine, or study revolutionary surgical techniques, or cope with the flow of new knowledge emerging from research. Yet being conditioned to a mystical position in society, like a priest, he must resent any suggestion that he is not infallible or that he does not know all the answers.

183

"Among the poor people of the West the old superstition still persists that 'the doctor' is above the masses and beyond criticism. That he is an aristocrat, and that it is bad manners to question his guesswork or his failure to produce solutions. It is insulting for a poor man to ask his physician for a second opinion. Only those who are richer than the doctor or of a higher social position are permitted to do this.

"With us it is quite different. The idea that a doctor should see himself as being in any degree superior to other people in the community is ludicrous. And the thought that the level of medical attention made available to individuals should be determined by their social or financial status is purely feudal.

"In our society the doctor is an integrated member of the community. He has particular functions for which he is specially trained, functions which are as important as those of a school-teacher, a brigade leader on a commune, a cadre, or a kindergarten supervisor, though the doctor's work is no more mysterious than theirs and of no greater significance.

"His efficiency will always depend upon how much he is willing to identify with the people he is sent to serve and how clearly, from personal first-hand experience, he understands their problems, their attitudes, and their point of view. This is why all of us, including the professors and the heads of research institutes and major hospitals, spend part of our time each year living with the mass of the people."

Suddenly he looked serious.

"Those of us who have lived in the West can see and understand quite well why you smile politely when we talk of being guided by the thought of Mao Tse-tung. But you must try to understand that what he teaches is the truth by which we try to live, and by which we hope to lead the world toward a new and better way of life in which justice will be done to all men. Not only to Western men or clever men, or men who are prepared to kowtow to the powerful, but all men, everywhere. In Asia, Africa, Europe, and America, and even in your own rich country."

My friend said, "What you have been saying is very interesting, but much of it is pretty theoretical. You don't as yet have a complete and ideal medical system set up all over China, and though

184

your ideas may be right there is a lot more to medicine than efficient organization and having your heart in the right place."

To this he replied, "You're right. We've a long way to go, both in the practical and the ideological sense. And we are human like the rest of men and have our problems of personality and individual character. All Chinese are not one hundred percent virtuous or idealistic, but because of Mao, we have a national sense of direction."

He told us of his visits to the countryside and sounded genuine when saying how much he loved living with the villagers, sometimes sleeping in the best bed and at other times on the ground, or even on a door. (He caught my look of surprise and in explanation said that in wet weather, when earth floors get damp and sticky, peasants in some places take doors from their hinges and use them as beds for the guests.)

"We go in teams to different localities and stay for six or eight weeks, depending on the needs of the people and the requirements of any special program that has been worked out between ourselves and the district committee.

"In the remoter places we usually do a fairly thorough check on everyone in the commune, working alongside the local medical people, so that we quickly become colleagues and learn from each other from the beginning. Then we use the information gained from this checkup as the basis for whatever special research or campaign is planned for the district.

"Maybe the local problem is liver fluke, or goiter, or some eye trouble that can be traced to parasites or dietary deficiencies, or old-fashioned habits and customs, or superstitious beliefs that have produced unhealthy traditions. We are concerned with such things as the purity of water supplies, with methods of manuring the fields, with the kinds of things people eat.

"We give health talks to the children in the schools and to adults in the village meeting places. Discuss birth-control methods and, if necessary, arrange for operations to be done on women who ask for sterilization, as many of them do after they've had three or four children.

"We hold classes, lectures, and demonstrations for all medical personnel in the area—doctors, clinical assistants, and nurses—

bringing them up to date with what is happening in city hospitals and research institutes. If we find people who need special treatment, we arrange for them to be boarded out to the nearest center that is equipped to deal with them.

"By living with the people, eating with them, fitting into the intimate routines of their daily way of life, taking part in their work in the fields and their recreation in the evenings, their discussions and conversations, their family problems and plans and hopes for the future, we lose any feeling of being strangers or in any way separate.

"When Mao tells us to go and live among the masses, to learn from them and then give back what we have learned in some form of service, he is not only talking benevolent good sense but is showing us how we can all become more practical, more complete, and altogether more useful people."

When we asked about salaries he said that the general run of qualified doctors would be paid $30 a month and the head of a major hospital or research institute would perhaps get $135, though there were many who refused to take this much. Looking at my friend the physician, I thought he seemed momentarily embarrassed.

In the afternoon we boarded a launch and, crossing a corner of Lake Tai, came to a small but high island where the Federation of Trade Unions has a workers' sanitorium, one of a dozen established in this province to provide union members with facilities for rest and convalescence.

Each province has similar institutions, usually located in places which, before liberation, were holiday resorts for the upper classes, or where the aristocracy maintained estates.

Patients may stay for two or three months if their doctors and cadres agree on this, still get their wages, and pay nothing but the equivalent of fifteen cents a day toward the cost of their keep. Medical treatment and the use of clinical and therapeutic equipment and facilities are free.

The most interesting case among the convalescent patients was a commune man named Chung: a big-framed, tough, and muscular brigade leader with a shaven skull who, a few months earlier, using a newly purchased and electrically driven chaff cutter, had turned to answer a friend's question regarding its efficiency and in a twinkling was missing half a hand.

They had taken him quickly to the commune hospital where a doctor gave him sedatives and applied a temporary dressing, meanwhile sending his friends to search for the severed section of his hand, which consisted of half the palm and four fingers. When this was found the doctor took it, together with the patient, by train to the provincial city, a journey totaling, all told, five hours and thirty minutes.

Had this happened six months sooner the man would have been treated on the commune or at the county hospital and would have lived out his life minus half a hand; but commune and county doctors and cadres had already heard much of the astonishing operations performed lately in Shanghai by which severed limbs had been reattached to victims of workshop accidents. Immediately, then, it had seemed to them medically worthwhile and politically sensible to see if a similar operation could be done locally.

When Chung and the doctor left the train at Soochow two surgeons with their specialist assistants had already arrived from Shanghai by airplane to make this operation a twofold demonstration, first of new surgical techniques, and secondly of social equality: an underscoring of the difference between life in old China, where a poor man might have died without any government official showing interest or lifting a finger, and life in the new China, where every single peasant is important in the eyes of the Party.

It was Chung himself who said this, speaking through Feng and telling us then that although the surgeons had replaced his hand only six weeks ago he could already wriggle his fingers; which he did, inviting me to take hold of them and see for myself that they could be moved, though only a little as yet.

He had this week begun to come to the sanitorium for a few days at a time, to make use of physiotherapy equipment which was better here than anywhere else in the area. And the doctors also thought it good for him to be able to share in the cultural activities that were a regular part of the treatment: the television and films, visits from theater troupes, and discussions of the works of Chairman Mao.

187

He was clearly fit and well and spoke confidently of being back on the commune within three months (though the doctor looked dubious) and said that he would be working by the next harvest, but would be careful in the handling of any new machinery.

My friend the physician seemed impressed, though many Western doctors who have not been to China suggest that there is as yet insufficient evidence to show that surgery of this kind is, in the long run, successful. I have no qualifications which permit me an opinion: only a photograph of Chong in which he seems happy enough wiggling his fingers, though his hand was still pinned and in plaster.

We spent two hours at the sanitorium, partly in wards and dormitories, all of which seemed well appointed and even snug by the normally austere standards of Chinese life, partly in the clinical and treatment section, and for a while in the gardens overlooking a little bay, where we sat talking with patients and members of the medical staff. Afterward, going back across the lake, the physician tried to clarify his mind about the place.

It seemed to me, listening to his tentative, cautious talk, that half his mind was excited by what he was seeing in China and the other half apprehensive, affected by what his professional friends and colleagues would think and say when he went home and spoke of the things he had seen—how most of them would listen with their faces fixed in conditioned disbelief, their minds closed tightly against anything good he might say about China; how they would talk about him in their clubs over lunch and in the doctors' rooms in hospitals, saying that he was a nice chap but naïve, an easy subject for brainwashing by the Communists, who were expert at it, in fact, something of a sucker.

I could see that he found these thoughts irritating, for he frowned without apparent motivation and made clicking sounds with his tongue, resenting in advance the judgment which awaited him at home, the frustration, the fact that he would be battling like mad to convince people that his opinions, even if incomplete, were sensible and founded upon the evidence of his own eyes. What made it worse for him was the feeling that he would have been party to equally stubborn judgments had he not made this trip; and this he admitted when, in the evening, we talked with our other friends about these things, over a drink.

He said then that although most of the patients at the sanitorium had seemed to be genuine postsurgical or physical rehabilitation cases, many of them might as easily have been classed as neurasthenics of one kind or another. A fair amount of hypertension was evident, nervous debility, assorted aches and pains, insomnia, gastric ulcers and the like, much of it being relieved by massage and acupuncture treatment given at the sanitorium (the chief masseur, he noted, was a blind man).

"Maybe some of these people find it difficult to keep up with the physical, mental, and moral disciplines imposed upon them by the Communist system. They get to feeling inadequate in one or all of these categories, especially cadres and ex-Red Army men who are given supervisory jobs beyond their competence in professional or specialist fields, then get out of their depth and develop complexes and aggressive resentments. Or men and women who are naturally slow thinkers, or lack manual dexterity and the temperament to keep up with pacemakers in the communes or workshops and factories, and either worry themselves sick or become stubborn neurotics.

"I've noticed, for instance, that many women in hospitals and rest homes are textile workers, an industry in which the competitive element is keen and personal achievement counts for a great deal in terms of prestige. Under such conditions women who are conscientious but naturally painstaking and slow, or just clumsy, are at an emotional disadvantage among the others, particularly if they are plain or lack personality."

The Communist in our group (who had come to China not only for a holiday visit but in search of medical attention) became restless and said that, although the physician tried to give the impression that he had an open mind, he seemed to be taking the standard capitalist line, refusing to admit willingly that any good could come out of a Communist country or that the socialist system was not only more just and fair than any other but in many respects technically better, and before very long would get better still and leave the West well behind, though people just simply didn't want to believe this in spite of the evidence. All of this he said without taking breath. Then, being a pleasant as well as a forthright man, he bought us all another drink and settled back to let the physician continue.

189

"I'm not suggesting that social and industrial neuroses are exclusive to the Communist system in general or to the Chinese in particular, far from it. We have similar problems at home and they span a wider range both socially and in terms of age.

"Here in China it seems to be mainly simple, middle-aged people of no great ambition who find the new competitive tensions hard to take, whereas we find in our own country that apart from the high-pressure section of the population, it is among the young adult and adolescent groups that the strain of keeping up with competition shows most, even in the late school-age group."

The professor, avoiding his wife's eye, interrupted, pointing at us with his pipe. "Chinese children are conditioned from kindergarten onward to adopt the revolutionary approach to work and service. They grow up in a prefabricated atmosphere of challenge, are given idealist incentives and visionary guidance. Just now they have this little extra dimension of inspirational strength that the West in general lacks today and which few of its leaders seem able to give: the sense of inspired rightness that men like President Kennedy, Pope John, a Mahatma Gandhi, or General de Gaulle have been able to generate.

"This special kind of imaginative genius has its practical limitations and may ultimately overrun its usefulness, but it is essential for the continuance of civilization that it exists and can occasionally take control, give impetus when the processes of social progress seem to reach an impasse. Though there is always the danger that inspiration may produce its own hazards, as well as its excitements and delights.

"This could be the case in China today, although throughout his lifetime Mao Tse-tung has shown an outstanding capacity to create and control complex revolutionary situations. And except for the approach of old age, which he disguises by swimming in rivers, there is no real evidence that he is losing his political grip, even though the Cultural Revolution is producing growing overtones of discord and considerable confusion."

He reached for matches to relight his pipe and seemed about to continue, but his wife looked up from her knitting.

"Perhaps you don't remember, Henry, that the doctor was telling us of his visit to the sanitorium."

"No, no. I've said all that's relevant." The physician refused to approve anyone's captious wife. "The only other comment I can make is that one cannot compare medical or any other social systems and services in one country with those of another without first knowing both the problems and the needs of the particular kind of society one is discussing. Our ways are obviously not suitable for this sort of society, and the Chinese system would not suit us in every respect. Though I wish that we could provide as benevolent a medical and welfare service for our low-wage-scale workers and old folk as the Chinese do."

To this the Communist called from the depths of his chair, "Hear, hear." And we drank his health politely.

CHAPTER

18

I WENT to a popular revolutionary opera, *Sister Chiang*, fell thoroughly in love with the leading lady, and asked to be taken backstage to make her acquaintance, thus throwing Mr. Feng into confusion.

Cadre Wang, smiling slyly, approved but took me first to meet the political leader of the troupe, a Mrs. Sun, who proved pale, glum, and discouraging and more particularly so when, discreetly dropping the leading lady, Ching Li-ping, a little way down the list, I first praised the director of the piece, the leader of the orchestra, and then many of the secondary characters, individually.

Her attitude was clammy.

"We are engaged in a collective enterprise. No person in the company is more important than another. We are pleased if foreign friends like the opera because this shows that they understand the purpose of our revolution, recognize the true nature of all reactionaries and their lackeys, and share our determination to serve the peasants, workers, soldiers, and the revolutionary masses. For us, only the audience is important."

It seemed somehow senseless to try to tell her then that I had really enjoyed the performance; that the standard propaganda characters, good and bad, had come to life, had moved outside the restrictive political framework within which the action was contained and, taking flesh and blood, had seemed to identify with personal human issues that came through clearly, issues that were bigger and more relevant than the ideological text and the simplified historical incidents of which the story treated.

I wanted to say that I thought the production excellent and deft, the coordination of music and action adroit, the players uniformly persuasive, and the leading lady not only lovely but a first-class artist who had reached out beyond the conventional boundaries of Chinese theatrical art, and the barrier of language, to make me see that Chinese people may be as deeply moved by the individual flux of love as by the bitter contemplation of collective suffering.

But this would have confused her, so I said that I would like her to thank everybody—actors, orchestra, and stage technicians—for an artistic and politically instructive experience and to convey to them the fraternal greetings of my countrymen, most of whom were sympathetic to the aspirations of the Chinese people. I felt depressed, however, as I said these things.

Then Wang prompted Mrs. Sun and I was taken backstage, where Ching Li-ping stood with the rest of the company in a corridor, all of them beaming and seeming excited because a foreigner had enjoyed their performance.

When I went toward her she came forward with outstretched hands, warmly smiling, not needing to speak, knowing that it was not politics or formal politeness that had brought me to see her, but true appreciation and pleasure.

Then the others crowded around to shake my hand, but Mrs. Sun brought an old man with a broom to speak to me, saying that he was the theater janitor, an old revolutionary who had helped all of the actors to reach true understanding of the characters they portrayed in their performance, and he began to make a speech.

While he talked I thought back, measuring the moments of pure pleasure I had met with on this visit to China: remembering the children in the parks of Peking on May Day, the uncovering of Feng when he had told me of his boyhood, the talk with the old railway workers, and the visit to the hospital where the good county secretary, Chiao Yu-lu, had died. These were human incidents that had broken through briefly and made me feel one with these people, and now this meeting with Ching Li-ping and her friends, which was already being vitiated by the old man's mumbling about other days while we all stood listening. Then Wang spoke and Feng touched my arm. The moment was over. We went into the empty street where the car was waiting in the rain to take us to the hotel.

The opera *Sister Chiang* has a stock story. It begins with a prelude played on the waterfront at Chungking in the spring of '48, at about the time when the Red Army was ready to launch its ultimate offensive against Chiang Kai-shek's Kuomintang.

Against a drab background of laborers struggling up gangplanks with bales of silk and cotton, an eminently respectable but impatient young matron waits for someone who doesn't come. She is watched by a newsboy and a peddler, both U.S. agents.

The lady is Sister Chiang. Her husband is the political cadre of a Red Army guerrilla group operating upcountry. A Communist agent from the Provincial Committee is about to bring a message which Sister Chiang must take to her husband. On the way she will masquerade as a new schoolteacher assigned to a small town in the mountains.

The agent arrives in a flurry, says that he is being followed. Quickly a paper is exchanged. The newsboy and the peddler fade. The game is on. The orchestra goes wild with excitement.

The first act opens tragically. Sister Chiang has not yet reached her objective when she meets men from her husband's unit who tell her that he has been caught up by the enemy and is already executed.

She sings a long and introspective aria in which she recalls his patience, with what affection and tender gentleness he taught her to be a good Communist, to love the Party more than life itself, eventually to be accepted as a member. Accompanied by her husband's men, she exits singing, "Never will I forget the true and beautiful words he taught me."

They bring her to a mountain hideout to meet their fighting leader, a woman called Two-gun Granny, who plays it tough but has a heart as soft as butter. Sister Chiang delivers the message intended for her dead husband, and Granny gives Chiang the old red flag that he used to carry. Pressing it to her breast, she vows to continue the fight to the bitter end.

But troubles never come singly.

The man who delivered the original message to Chiang on the wharf at Chungking was followed by U.S. agents (tipped off by the newsboy), was captured, and has cracked under questioning. He now returns to the story as a running dog of the Kuomintang (wearing a gold watch) and, Judas-like, delivers Sister Chiang to the chief of police.

She is cast into a prison controlled by the S.A.C.O. (Sino-American Cooperation Organization) and is interrogated by a senior official of the Kuomintang (in U.S. uniform) who tries to bribe her to betray her comrades. Indignantly she sings, "I will never be part of the crimes which you commit in the name of peace and freedom."

He threatens her with death. She smiles and sings back at him, "I shall gladly die as the Red Dawn rises on our land."

In a cell with other women, she calmly awaits execution, soothing those who weep for her. A note, thrown in through a high window, tells them that the People's Republic of China has been proclaimed. Sister Chiang unwraps her husband's red flag and together the women stitch the five stars of the Republic onto it.

Guards come for her. She is taken away, singing to her dead husband that she had been true to the lessons he taught her. There is a volley offstage. The lights dim and the theater is in darkness. Only the frangible, fluttering sound of women weeping wanders in the quietness like a lost moth. In the audience we are all crying.

Then slowly red dawn rises to reveal Sister Chiang standing on a rocky crag, among spring blossoms—a symbol of the indestructibility of man. Triumphant music rises. People in the theater sigh, as men and women in their millions have sighed since time began, satisfied, at the dramatic climax of some esoteric ceremony, that man is more than body and mind, that he is mysteriously linked to all things from the beginning through all civilizations, and for all time.

Before we left Soochow we were given an official dinner and I was surprised to find that Mrs. Sun had been particularly invited for my sake because, Feng said, "You are interested in the opera and she is anxious to answer any questions that you would like to ask."

Shamefully I admit that for a moment I had wished it were Ching Li-ping being placed beside me, but remembered that I had not come to China for pleasure but to tighten the bonds of friendship and to learn. So I smiled and said that it was kind of her to come when she had a husband and two children at home. To this she replied that she had her work and her husband had his, and the children were well looked after while the two of them were busy; it was her duty to help foreign guests understand the message of the revolutionary theater.

I told her that I had seen the opera a second time and had left with the feeling that the whole production created a sense of reality around the plot and situations, so that each character seemed completely convincing, even Two-gun Granny. Then taking the bit between my teeth, I said that to my mind Miss Ching had brought to her part a simple nobility which gave the character of Sister Chiang the stamp of universality, so that she would seem a heroic figure to people of any language and place.

Mrs. Sun helped herself to a piece of glazed fish, picking at the dish with her chopsticks. Then she said that the troupe I had seen was a good one, but not the best of the five operatic companies in Soochow, and that Ching Li-ping, though popular with certain elements among the masses of the people, tended to bring to the parts she played an interpretation that was too personal.

She ignored my surprise and went on to say, still picking at the fish, that in the opera I had seen, Miss Ching made it seem that her devotion to socialism was based more upon a private and personal loyalty to her dead husband than upon the political truths established by Marx and Engels and brilliantly developed by Mao Tse-tung.

"She has a natural habit of individualism which she recognizes and is trying to overcome." Primly she added, "I do my best to help her. It is my duty. Every day we read the works of Chairman Mao, especially the essay *On Individualism*."

I said that perhaps the mass of the people would soon lose interest in the theater if every actor and actress gave set, puppet-like performances. (Feng sighed, translating this, raised his eyebrows, and seemed to be explaining that I was a difficult and stubborn case of ideological blindness.)

She replied with no emotion, saying that in a socialist society the function of art and culture is not to provide means for self-expression but to serve the masses by educating them politically. This leaves no room for sentiment. Writers and artists should not praise weakness of any kind, create paper tigers, or lead people to believe that a choice between right and wrong may be left to the individual. Nor should they manufacture sugar-coated bullets with which to shoot down the truth. A good Communist must have more love for the masses than for any individual.

"Chairman Mao has told us in his talks at the Yenan Forum on Literature and Art that in a class society there can only be class love, but some comrades like Ching Li-ping can imagine a love that is above class. They believe in love in the abstract, truth in the abstract, human nature in the abstract. They must rid themselves of this influence and with proper modesty study Marxism-Leninism."

The food was good and the company, excepting Mrs. Sun, in good humor. I could see Wang watching me across the table, his face straight, but his mind betrayed by a smile in the eye. So I raised my glass and called to him, *"Kanpei,"* and the others joined us in drinking, while Mrs. Sun bent her head and spat fishbones onto the tablecloth beside her plate.

Talking then in more formal terms about the Soochow theater, she told me that each of the five companies has its own headquarters (four of them use converted cinemas) and each has its own style of entertainment. They all play two seasons a year, including a country tour which takes in small towns, communes, educative and technical training institutes of various kinds, and pioneer rural and industrial settlements.

As with other cultural and sedentary workers, members of theater groups spend several weeks of each year living in factory complexes or on farms; and sometimes when rehearsing an opera with a new thematic or locational background with which the players are not familiar, they go to live and study for a while in the area or among the kind of people to be portrayed in the play.

Wages for these provincial players seem to range from U.S. $30 to U.S. $50 a month, though Feng thought that a dozen or so of the

197

most popular performers in Peking and other big cities might earn as much as $80 a month. The thought seemed to aggrieve Mrs. Sun, who picked up her rice bowl and, holding it under her chin, resumed eating with determined detachment.

She seemed peeved, and to please her I said that great changes had clearly taken place in the Chinese way of life since liberation and that visitors could find little to criticize.

She answered without raising her eyes from her rice bowl or setting it down, but continued to scrabble around in it with her chopsticks while speaking.

"We need more time. The revolutionary struggle has yet to be won."

Wang nodded across the table, giving encouragement, though Feng, beside me, helped himself to more food, content to take advantage of the chance to eat something while this woman made the long, predictable speeches which he would be able to translate parrot-fashion, without having to think, having mouthed them more often than she had.

"The old exploiting classes no longer have any authority, but their reactionary ideas have not yet been completely eliminated from our society. A handful of anti-Party thieves, cheats, and opportunists, masquerading as comrades of Chairman Mao and holding high places in the Party, are using their influence to confuse the masses and to keep a way open for the return of capitalism. This is why we must carefully study and work hard to remold our thinking."

The words fell pat, though flatly, with no gesture or expression to lend emphasis, to suggest sincerity or conviction, until she put her bowl and chopsticks on the table and looked at us all, blinking like an angry hen.

"We are the guardians of the future. We must not let the enemies of our socialist revolution use official positions to further their own private plans. All artists, writers, and intellectuals must join the peasants, workers, and soldiers to beat back and eliminate those traitors who wish to follow an anti-Marxist bourgeois line and lead the people with them, away from the true goal of the Party and the revolutionary masses."

Dimly, and with a certain sadness, I could see Ching Li-ping and the others of the cast of *Sister Chiang*, gathered each day

198

about this thin-faced, pale, fanatically anxious woman, hearing her, in the breaks between rehearsals or before a performance, read Mao's holy writ, and afterward, when the audiences had gone from the theater, participating in sessions of scarifying self-examination and individual criticism.

Now our host, the local secretary of the Association for Cultural Relations, picked up her theme and, leaning forward across the table, filled out the framework of her thesis, speaking reasonably.

"When the Party liberated us not many of its members had been trained in government or administration, so that many of the old Kuomintang officials and functionaries, and members of the so-called upper classes who had rejected Chiang Kai-shek, were allowed to stay in their places. Most of them learned to think differently, saw their mistakes and changed their ways. Some became good members of the Party and held important positions.

"Now, almost twenty years later, China is stable and many believe that the revolution is finished. They begin to think that they may go back to the old ways again; that they should be able to enjoy the luxuries and comforts of the positions they held in the old society. They begin to behave in the old ways—to put themselves above the Party and the masses of the people, to hand out jobs, take bribes, buy wives, deal unfairly with the simple peasants on the communes.

"These people do not understand the nature of revolution. They do not realize that although the masses have won the basic victory by taking over total ownership of all materials and means of production, the final ideological victory has not yet been won.

"It may take several generations, perhaps centuries, to change human nature, to completely stamp out the old evils and create a new kind of society in which selfishness is unknown and no longer an obstacle to progress."

He looked down at the table, hesitating, as if remembering days gone by. (Feng, beside me, said quietly that this man was once a revolutionary leader in the south but now had stomach trouble and was sometimes very sick.)

I liked him, this thin, wispy, frugal little man of modest manner, and knew that what he was saying was sincere even if it was wrong and all one-sided, as my friends at home, being impartial, would point out when I told them about it: going to their homes with a pressing invitation to talk to them and their friends about my visit to China, aware that they did not want to hear anything that would conflict with beliefs already entrenched in their heads, truths told to them by their teachers twenty or thirty years ago when they were children at school.

So I watched him closely while he spoke and heard Feng beside me turning his words into English:

"We must learn from the example of Russia that this is not the time to relax and to give up our disciplines. It has taken a generation of total effort to revolutionize China. How much longer must it take to save the rest of the world, how much more effort, how much more sacrifice?

"These are great days. Days in which sacrifices even greater than those already undertaken must be made by and for the masses. This is the time to renew the revolution. To clear out of our political and administrative system all reactionaries and back-sliders. To purify the Party and the people, especially the young, so that the long march toward our socialist goal can go forward with new strength, new courage, and new understanding."

Perhaps he was trying to convince himself of something, or it may have been the stomach pains that made him hesitate and seem uncertain. For suddenly he stopped, then smiled and made signs to the waiters that they should refill our glasses. He pointed to the innumerable dishes on the table, insisting that we should put more food onto our plates. But although we politely complied we were quiet, a little confused, feeling that what had been said was in some way tremendously significant for all of us, even if the phrases did seem stale, familiar from continuous repetition, and in our own political idiom meaningless.

But when the wine was poured Wang, standing, bid us drink to friendship, emptied his glass in one gulp, and held it upside down, smiling. We were relieved—satisfied that what we had heard was merely the usual bit of Peking propaganda which goes with official dinners on the tourist route.

In the morning at the railway station, as we waited to board the train that would take us to Shanghai, the talk was of atomic tests and rumored news that another nuclear device had been exploded somewhere in Sinkiang.

Even Wang, usually noncommittal and a little aloof except at dinner, seemed animated, standing with officials who had come to see us leave, all talking at once with their heads together.

Our capitalist stopped his stately promenade along the platform and stood looking at them. "Feng says that they've got their own atom bomb. It seems a pity to have to waste money on making those useless things when there's so much else to be done before everybody in a country like this can have a suit of clothes and a decent place to live in.

"But I suppose they feel that they have to do it. It's the only way to get other people to listen, to give you a bit of respect. There's nothing new in this. All people, poor or rich, want to be treated decently. You'd think that the brainy ones who run us would wake up to these simple things and do something about it, instead of stirring up strife and making us all afraid of one another.

"We're enjoying ourselves here even if we don't agree with everything they tell us or appreciate everything we see. They're not bad people if you treat them the same as you want to be treated yourself. It beats me why we always have to be fighting. Maybe the next generation will have more sense."

But I had seen Mrs. Sun and was really not listening to the capitalist, he being a much too simple man to have anything significant to contribute to a serious discussion of the world situation.

She came from the waiting room, looked around, and then made her way quickly among the people on the platform and came toward us holding a bunch of flowers in her two hands, like a bridesmaid. She found Feng, and when she spoke he seemed surprised and looked at me. Then they came together, and Mrs. Sun, without speaking or smiling, gave me the bouquet.

Feng said, "Madam Sun wishes you to have this appreciation of your interest in the Soochow Revolutionary Folk Opera Group. All members of the group hope that you will remember them and that your visit will help to bring closer friendship and better understanding between your friends at home and the Chinese people."

When he had finished she took my hand and spoke, looking at Feng as he translated:

"Madam Sun says that China now shares the secret of the material atom bomb with other countries, but she also has the spiritual atom bomb of Chairman Mao's thinking, which the enemy does not possess. Therefore we are able to beat all revisionists and aggressors and will one day rescue the world from Western materialism."

As the train pulled out she stood stolidly waving, and I wished that I could have liked her as much as I had liked the actress Ching Li-ping.

CHAPTER

19

WE WERE in a bus, returning from a workers' settlement in the suburbs of Shanghai. In two days we had also seen a machine-tools factory, a middle school, a film about progress in Tibet, and a friendship store, where foreigners may buy luxury goods at moderate cost. We had spent all morning at an industrial exhibition, collectively marveling at China's apparent capacity to manufacture practically anything from huge electrical power-generating equipment to surgical needles so minute that they can be used only with a microscope.

The women had been ecstatic about ceramics and fabrics, the men impressed by almost everything. The capitalist had surprised us by playing on a plastic cello (trade price $30), giving a determined performance of the Boccherini A major minuet to a wide-eyed audience of Young Pioneers on a tour of inspection with their teacher. When they clapped he gave them Gounod's "Ave Maria" for an encore.

Now, driving along the bund with the river on one side and a nineteenth-century façade of banks and business houses on the other, the professor was saying, with an air of vague amazement, that nearly twenty years after the Communist takeover Shanghai is still a monumental symbol of the Western presence.

"It was never a truly Chinese city, and few of us who lived here in the old days would have been surprised if the Communists had pulled down this mercantile section and rebuilt it as an expression of their own economic strength and independence, just as they built the Great Hall of the People in Peking as a political symbol.

"Perhaps the gesture would have been too prodigal, though the Party must have been very tempted to do away with this reminder of a century of almost total Western dominance. As it stands now, with this completely Westernized skyline so unlike any other Chinese city, it must seem to many of the old-time Communists not so much a relic, not so much a mausoleum containing the corpse of imperialism, but a rather provoking and somewhat worrying reminder that there is another and quite comfortable way of life."

The modern history of Shanghai, a city of seven million people currently, goes back not much more than a century. Before then it was a drab, small, and unimportant provincial town with no outstanding characteristics or particular history.

It began to be a city of significance in 1842 when the British, having won the trumped-up Opium War (one of the most hypocritical iniquities in the history of any civilization), forced a bewildered Emperor Tao-kuang to sign a treaty which gave them Hong Kong and also established the principle of allowing foreigners to set up trading centers and to use certain sea and river ports on the Chinese mainland for their own commercial purposes.

So began a hundred years of national embarrassment for a China stripped of her mystery, a century during which her internal decay was openly uncovered, her senility made evident to a world which had been kept arrogantly at arm's length for several millenniums. She was shamed like a rich, but sick old woman who, the walls of her fine house fallen, gates hanging on their hinges, finds her decaying state exposed to the gaze of strangers.

They came, the British, French, Americans, Russians, Germans, Japanese, and the rest, came to strip the old lady's estate and to filch her riches. Like hucksters they marked out their pitches, set up shops, warehouses, money-changing booths and banks in the most favorable places, one of which was this little town built on the silt at the mouth of the great Yangtze River system.

It became a drain, a duct through which these foreign traders (these gypsies) siphoned the lifeblood from almost the half of China—down the thousands of miles of the big river, out of faraway provinces linked in by its tributaries (places where the foreigners never went), by the canals, the little coastal ships, and the inland railways.

In less than a century the dismal little town was a city of four million. The biggest and richest in all China, it was also the most squalid, sinful and filthy—a city containing a more concentrated conglomeration of luxury and suffering than any other in the long history of the Chinese dynasties; a city in which the power and privilege of a few foreign families matched that of the Emperor in Peking.

Four-fifths of this city belonged to the interlopers.

In it they built workshops and factories and introduced their Western technology. They trained several generations of peasants and village artisans to be mechanics, machine-minders, process-workers, and clerks in various kinds of industry: in textiles, ship-building, metal trades, and minor manufacturing. Rich Chinese watched the foreigners, then copied them. Together they created a huge new class of semiskilled and underpaid industrial workers and laborers, a million underprivileged people who lived in unserviced mud-and-matting slums without water or sanitation, on the fringes of this sprawling, parasitical foreign metropolis. Some, to keep themselves alive, sold their girl children into harlotry at the age of eight.

Had the Western invaders been a little less rapacious, a little more civilized and benign, and had the misery, brought about by their amorality and their gluttony for money, been more thinly spread, less intensely concentrated than it was in this one city, it is possible that Communists would not now be governing in China.

As it was, the foreigners and their Chinese imitators (who were even more avaricious) created, without knowing what they were doing, the necessary social situation and environment in which communism could, and did, take root in China.

So Shanghai was never, in the classical sense, a Chinese city. Nor was the communism which originated here in May, 1921, with the foundation meeting of the Chinese Communist Party, a home-grown revolutionary movement of the kind which from time to time had erupted to overthrow decaying dynasties. It was, like the city itself, a foreign thing which did not fit naturally into the overall panorama of Chinese history.

The Party Central Committee, meeting regularly in Shanghai to lay its revolutionary plans, was guided by Russian advisers and followed patterns of activity which had been designed to meet Russian cultural and historical economic situations. It set as a first objective the political organization of urban industrial workers and students, especially in Shanghai, thus flying in the face of Chinese history by ignoring the traditional and fundamental role of the peasants, who had provided the revolutionary strength of every Chinese uprising for three thousand years.

At least one member of this original committee, Mao Tse-tung, then a young man not long from the country, saw this hand-me-down Russian plan, hatched in the least Chinese of cities, as inadequate and inapplicable to China. He believed then, as he does now, that the peasant represents the ineffable strength and the substance of this enormous and enigmatic country; that the cities and their technology exist to help and support him; that philosophically and politically the urban proletariat is of secondary significance.

This proposition, seen through Chinese eyes, is logical. Any Asian arcadia must chiefly consist of well-fed, healthy, and contented peasants living comfortably on and mainly off their own land with the help of such twentieth-century accessories as are beneficial but not overexpensive.

The concept is sensible. Put into practice, it could create a balanced culture and economy, halt the population drift to parasitically swollen cities, and bring spiritual stability. With this vision in his head young Mao Tse-tung went from Shanghai to become secretary to the Hunan provincial branch of the Party, leaving the city work to his colleagues.

Genius, born to lead (especially in politics), is inevitably perplexed at some stage by the dilemma of split or conflicting loyalties, and to this premise Mao was no exception.

He was an intellectually convinced Marxist, profoundly impressed by the world-changing achievements of the Russian Communist Party. He revered Lenin as a major philosopher and politician and later admired Stalin as a master tactician. For him Marxism was, and still remains, the means by which the Chinese peasant will achieve dignity and become politically potent.

But even in the early days of his conversion, and at the starting of the Chinese Communist Party, he suspected that this Russian way of salvation was not precisely the right way for China; that with its emphasis on the urban proletariat, the Russian way of revolution was, technically, an incorrect way for a country of six hundred million peasants.

He went, then, to the peasants and urban workers of Hunan to search among these truly simple people for a Communist-colored truth which would satisfy the Chinese mind. He went also to commune, to meditate, and in solitary contemplation to hammer out a Communist assessment of mankind's destiny in an idiom that any Chinese peasant could understand, accept, and fight for behind Chinese leaders.

Today, when his own way is subject to critical discussion, he insists that the Russian way is still the wrong way, not only for China and for the rest of Asia, but that its inbuilt errors have led it to betray the whole of hopeful humanity.

"You see, then," said the professor, "that the present rift with Russia was already a hairline crack from the day the Party started, almost fifty years ago, when Mao was a young man and the Chinese Communist Party was holding its first meetings in this city. So it is in Shanghai, as well as in Peking, that you must look for answers to most of the questions that the outside world is asking about China."

We continued, in the evening, to talk of these things, for he planned to leave next day for Changsha in southern Hunan to see a new collection of inscribed bronze vessels unearthed during the reconstruction of the railway; and I was anxious, before he went, to have his guidance and opinion because it seemed unlikely that we would meet again on this trip.

His wife, going with others of our group to see a famous troupe of acrobats at the Workers' Cultural Palace, said as she went that she left us without regret, since there was little pleasure in our company once we got lost in politics.

They left, and the professor read some passages from *Selected*

Works of Mao Tse-tung, saying that nobody today need wonder what plots the Chinese leader was hatching since Mao himself had outlined them clearly in his writings for all to see and read. And although most of this writing was early work, it was as relevant now as it was during the days of the Party's early struggles.

"Listen to this piece, written in answer to Party leaders in Shanghai who were critical of his work among the Hunan peasants, and catch a glimpse, if you will, of the vision that he saw. The vision which stiffened his resistance to the Russian belief that revolutionary activity must begin in the cities."

Then, clearing his throat and putting his spectacles straight, he read from Committeeman Mao's report on the peasant movement in Hunan, written to the Central Committee of the Party in 1927:

"In a very short time . . . several hundred million peasants will rise like a mighty storm, like a hurricane, a force so swift and violent that no power, however great, will be able to hold it back . . . every revolutionary comrade will be put to the test, to be accepted or rejected as they [the peasants] decide. . . . There are three alternatives. To march at the head and lead them? To trail behind them, gesticulating and criticizing? Or to stand in their way and oppose them? Every Chinese is free to choose, but events will force you to make the choice quickly."

He looked up. "That was written forty years ago and was aimed at Party members with whom he was in argument, but it could as easily have come from this morning's editorial in the *Liberation Daily,* commenting on the Cultural Revolution.

"And now listen to this piece, telling the Central Committee how the members of his Peasant Associations were dealing with uncooperative landlords."

"They fine the local tyrants and local gentry, they demand contributions from them, and they smash their sedan chairs. People swarm into the houses of local tyrants and evil gentry who are against the peasant association, slaughter their pigs, and consume their grain. They even loll for a minute or two on the ivory-inlaid beds belonging to the young ladies in the households. . . . At the slightest provocation they make arrests, crown the arrested with tall paper hats, and parade them through the villages . . . sometimes he is led by a rope and escorted with big crowds in front and behind. Sometimes brass gongs are beaten and flags waved to attract people's attention. . . . Doing what they like and turning everything upside down, they [the peasants] have created a kind of terror in the countryside. This is what some people call going too far."

He turned a page and read on awhile, then looked at me quizzically. "I wonder what your friends would think of this?

"To put it bluntly, it is necessary to create terror for a while in every rural area, or otherwise it would not be possible to suppress the activities of counterrevolutionaries!"

He put the book on his knee and tapped the page with one finger.

"It would not surprise me if there's a memorandum on these lines circulating in Washington right now, in the Vietnam file. But it will be marked Top Secret. Certainly not for publication. Politically and philosophically we do not subscribe to violence.

"One of the differences between these Eastern people and ourselves is that in such active matters of conduct and self-expression we Westerners are more refined, more discreet than some Asian races, even though we have a reputation for being ugly, vulgar, and brash by comparison.

"We do not like to speak openly of violence. We are diffident in these things, perhaps because we are a little ashamed at being unable to live up to our Christian principles, which are, of course, very difficult to follow, especially in politics. Yet we don't want to admit this, or to abandon these principles because in an age of efficiency the only real alternative is some compromise with communism, and mentally we are not yet ready for this. So we have to invent explanations which will satisfy us when we deviate from the letter of our gentle Christian teaching.

"We just cannot be as frank as the Communists in this matter because we can never admit that anything we do is sinful (meaning anti-Christian) or that crime may sometimes be justified. We have at least to convince ourselves, if nobody else, that all our actions are perfectly in accord with these superior Christian teachings and principles which we have accepted as a kind of spiritual gold standard, even if we have no practical or creative use for them.

"Mao and his followers, especially the younger ones, see things differently and are not so inhibited. When even the leading

Communists (Peking academicians) complained that the behavior of the peasants in Hunan was terrible and that it was going too far, Mao replied, 'It is not terrible at all. It is anything but terrible. It is fine!' "

The professor said, "You can't imagine any decent Westerner saying a thing like that about dropping atomic bombs or about the war in Vietnam. However much we privately deplore our behavior, we must justify it in public.

"Yet it was the gentle Jesus, our teacher, who said with simple practicality that it is better to chop off a hand, or pluck out an eye, than to be diseased. Who insisted that once a man makes up his mind about an absolute truth he must pursue it without counting the cost of making excuses. And who said without equivocation, 'Do you think that I have come to bring peace on earth? No indeed, I have come to bring division.' "

So we talked about this man Mao who, perhaps more than any other, now has the world on edge—this latterday prophet, this Moses who, having led his people for twenty years in the wilderness and brought them in glory to their land of promise, knows that he must soon die and is fearful (as prophets, knowing the weakness of man will always be) that the way he has laid down for their salvation, and for the ultimate salvation of the whole world, will prove too difficult for those who take his place; this man who now seems to be saying desperately, "Let the children, at least, follow me, for theirs is the kingdom that I saw in my vision."

When we had done, and I had brought the professor a drink, which seemed reasonable after all his talking, I asked if he saw any connection between the attitudes and events of these early days of the Party in Shanghai and the present trends in Peking. Was there, in his opinion, a consistency in all that Mao Tse-tung had done and said since 1921?

The professor admitted that he had a theory, and since it is as neat and plausible as any I have listened to or read in its assessment of Mao's thinking and the present China situation, I will pass it on, having nothing of my own to offer which is as solidly based on scholarship and knowledge.

But as this account of my travels is meant for the general reader and not for experts and specialists, it may be sensible (at the risk of irritating these) to recapitulate briefly some history and to sketch a little background against which the trend of his thinking may be seen and its validity assessed.

It is first necessary to accept as fact (and there is evidence in plenty to back it) that when the Communist Party was formed in Shanghai, China was in a state of chaos.

An ineffectual government in Peking, intimidated by foreign powers to whom the country owed money, and lacking any general support, could not control the motley gang of warlords and bandits who between them kept the whole country (including Peking) fragmented into spheres of personal servitude.

In opposition to the government was the Nationalist Party (called the Kuomintang) descended from the patriot Sun Yat-sen and led by his legatee Chiang Kai-shek. Based on Canton in South China, and advised by Russia, the Nationalist army planned to march northward in an attempt to clean up the country and humble both the warlords and the foreigners, then to establish a Republican government.

By arrangement with the Russians the new Chinese Communist Party was accepted into a coalition with the Nationalists, both parties having the same immediate aims and the common encouragement of Moscow.

This alliance, although at first one-sided, was successful. The Communists were free to operate and were effective in organizing support, among both the urban workers and the peasants, and for six years there was considerable progress. In 1926 their integrated forces overran and occupied most of southern China. The Kuomintang was able to move its government headquarters to Wuhan on the Yangtze river. Next on the list of occupation were Nanking and Shanghai.

Shanghai, as we have already said, was four-fifths foreign and one-fifth Chinese. The Communists in the city (with Chou En-lai active among the leaders) had been busy, and before the Kuomintang army could reach its target the one-fifth of the city was already captured and its warlord in Communist hands. Only the foreign garrisons stood between the Reds and the rest of the city.

At this point history took a sudden and sharp turn not yet satisfactorily explained by Chiang Kai-shek or his apologists, but called by the Communists "The Great Betrayal."

Without warning Chiang dissolved the alliance, rounded up as many of the Communists as he could lay hands on, and executed them: in Shanghai, Canton, and Wuhan and in all the provincial cities and towns that they had overrun together. The Peasant Associations were broken, the unions smashed, the Communists everywhere on the run. Perhaps one in six or seven of the Communist officials escaped.

To put the rest of the matter briefly, all that need now be said is that Chiang Kai-shek no longer persecuted the foreigners or the rich Chinese of Shanghai, but formed an alliance with them, and with their approval went on to take Peking and become the nominal ruler of China with his capital in Nanking. Shanghai remained as it was before the Communists took it. Thirteen years later, after Pearl Harbor, the Japanese took the city and put the other foreigners into prison.

From this point we can pick up the thread of the professor's theory, which goes like this:

With the finish of World War II (the Japanese being defeated) China was handed back to Chiang Kai-shek. The foreign businessmen had gone from Shanghai, but their place had been taken by retired warlords, rich refugee landlords, bankers, businessmen, and a motley lot of gangsters who together continued the tradition of unprincipled moneygrubbing which had been established by the foreign founders of the city a hundred years previously.

Four years later the Red Army drove Chiang Kai-shek out of China and the Communists were back in Shanghai where the Party had started—back in a city of bitter memories, where it had been betrayed and many of its leaders hanged in public; a city which was now even more corrupt than before, more rotten, more unjust; a city run by thugs; a vicious city in which the price of human life could be reckoned in cents.

Had they rounded up the rich and hanged them nobody would have been surprised. Had they stripped the rich and put them into prison it would have been considered no more than rough justice. But these Red Army peasants had a country to run. They needed not only the factories and workshops and the continuance of foreign trade relations which were based on this city; they needed, as well, the sophisticated knowledge of industry and commerce, the foreign connections, the experienced engineers, technicians, and skilled labor, even the capital and the capitalists: just as in 1921 they had needed Chiang Kai-shek and the Kuomintang.

In those early days of the 1920's many of Mao's critics within the Party (in Shanghai and in Moscow) had blamed him for precipitately inciting the peasants to demonstrate against the rural gentry and urban workers to strike against their employers. There were suggestions that these activities had swung the balance of influential opinion against the Communists and, in part, had been responsible for The Great Betrayal and the long fugitive period of proscription.

This time, in 1949, there could be no such criticism. The capitalists and the gangsters were themselves surprised by Mao's mildness, amazed how easy it was to be forgiven. One needed only to confess (*mea culpa*), to do penance, promise to sin no more, and one could continue to be a capitalist.

Many who remember that time have remained skeptical, have said from the start that in Mao Tse-tung's reckoning twenty years would not be too long to wait for a final accounting. These say that the Cultural Revolution is a euphemism for this day of judgment. With time running out Mao now wishes to finish the business he began in 1921.

The old-time capitalists, the intellectual bourgeoisie, the "poisonous weeds" must go now. They have served their purpose. Their influence and their example must now be rooted out. It is all written in *Selected Works of Mao Tse-tung* and repeated in the editorials, on the wall posters, and in the slogans:

Sweep away monsters of all kinds and all forms of decadent and feudal ideology.
Down with those landlords, rich peasants, counterrevolutionaries, bad elements, and rightists who have not reformed themselves sufficiently.
Eradicate all vestiges of the exploiting classes.

This time Mao leads from strength. Using a new generation of indoctrinated revolutionaries as shock troops, he aims to eliminate all traces of the old order—to purify China before he dies.

213

We did not know then, as we spoke about Mao, that the Red Guard movement would erupt within a few days, but nothing that has happened since that evening in Shanghai seems to invalidate the professor's assessment or make it seem obsolete and untenable.

A recent editorial in the Shanghai *Wenhui Pao* stirs echoes of the pieces he quoted from Mao's early works that night:

The great proletarian revolution in the Shanghai area has advanced to a new stage . . . the situation is getting better and better! . . . more than three million peasants of Shanghai's outskirts are plunged into the mighty revolutionary torrent of gigantic revolution against the handful of persons in the Party who are taking the capitalist road . . . its revolutionary actions are splendid. Its general orientation is entirely correct.

But it was quiet in Shanghai that night when we walked for a while in the wet and empty streets to stretch our legs and to smell the freshness of the air. We stood to watch a long and loose procession of men and women coming from the bund, some pulling handcarts and barrows of different kinds and size, some riding or wheeling pedicabs grossly overloaded, and others with baskets hung on shoulder poles, all hurrying. Those with lighter loads called encouragement to others or ran along the line to help shove a heavy load past a puddle. Among them a woman with a harsh, rasping laugh cracked jokes as she passed.

We went into the Seamen's Club (a crewman friend from a wheat ship was staying there). He told us that the people we had seen coming from the bund belonged to a stevedoring or a transport workers cooperative. They worked through the night when streets were otherwise empty and so could make their trips between ships and the city stores and warehouses more quickly than during the day.

He showed us the upstairs room which he shared with two others, a room of heavy elegance big enough to accommodate half-a-dozen guests and with a marble bath. Then the billiards room with four tables, all busy with sailors playing. A cinema, where a film of the fighting in Vietnam was being shown to a crew of Indonesians. The reading room and library, with *Selected Works of Mao Tse-tung* in eleven languages. The PX, and finally the long bar, famous for its stateliness when the club was exclusive to English gentlemen and their friends, but now clamorous with the multilingual conversations of a hundred sailors buying drinks for each other.

When we came back to our own hotel Wang was waiting for me, with Feng, both seeming secret. And having said good night to the professor, they took me aside to say that someone from their office in Peking had telephoned, giving permission for me to visit the city of Nanchang in Kiangsi Province and the border country about Hunan. Feng and little Ping could go with me.

CHAPTER

20

THE new hotel in Nanchang, capital of Kiangsi Province, is ten stories high, marble-lined, and impressive. Each day of my stay the sitting room was filled with bowls of fresh flowers. Each time I came in from sightseeing the bellboys hurried to bring tea, to take my shoes for cleaning—and would not accept tips.

But the old hotel on Sun Yat-sen Street belongs to a different period. It has stone water jars in the unpaved courtyard, at which guests coming in used to wash the dust from their hands and faces. Its plaster walls are whitewashed, there are potted plants and a single hand-crank telephone. The furnishing is sparse and old-fashioned. In preliberation days it was a respectable place at which to entertain on notable occasions. Wedding receptions were a specialty.

It is a hotel no longer.

It is now the Museum of the August 1st Uprising because, for a little while in 1927, its ground-floor rooms (where the wedding receptions were held) were the battle headquarters of the Communist Party in Kiangsi Province. It was here that Chou En-lai, aged twenty-eight, together with Communist officers of the Chinese Nationalist army conspired to capture this city from their colleagues who were holding it for Chiang Kai-shek.

Chou, lately escaped from Chiang's massacre of the Communists in Shanghai, had come to Nanchang to pursue the fruitless policy of trying to take and hold provincial cities, to make bases of them from which the Party might, when strong enough, overrun the country.

Simply as a short-term military objective the taking of Nanchang was not a difficult problem. Of 40,000 soldiers in the city some 30,000 were commanded by officers who were either Communists or sympathizers. Among them was General Chu Teh, head of the city police and afterward commander-in-chief of the Red Army. Another was Colonel Lin Piao, one of Generalissimo Chiang Kai-shek's most brilliant students at the Military Academy —and now Mao's heir apparent.

The political objective, which occupied the mind and time of Comrade Chou En-lai, was to have these professional military men abandon Chiang; to convince them that the time had come to make a break from the vacillating and traitorous Kuomintang and to take the uncompromising Communist way to national unity and independence without further hesitation.

His arguments, taken together with the temporarily favorable situation, were persuasive. On August 1, by arrangement rather than by battle (although there were three hours of excitable street fighting), troops officered by the Communists took control of the city.

Chou made speeches to the townspeople from the steps of the hotel. The Women's Auxiliary, using a Singer sewing machine in the back room, made red neckties for soldiers who wished to change sides, and make do uniforms for seven hundred new Communist recruits. Students wrote slogans on walls, while boys and girls of the Children's League arrested local reactionaries and led them through the streets with penitential notices hung around their necks. There are pictures of these incidents in the upstairs rooms of the museum.

A week later, when Chiang retook the city, most of the soldiers who had switched removed their red neckties, many of the recruits hid their new uniforms, students altered the slogans on the walls, and the children went back to school.

Chou En-lai and the rebellious Red soldiers left Nanchang and, still persevering with the Central Committee's Moscow-made directive, moved on to attack other cities and towns with even less effect, losing many of their men in rear-guard engagements and uneven encounters with units of the Kuomintang.

In terms of military achievement this capture of Nanchang by the Communist mutineers seems a meaningless and extravagantly melodramatic gesture. Materially much was lost at a time when the Party was poor, short of both men and equipment. Nothing was gained but a glimpse of the glory that came twenty years later.

Superficially, then, it would seem to have been a pointless operation, stupidly conceived and undertaken in ignorance. But when I said as much (though less bluntly) to the woman who took us through the museum she was obviously astonished and questioned Feng. Then she took us to a bench where we sat under another great painting: a crowded street scene with Communist soldiers pasting up proclamations, Kuomintang prisoners being led away, a captured fieldpiece being drawn by prancing horses, joyful boys parading with banners, a fruit seller handing out wedges of watermelon—Nanchang happy at being relieved.

She dragged another bench into place, came close and faced us, leaning forward—a big-boned village woman (from the mountains, said Feng), plain, able, anxious to explain. Ping opened her notebook and waited.

"The taking of Nanchang was not such a wonderful military victory, but it was a great political achievement, a step forward in our revolution.

"We were not yet ready, not strong enough to win big victories against the warlords or the Kuomintang and its foreign bosses. But we could stage these battles against cities, and peasant uprisings in the countryside such as Chairman Mao was organizing. We could lead local rebellions against corrupt officials and rural gentry all over the country. We could arrange strikes and demonstrations to show the people that if they were determined they could overcome their enemies and one day establish a government of their own.

"In these ways we helped the people to discover their own strength. They learned to trust the Party and its officials, to see that if they worked together under its guidance it would eventually lead them to victory."

I thought it odd to hear this woman, forty years old at most, speaking as if she had taken part in the events of 1927. But listening, I began to understand that in this part of China the Party first took real root, grew, and gathered its genuine strength. Here it found its true place, its identifications with the people; here it was caught up in the ancient and continuing stream of China's history and so became a reality, acceptable to the millions.

By her very possessiveness, her speaking of "our revolution," this woman let me see that the villagers of Kiangsi, Hunan, and neighboring provinces were the foster parents of this city-born child thrown out by its rich relations in Peking, Shanghai, and other urban centers. And I could also see now that Mao had been right to insist that those who would rule China must first win the villages, whatever they might do afterward.

So, although his mountain woman was only a baby when Chou En-lai and the rebel generals took Nanchang, she spoke as if she had been there, directly and personally concerned in all that had happened in the old hotel.

"We needed professional military men to lead our army of peasants and workers, but the Party had nothing to offer anyone. We could only promise hardship and struggle, a life of hiding and being hunted, and sooner or later execution. So, for the officers listening to Chou En-lai, this was the moment of truth, the time to finally decide whether they were for the people or for the enemies of the people.

"Our cause seemed already lost. And because these men were officers of the Kuomintang, friends and colleagues of the Generalissimo Chiang Kai-shek, they were comfortable and could have continued to live very well on foreign money.

"But they chose instead to join the people and to support the struggle of the peasants and workers with military action. To give encouragement to the masses and show them that they were not alone. Here, in Nanchang, in this hotel where I am speaking to you, dear foreign guest, the partnership between the people and the Liberation Army began."

She stopped to let this sink in, laying her firm, masculine hand on my wrist for a minute and looking into my face to see if I had understood. The rest I knew, for I had read it in a dozen books: How in the following months the Communists were harried by the

Kuomintang (so much stronger with the foreigners supplying all their wants), battered and scattered about in small bands. Men like Chu Teh, who had commanded whole armies, now roamed the backcountry with a few hundred homeless men. The failure of the city-based Central Committee to organize rural support was paying its dismal dividends. With winter coming the Communists were in a sorry way.

The woman leaned back, watched me write my notes, and when I had done went on again. Feng, carried away, was at his most dramatic:

"They had no friends, no supplies, no clothing, no place to rest or to sleep, no medicine. Their sick lay down in the evening and were dead when the sun rose. Still Chu Teh did not despair. He told them, 'It may seem that we have already failed and must soon be beaten, but in the end we will win. Even if every one of us must soon die of sickness and starvation, or be taken by the enemy, the final victory will be won by the people.' "

I said, "Where, at this time, was Mao Tse-tung?"

Her eyes opened wide, were bright, and like a child she spun around on her bench to face the opposite wall. And there he was, in a copy of the painting that is in Peking, sitting on a stone, on the side of a mountain, thinking.

"There was light burning in the mountains. A small light, but bright, shining like a lantern in the darkest days of our oppression. A beacon to give courage and hope to the people."

She spoke softly, gently, motherly, like a woman in love—this rough mountain woman with the strong, masculine hands.

Feng looked seraphic, and little Ping was sniffing, trying not to cry while writing.

Afterward, when we had seen everything in the museum and had become good friends, we sat together in the reception room to rest.

Then she asked Feng if I had more questions and I said that I would like to know more about her own life. At this she laughed and said that it was not so interesting; that there were many more important things for me to see in Nanchang and in the Kiangsi countryside and to write about for my friends.

But I persevered, finding first that she had been married ten years and had three children; that her husband, a local man, worked on a State Pioneer Farm in charge of fish harvesting and marketing and the collecting of lotus seeds and roots, which are a big part of this farm's production.

The fish, salted, are sold in the market. Part of the lotus-root crop is processed for starch and the rest used for vegetable. The seeds are a popular sweet, said to encourage love, though the leaves, burned and turned into a powder, prevent pregnancy. The woman did not tell me this. I read it in a Chinese medical book.

Her own work in the museum kept her busy lecturing to adults and training junior guides to look after children, who came in classes to learn about the August 1st Uprising, not only from city schools, but from the communes. She also talked on the radio and in the evenings wrote stories and behavior plays for children, to help them be good revolutionaries.

She said this modestly, not claiming any special talent, but saying that her writing was simple and only for little children. She tried each new story on her own three and those of her neighbors and had learned from them how to work for the revolution and serve the Party in this way.

When I asked if she had spent much time at school herself she shook her head and smiled and said that most of her early life had been spent in the village, where she learned very little, but she had lived for a short time in Shanghai and there had been taught to read and write and name the cities and big rivers, not only of China, but of the United States of America.

Even Feng seemed surprised, listened to Ping whisper, then turned to the woman and talked to her for several minutes, at the same time making notes while I waited. Then satisfied, he told me what she had said.

"The parents of this lady were poor peasants. Many times they were hungry. Her mother became blind because she did not have enough to eat. One day she fell into the river and was drowned.

"There were American missionaries in the town where this lady lived. They were sorry for her father and gave him work to do. Afterward, when they went to Shanghai, they took him and this lady to work in their house. They taught her the names of the big cities and rivers in America.

"After a little while her father left the missionary because he had found some other kind of work. At first he was poor but afterward began to do business for the Japanese soldiers in Shanghai and then with the U.S. soldiers. He became a little capitalist."

Ping made a clicking noise with her tongue, colored with embarrassment, and coughed into her handkerchief, while Feng went on.

"Shanghai was not a nice city when the Japanese and the Americans were here. No Chinese family would let their children come into the city. No lady would walk by herself along the bund unless she was a prostitute."

He stopped, and I asked the woman, "How old were you at this time?"

Feng listened and answered for her. "She was a junior at middle school. The students wished to make a demonstration against this bad behavior of the foreign soldiers, but the Kuomintang officials told their teachers that they would be dismissed if they allowed the students to do this. So it was forbidden.

"Her father was busy and did not want her to be with him. So he sent her back to Kiangsi to live with his own sister."

We were all silent for a while, and they sat expressionless, watching me write. But when I had done, the woman looked at little Ping and Feng and began to speak again, slowly at first, then passionately and at length, as if exasperated. And when she finished and was sitting back, part angry, part ashamed, Feng sighed and shook his head.

"The lady asks you, why are the American people afraid of us and why do they try to make you others afraid? She says that we in China have suffered much and do not wish that others should suffer also. We do not hate anybody because it is not good to hate, and it is bad to make other people hate one another.

"It is not people who are evil. Power is evil and makes people afraid. People are all the same. They hate what they are taught to hate. We are sorry for the American people because their leaders try so hard to make them afraid and to hate us. We are sorry for them because the rest of the world has abandoned them and only wants their money.

"They say that we who are Communists wish to make everybody the same, but they hate every nation that does not wish to follow

222

the American way of life. It is they who want everyone to be the same. They cannot understand that in China we are very busy making a Chinese way of life. If every nation will please follow its own way of life, we will all walk side by side and one day will meet together with much pleasure."

Feng was speaking evenly, almost pleading, trying to be kind, but suddenly I felt tired and empty.

It has all been said so often. On television, on the radio, in every newspaper, in books, at lecture desks, even from pulpits. There seemed no point in going over it again, in saying to them that all people of all races feel the same; that we of the West are not so much worried by what our leaders preach, for at least we can answer back even if they do not listen. It is what the Chinese leaders preach that worries us, even though we want to believe that we have no need to fear their threats, that their warlike language is empty of malevolence.

But I said it, knowing that I need not listen to the answer that Feng gave on behalf of this woman, himself, and little Ping, because, like my speech, it was also a repetition: an enumeration of foreign bases, subsidized by the U.S.A. to contain China; the statement that there are American military men on every continent, American ships in every sea, American aircraft watching the whole world. While China's soldiers stay at home, minding their own business.

I was about to ask, "For how long will they mind their own business?" But it seemed a pity to leave the woman in this way, for she had been generous with her patience and her time and I liked her very much. Nor did I want to seem afraid, because I do not think I am.

CHAPTER

21

AN OFFICIAL in Shanghai had told me that since liberation more than a million people had gone from that city to settle in other provinces, some singly or in family groups, others in pioneering teams; that they leave the comfort and pleasures of the city and go into the most remote and difficult parts of every province and to the autonomous areas of Mongolia, Sinkiang, and even Tibet.

One in four is a specialist concerned with some aspect of national development, management, research, or education (including culture and politics). These busy themselves with public health, agriculture, soil and water conservation, animal husbandry, afforestation, geological and industrial research, communications, and other categorical matters.

The others go simply to help where help is needed, or to find fulfillment as individuals with some special aptitude or skill to contribute to an established community, or as members of a pioneer work group. They go, not only from Shanghai, which has the largest pool of educated labor, but from Peking, Canton, Tientsin, and most other big cities.

In Kiangsi Province alone there are a quarter of a million of these "foreign" specialists and voluntary labor immigrants working on provincial projects. Each project fits into an over-all scheme of national development that has two principal objectives: first to make each region fundamentally self-sufficient; secondly to simplify the interchange of basic foodstuffs, domestic commodities, and industrial items which can be produced in surplus in particular regions.

The official had said that there were four general aims:

(1) To equalize levels of regional development.

(2) To spread talent effectively across the whole country.

(3) To develop regional self-sufficiency, particularly in matters of finance and defense.

(4) To expand national productivity in all categories, and raise the living standards of the masses.

"When you get to Kiangsi Province you will be able to see something of how this works. We have spoken to our office in Nanchang and something will be arranged."

So when in Nanchang they said benevolently that I would be taken to a State Silkworm and Mulberry Comprehensive Reclamation Farm I felt at first dismayed, for I have seen silkworms in several countries and have not so far been excited by them; nor could I see any evident connection between mulberry trees and large-scale national development.

But in two months of dealing with officials of the China Travel Service I had not been disappointed in any arrangements made to enable me to see things in which I had expressed some special interest. It seemed best, then, to show enthusiasm. In any case, to be allowed to travel around in the backcountry was in itself satisfying.

The red earth of Kiangsi reminds me of the almost empty cattle lands in the center of my own country. The coarse, porous soil is gritty and rough like crushed rock—deathly dry in summer, glutinous when wet. Our aboriginals use it to paint their faces. Yet cattlemen, letting it trickle through their fingers, say that it will grow almost anything if looked after and given water and a little attention.

These Chinese hills through which our road winds have bald and seemingly sterile heads. Erosion has uncovered the yellow structure of the country's skull. Millions of seedling pine trees planted on their sides seem sick and apathetic. Yet in the earth's wrinkles and cleavages where water has been lying, strips and scarves of grass are vivid green.

Feng and little Ping sit in the back seat with young Mr. Kuo, who has been appointed by the office at Nanchang to be our guide. In another country he would be a backslapper, but here, where such public intimacies are regarded as indecent, he just talks continuously, proffers cigarettes, gives unnecessary instructions to the driver, who takes them amiably, and works hard at making little Ping laugh.

This is not difficult. Both she and Mr. Feng are pleased to be in country that is new to them. Constantly they interrupt the flow of Mr. Kuo's patter with quick questions. A bird, darting across our path, excites them as they follow its startled flight. They demand to know the name of it. Mr. Kuo, making a show of confidence, gives it a name and continues talking.

I say to Feng, "We call it a quail." His eyes open wide with surprise. He repeats the name, then he and Kuo and Ping repeat it to each other. Notebooks are produced and they write slowly as I spell out the letters, though Kuo must copy from Ping because he has no English. We are all happy with this educational collaboration, which Kuo explains to the driver, first turning back to Ping to check pronunciation.

The driver speaks this strange foreign word to himself, then nods and grins and gives me the Chinese. We are all very happy indeed and play this game for an hour or more, learning new words and enjoying each other's company. It all seems so easy.

Somewhere we must leave the highway and follow a subsidiary road. Kuo says that there will soon be a signpost and we must watch for it. We all look ahead, concentrating, except little Ping who, being myopic, will not be able to see it anyway. She pouts, finding the hiatus irritating.

Although this part of China is as new to Feng and Ping as it is to me, it has more meaning for them historically. Feng, at least, is aware that Chairman Mao moved among the people of these parts, helped them in the early days to set up their local Soviets, their Peasant Associations and Party units in the villages.

It was here and in neighboring Hunan that the first experiments in socialism took place, where peasants were educated literally and politically by the Communists, taught to organize, to face the landlords and the autocratic gentry with collective strength.

And it was here, when Mao's amateur army of workers and peasants had been decimated, and its remnants chased into the borderland mountains by the Kuomintang troops of Chiang Kai-shek, that this early glimpse of a poor man's paradise was snuffed out, trodden into the red mud, devastated in a deliberate lay-waste campaign put in train to eradicate all traces of the Communist experiment. It was one of history's great exterminations, pursued ruthlessly by the Methodist Generalissimo, who spurred on his troops with the battle cry, "Better a thousand dead peasants than one Communist left alive."

The driver spoke and, coming to the signpost, slowed, turned in, and followed a winding road through wild hills thinly thatched with bracken. There were small patches of rice in paddies where the ground was flat, and here and there a lonely grave in a landscape without habitation. Then, crossing a low ridge, we came into another land—a long valley, entirely cultivated, its sides lined with mulberry trees, and the flatter lands a patchwork of ripe wheat and the delicate green of freshly planted rice, as far as one could see. In the gullies running ribwise from the valley there were fields of flax and rape, orchards of orange trees, stands of tasseled maize, melon vines, and groundnuts; men were plowing. And ahead of us there was a new town.

We stayed all day talking with the men who manage the fifty-four square miles of what, eight years ago, was an uncultivated, uninhabited wasteland and is now a settlement supporting twenty thousand people, only one half of whom are native to Kiangsi. And for my part I would have been happy enough to spend a week with them, for there was much more to be seen than could be fitted within a single day.

However much I recall the warnings of my country's leaders, I am not able to feel afraid of these friendly, unassuming, yet enthusiastic men and women who manage the new institutions, the communes, the huge industrial undertakings, and the pioneer projects of China.

For the most part their origins are modest, their formal education scant. Some of them ran messages for Red Army guerrillas in

227

the difficult days, when they were village children. Others, as teen-age lads, had fallen in behind the red banners and straggled all over China until at last they marched into Peking, Shanghai, or Canton, already veterans within a decade of their adolescence.

Three such as these received us at the Mulberry Farm. Office Manager Sun was an unmistakably village-born ex-corporal of infantry, one accustomed to taking orders from almost anybody and translating them into instant and practical action without seeming to fuss or to puff himself up. Tai was a Mr. Fixit—handy with a spanner, a plow, or at making a speech, but good-humored. A younger man, Li, neater than the other two, had been through school, read easily, remembered to slip in the proper phrases when the others forgot, but he loved them and was proud to be in this outfit.

At first, in the meeting room, with tea, sweets, and a huge dish of home-grown groundnuts, Sun explained the general scheme, its history and present situation, with Feng our go-between and Ping assisting.

Sun spoke slowly, the others reminding, adding bits, making things clear when he drifted or took for granted that we under-stood certain basic facts and phrases. Tai tossed peanuts between his strong teeth, urging us all to do likewise. Li sat poised to assist his leader.

"We came here at the end of 1957, five hundred demobilized men from the Red Army, and built a base, living, to begin with, in tents. Then in the spring of 1958 five hundred youngsters came from towns along the river, most of them middle-school students from Shanghai.

"No other people lived here then. Nothing grew on this ground. The villages and the pine forest that were here in our fathers' time had been burned down by the Kuomintang. We began with bare ground and a loan of eleven million yuan [about $5 million] from the provincial government. To begin with we studied the works of Chairman Mao, especially the story of the foolish old man who moved mountains. When things were diffi-cult we read this story to each other at night, then went on work-ing, sometimes going out in the dark to get on with the job. If the old man and his two sons could move a mountain by working diligently with pickaxes, we could make this land produce food."

He said that the loan had been paid back to the government in nine years and that the first one thousand pioneers were still here, together with nineteen thousand other people.

Ping wrote all this in her notebook, learning, like me. Together we checked and corrected with Feng, then scribbled, she in Chinese characters, and I in English script, reducing these human achievements to simple figures: 3000 acres under mulberries, 3500 acres under rice, 5000 pigs raised last year, 6000 this, not counting those kept by individuals. One million meters of silk processed in 1960, four million in 1965. Per capita income for peasants in 1960 was $8.00 a month. By 1965 it had risen to $13.50. Cadres and industrial workers were now being paid $20.25 a month.

I dug my toes in and stopped them. I apologized for being unable to speak Chinese, for being slow to follow explanations; but with diffidence I insisted that I wished to be quite clear about all this, about these figures and what they meant. For instance, what were these differences between peasants, industrial workers, and cadres?

For five minutes or more Feng asked questions, made notes, checked and rechecked until at last everyone was satisfied that he, at least, understood. And so, I think, did Ping, since the dull, defensive expression on her face had been erased by a smile while Feng told her what had been said. And when, at last, I understood they smiled. Tai took a handful of nuts. Sun sent for more tea water. Li grinned and nodded and nodded like a mechanical toy.

And this is what Feng said:

First the army men came, then the students, and together they set up a State farm, working for the provincial government. At this stage they lived very much as the army had lived on the Long March, in tents and shelters, making do with little food, sleeping on the ground (remember that they were paid little more than a ration of rice, salt, and oil for lanterns).

They planted vegetables and rice to provide more food for themselves, and mulberry trees which grow well in this red earth. They plowed other land for fodder crops, which were turned back into the earth to nourish it. Meanwhile scientists took soil samples,

229

analyzed them, checked with experiments made elsewhere in China where there are similar conditions (all this information is recorded in Peking).

They set up pig and poultry sections to produce both food and manure; planted orchards and vegetable gardens, and began to work on fishponds and irrigation ditches. Being close to a lake, they have no shortage of water. An industrial brigade set up a brickworks, metal and woodworking shops, and an electric generating plant. They laid down roads, built and equipped a silk mill.

This preparation of the land, the establishment of basic amenities and a local industry was, roughly speaking, stage one of the reclamation and resettlement project. It engaged the pioneer one thousand and others, including their families, who came later as houses were built; and the work progressed until there were ten thousand people on the place.

Then, when much of the total land had been ready for cultivation, and housing, amenities, and the beginnings of industry had been established, stage two brought in ten thousand other people, mostly landless peasant families previously dispossessed. These were settled in villages on the commune system so that the total project now became a combination of State and community enterprise (the subject calls for a complete textbook).

There was some excited, emphatic talk between Feng and the other three. Then he said that similar activity had been taking place simultaneously in two hundred other locations in this one province, beginning at a time when most of the Western press was cynically jesting at the failure of the Great Leap Forward, and Western politicians were saying to their people that the Chinese government was sending millions of helpless peasants and political prisoners to forced labor camps, separating men from their families and mothers from their children.

But of the thousand who had first come not one had left, except of some necessity, or when health was affected. And as for the separation of families, those who were married had built homes for their families and were now well settled, while many of the students had married each other or found husbands and wives among the newcomers. Some had even sent for friends back in the cities to come and marry them. And one million acres of Kiangsi's red earth had been brought back into production.

Ping, blushing and looking angry, turned to me and said, "Western writers have no interest in the truth, only in what they call news." And when this was translated for the others they all approved Miss Ping's sagacity, making her blush still more.

With this background I could anticipate part of the answer to my next question.

"Why do the State-paid cadres and industrial technicians earn more than the commune peasants?"

To this Feng, having checked, said that the peasants now have communal ownership of their part of the land and can produce their own food. The amount that they earn, both in produce and in cash received for salable surpluses, will depend on how well they run their commune—how much they produce. But the State Farm runs in a different way. Its main purpose is to produce rice, silk, timber, and tree oil required by the national trade and merchandizing organizations, and also to maintain social and industrial services for everyone in the area. This means that most of its four thousand workers do not produce much of their own food but must live on wages earned as industrial craftsmen and artisans, administrators, teachers, doctors, agricultural experts, and so on.

They mentioned then the hospital with 130 beds, dental and ophthalmic services, and an elementary medical-training section; also thirteen primary schools, several kindergartens, and a "Labor University" specializing in practical engineering and agricultural sciences and, of course, politics. A plant and fruit-tree nursery. A veterinary center which attends to the farm's one thousand working animals, runs a stud of English pigs and provides a service of insemination to improve the local stock.

Then, called to the canteen for a meal, we walked through a vineyard and an orchard where pears and apples were coming ripe, though the peach trees were already stripped. And Li, walking with Ping, told us as we went that this combined enterprise of State Farm and commune system is an experimental step toward an integrated society, in which urban workers and peasants will together achieve a cultural and economic unity and an irresistible political partnership.

"It is something new. We feel that we are walking a little ahead of everybody toward a new kind of society, a new way of life for generations to come, not only here, but in other parts of the world."

And I could see that they both believed this, deeply.

The canteen food was good: goose and noodles, a fish, rice, fruit, with beer and homemade wine for the guests. The cook came to shake hands, and the people in the canteen clapped when I said that I had not fed so well in Peking.

We went then on a little inspection.

Children going to afternoon school followed us through a village of newly built brick cottages, small but neat, and each with a garden. Then four young men came past, going gravely, carrying a miserably sick old man who sat in an armchair carried on poles which rested on the young men's shoulders, so that he might have been a village mandarin. Feng said that they were taking him to the clinic.

At the silk mill we met a man who had come originally from Shanghai to help set it up, then stayed to teach promising young men and women how to maintain and to create equipment. The first machines had come from factories in Soochow and Wusih and were reconditioned, but much of the new machinery was being made in the farm's own workshops.

Of the thousand people who work in the factory a hundred are work-study students from the Labor University, making silk for peasants to wear (said Ping) instead of for rich foreigners and emperors. But Feng said that it still went to foreigners because silk is a major item in China's export trade.

In the nursery, attached to the factory, young mothers were taking time off to feed and clean their babies. And outside in the courtyard a squad of State Farm militia was drilling because, said Sun, "The imperialists do not want us to make progress and are trying very hard to crush the new China that is arising to lead the masses of the world's workers."

CHAPTER

22

In 1927–28 the condition of the Communist Party of China could have filled its followers with neither confidence nor hope. Its leaders were fugitive, in hiding. No railroad train or rivership went unsearched by the Kuomintang police. Yet the Central Committee, undercover in Shanghai, continued to send instructions to regional groups insisting that the main objective must continue to be the securing of cities which would, in time, become bases for a nationwide uprising.

Small, almost vagabond armies, mostly led by Communists, roamed the countryside, attempting, whenever possible, with loyal determination but disastrous result, to follow these instructions; but more often preoccupied with the practical problem of finding supplies, and of avoiding uneven encounters with fully equipped units of Kuomintang or local warlord armies.

The military failures at Nanchang, and a little later at other places, brought further fragmentation, desertions, and battle casualties, so that the whole revolutionary movement seemed likely to disintegrate.

It was becoming clear that somewhere, soon, a place should be found where scattered fragments could be assembled to consolidate, gather strength, and plan.

Mao Tse-tung's own rural uprising, after the 1927 harvest, was crushed and Mao himself was lucky to evade decapitation. With less than one thousand men, the remnants of his Peasants' and Workers' Army, he withdrew from the lowlands and made for a hideout in the Chingkang Mountains, a traditional base for bandits, on the borders of Hunan and Kiangsi.

LITTLE PING, looking neater than I had previously seen her, had a new blouse and fresh red hair ribbons and was humming "The East Is Red" as we left the little river town of Kian, going south to the mountains. She was sitting in the front seat of the car as a special gesture.

For she had said as we prepared to set out, "I am glad today that I will see the birthplace of the People's Liberation Army and the cradle of our People's Republic." Then we said that she should sit in the front seat and so be first to see each new sight as we approached the place, though none of us had been here before, not even Feng.

He, in the back seat beside me, read verses from the works of Chairman Mao, archly, with hand raised in a delicately imperative pose:

. . . we were encircled by the enemy's men in their thousands, yet we stayed here at ease on the mountain, without anxiety. . . .

Kuo told the driver to turn on the radio so that they could listen to the morning "editorial" from Nanchang. But I protested, being content to let my mind rest, to be quiet, to watch the countryside unwind, knowing that these others were in duty bound to listen to the session, and may have wanted to (had I not been so rude), and would mention the omission in their evening self-criticism, though they could plead deference to a foreign guest. But I was tired of the continual din of a radio shouting at me all day in a language that I could not understand, and the jangle of jingoistic music.

So there was a moment of hiatus, they silent, uncertain, while I watched a white egret hover, then settle at the edge of a pond like a large English lady arriving at a garden party.

This is the China that has been stitched into millions of tapestries, silk scrolls, and screens, engraved, carved into jade and ivory, painted on numberless fans and lampshades, on jars and vases: these villages half hidden in trees, blocks of gray black brick (the color of Chinese ink) with step-rising eaves outlined in white; bowed women flailing grain; men carrying plows; oxen with swinging heads being led by nose ropes; children fishing under willow trees; regiments of worried young ducks hurrying through stubble; pigs snuffing in rubbish; geese dabbling dubiously in little streams.

234

A small boy in a ditch turned to watch solemnly as we went past.

The road climbed a hillside. Two men, carrying a coffin tied to a pole, stopped, moved aside to let us through. An old man, ahead of them, continued to play upon a flute while lifting his eyes to watch us. A young man set down the wheelbarrow that he was pushing. An old lady was sitting in it, holding up an open umbrella. Two other people and a child followed. When we had gone past the young man lifted the handles of the wheelbarrow and the cortege moved on up the hill.

Further on a girl with a willow switch drove a dozen calves. A man on a bicycle pedaled leisurely. Three live ducks in a sitting position were perched on the carrier bracket above the back wheel. We passed a small school, and the children waved at us. With a rattle of planks we swiftly crossed a wooden bridge, surprising women washing clothes in a little river. We heard their quick screams, then laughter.

The long, shallow valleys were summer lovely, vividly green with second crops of rice. Every little while a lake or pond was filled with blue and white sky reflections. The air was dragonfly lively. Sturdy, barelegged girls spread lime in unplanted paddies, then trod it into the slime. Behind them the hills began to rise, a dark line of fir trees, then the vague, hazy bulk of a great range.

A stone arch spanned the road ahead of us, so large that even Ping could see it fifty yards away and turned to tell us. Coming closer, Feng translated the inscription on its architrave:

"THE FIRST MOUNTAIN UNDER HEAVEN"

Once through it we climbed steeply and began to wind through hills that crowded one upon another, pressed together, reared up wildly, tightly, sheer, so that the road must twist and writhe and turn upon itself in sudden loops and bends, the car swinging left, then right, and always climbing.

Ping was sick, but until the road straightened there was no place to pull aside safely. Kuo sympathetically clicked his tongue and looked worried. The driver handed her a rag, and Feng watched for a place to stop. All around us now was a thick forest of cedar, fir, and huge bamboo.

It was huge and beautiful.

We stopped where a spring spilled into a cool cave and rested there while Ping bathed her face and tried to smile. I found tablets in my bag and made her take them, which she did, dubiously.

The driver, instructed by Kuo, caught the clear spring water in a tin to fill the radiator. Feng and I waited, standing at the edge of the roadway and looking at the horizon, then down into the plain where far away there was a strip of silver ribbon which was the river we had crossed at Kian. The yellow road and the villages and little towns looked like models.

Feng said, "When Chairman Mao came to the Chingkang Mountains there was no road like this, which we have made since liberation. There were only footpaths made by peddlers from those towns who came up with things to sell in mountain villages. The few rich landlords and timber merchants who lived up here had sedan chairs and were carried up and down by servants. But Chairman Mao and Chu Teh walked with their men."

Kuo, coming to us, added, "There are wild tigers and other animals up here. Very dangerous."

He looked over his shoulder.

A bus was coming, creeping its way up through the first few coils of this climb. Seeing it, our driver said that we should go again, to keep ahead of it. So we went, but switched on the radio so that Ping could keep her mind occupied.

In an hour, pushing past tassels of cloud, we dipped over the rim of a great crater, an amphitheater with a village on one slope and, facing it, the beginnings of a city.

Tseping.

There was entertainment in the evening, in the village hall, given by a visiting drama group from Changsha, capital of Hunan Province.

The players were staying, said Feng, for six or seven weeks, and their first purpose was to produce the script of an opera based on the story of Mao's coming to Chingkangshan and the events which followed upon this.

Before coming to Tseping they had studied the history of the period, the significance of the Chingkangshan episode in the total panorama of the People's victory. Now they would try to relive each incident, each detail of the way of life of Mao and Chu Teh and their men.

They would interview old revolutionaries. They were already seeking them out, in fact, walking the mountains from one village to another by the peddlers' paths. They planned to stay for days in caves, eating rice and pumpkin stew, the same scant rations that Mao's men ate when the Kuomintang had surrounded the mountain and hemmed them in. Much of their information would come from Mao's own reports to the Central Committee hiding in Shanghai:

. . . in addition to grain, each man receives only five cents a day for cooking oil, salt, firewood, and vegetables . . . all of us share the same hardships; from the commander of the army to the cook everyone lives on the daily food allowance . . . consequently the soldiers have no complaints against anyone.

There was a woman with the drama party, a Mrs. Liu from the river town of Kian, who had studied these things for many years and would guide them. She had been a primary-school teacher and now aspired to be a cadre as her father had been. As a lad, working for a timber getter on the mountain, he had been secretly a courier for Mao's men.

While still a teacher she had studied the history of the Chingkangshan campaigns. She had come to live in the mountains and, being capable, was often asked by the local leaders to guide visitors and explain things to them. Now she was an official lecturer at the Tseping Museum of the Revolution.

"You see," said Kuo, "before liberation there were only two thousand people in the five villages, but now we have a Pioneer State Farm and a State timber industry up here and there are sixty thousand people. And since the road has been made there are many visitors, even foreign guests who come to see where the Red Army was born. So Mrs. Liu is very busy, always explaining about the war in Chingkangshan."

When I talked to her in the evening and asked why she had given up teaching to be a guide, she said that a good Communist always strove to meet the needs of the people. "The Party needs our willingness."

The village hall was packed to overflowing for a show, which fell into three parts: two playlets and a group of musical items and dances from the revolutionary repertoire.

Six sprightly grandmothers, made up bravely with rouged cheeks and lips and wearing neat gray slacks with white blouses, sang an action song of their own composing, called "All of Us Are Energetic."

> We remember the dreadful days
> When we lived in straw huts
> And the tyrants whipped us:
> Then, led by the Party, we overthrew them.
> Now we are getting old
> But are still energetic for the revolution.
> We old ones
> Will always answer the call of the Party
> And play our part.
> Look after the home,
> Keep the gardens tidy,
> Help the street committee keep the pathways clean,
> Bring up the children in a proper way.

A young man sang two songs which, he said, he had learned as a child, hearing a peddler sing them in his parents' home. They were songs of sorrow, catalogues of woe, in which the beauty of little things, a feather, a flower, a falling leaf, alone brought pleasure to a peasant's tired life.

But he had added a new verse to this plaintive, almost primitive recitative of sorrow—a stirring affirmation of faith, of hope, of new life waking when Mao Tse-tung came to live for a while among the people of the mountains.

They made him sing it again, and then again, and when he had done the hall hummed, until the leader of the drama group came onstage to say that the company would now perform a short play, written in the past few days, about a famous incident in which many of the old men in Tseping had taken part. It was called "Keeping the Mountain Pass Against the Kuomintang Bandits."

The stage lights dimmed. A woman stepped from the wings and spoke a prologue. We were silent, except for Feng's whispered explanations and the sibilant translating which always embarrassed me.

We are in a rich house, in a town at the foot of the mountain—

238

the house of the commander of the Kuomintang. Two soldiers enter with an old peasant, a man who has lived his life on the mountains, gathering herbs for the town's apothecary, a man who knows every pathway, every track.

But poor, with never enough money to feed his children decently. Always in debt, and not enough saved to pay for his burial. Timid, afraid, and ashamed.

Ashamed because he is about to betray the brave revolutionaries on Chingkangshan; men who have given up the comforts of a home, the company of family and friends, to fight his battles for him. In a moment of weakness he has agreed to lead a Kuomintang army by back ways into Mao's camp and has come for his pay.

He shakes his head. Shrinks back, mutters, wrings his hands. But his eyes cannot leave the heap of silver dollars on the table. The Kuomintang commander picks up a few; lets them trickle through his fingers; then, when three or four are left, throws them to the floor at the old man's feet.

How can a poor peasant with hungry children see silver so despised, treated with this disdain? This waste?

Slowly he bends, gets to his knees to pick up the silver pieces. Stands up again slowly and goes to the table. The commander hands him a little cotton bag. As the lights dim we hear the chink, chink, chink of silver being counted.

The next scene takes us to a cave where three soldiers in thin tunics sup vegetable soup from pannikins. They are cold and hungry but full of brave humor. One, better dressed than the others and wearing straw shoes (they being barefoot), was previously a soldier of the Kuomintang, taken in battle and as a prisoner of the Communists given a choice: to leave unharmed, or to stay and become a comrade. He comes forward and sings.

> "I will never regret the choice I made.
> I always will be grateful.
> Because now I share hardship
> With good comrades
> And fight to free the people from their oppressors.
> I can hold my head up."

There are sudden sounds outside. The three soldiers snatch at their weapons—one gun, two bamboo spears, and some stones.

A young man stumbles into the cave, exhausted. Says that he is a timber cutter's apprentice. They give him soup, gather round, listen to his story told in breathless snatches.

Yesterday, in the town, he saw both Kuomintang and warlord wagons being loaded high with supplies. There were no soldiers walking in the streets. People were whispering. Toward evening a small group of officers went riding out toward Suichwan, a village on the south side of the mountain from which a track goes by back ways up to the crater. Clearly the Kuomintang were planning to attack. Mao must be told, and Chu Teh.

Mao Tse-tung is seldom represented in the flesh. On stage a red glow lights the horizon. Shadow figures hurry back and forth, suggesting preparation. The woman steps out from the wings again, quotes from "The Struggle in the Chingkang Mountains," Chairman Mao's report to the Central Committee hiding in Shanghai:

". . . enemy forces jointly attacked the Chingkang Mountains . . . attempting to destroy our base by military attacks and economic blockade . . . all country towns and the plains in the border area were occupied by the enemy. The enemy's jackals . . . ran amuck and white terror raged throughout the towns and countryside . . . but the enemy has never been able to capture the mountain areas . . . we are preparing to defeat his attack. . . ."

The red glow diffuses. Dawn breaks and we see men in twos and threes scattered about the mountainside, some planting bamboo spikes where the enemy will walk, others fixing trip strings that, when trodden on, will cause bushes to bend or shake and so betray the coming of strangers.

The young singing soldier is in a shallow pit, hidden by stones and high grass, with his two friends, fussing over a makeshift mortar. This, with two machine guns, is Mao's total artillery. Additionally the regiment has sixty other firearms, the rest of the men being equipped with sticks and stones. The enemy comes with four divisions and is defeated.

The battle scene is spectacular in the Chinese manner: noisy and full of exaggerated action. To untrained Western ears and eyes a mixture of mad music, outrageous mime, and spirited acrobatics.

Bugles and drums, banners blowing in the wind. Shouts and shots and the beating of gongs. Men moving quickly from place to place, shouting and screaming to simulate a big army advancing. The mortar fires its few shells, killing two men. Sounds of terror. Then the rest have fled.

The audience is astonished, the old people speechless. They have seen themselves as others see them. Have discovered that what they did that day is fixed in history. Cannot be undone. Is.

I was exhausted, and so was little Ping, and glad, then, that the next drama was for children, less tense, did not grip or leave one limp.

It was a simple story of a boy whose playmates called him Flying Legs because he could run faster than any other child in the village. His father, a veteran of the Korean war, had married a Korean. She was shot dead by foreign fliers while planting rice. Early every morning the boy went with his father and ran right around the village because, his father said, "You must begin to train as soon as you can and be ready to avenge your mother when the aggressors come to China."

I woke a little after midnight to the sound of men singing and went to the window. I saw a black bulk of mountain, a fringe of thin mist circling down from its ridge like an old man's wig slipping, and in the middle of the valley, on a hillock lit with yellow lights, the stone monument which is a memorial to the Red Army and the victory at Chingkangshan.

A company of soldiers marched by swinging their arms and singing.

CHAPTER

23

Kuo said, "This road is twenty-two miles long and was built in six months by twenty-five thousand men and women. They began when the snow melted in spring and finished before winter came again."

This mountain road is Mao's Way, and those who follow it make a pilgrimage. It goes from Tseping up onto the ridge, encircles the crater, links five villages, then winds steeply down to the plain where it joins the highway.

Going from the hotel, we pushed up slowly through mist, stopping so that I could take pictures, and to keep Ping from sickness. We went leisurely, having no need to hasten.

On the flank of the highest peak huge character posters spelled out China's message to mankind:

WORKERS OF THE WHOLE WORLD
OPPRESSED NATIONS
ALL OPPRESSED PEOPLE
UNITE.

At the top of the mountain there was an old inn, and near it another monument to mark the pass where Mao's ragtag regiment routed the Kuomintang.

Two old men came and talked to us. Both had joined Mao's army in 1928, Cheng being fifteen and Lo twenty-one. Both had been wounded in skirmishes with the Kuomintang; and when, in 1934, the army left Kiangsi to begin the Long March, both had been left in the mountains to fight on as guerrillas.

They took us to see where they had watched for the enemy, and we stood with them in a little pit fringed with grasses and wild-flowers, where the mortar had been hidden. Then we walked around the crown of the mountain to be shown how a few spry and lively men could see the enemy coming from any direction.

Standing there, we saw a company of soldiers coming up, following an old track as Mao and his men had done. A flute player led them, then a man with a gong and another carrying the red banner. We waited, watched them, smooth-cheeked youths carrying rifles and full packs, each with a rolled sleeping mat, blanket, washbasin (used also for mixing food); a few with umbrellas, water jars, rice baskets; some carrying blackboards and easels.

They stopped beside the inn, stacked their packs, then gathered in a group and sat on the ground. The blackboards were set up. An instructor drew diagrams and maps, pointing at the landscape as he filled in each feature. Another instructor, standing by him, spoke through a loudspeaker, explaining the strategy and tactics, the action of the same battle that we had seen enacted by the players in the village hall.

Feng said, "These soldiers have marched from Tseping this morning and will sleep tonight in another village. They will learn the history of the struggle on the Chingkang Mountains and understand the suffering of the masses."

Then Cheng told us that companies of Red Army men came here often; that he and Lo and other local veterans were sent up to this place to talk to the young soldiers about the days when they fought against the Kuomintang. They told them of the hardships and the sufferings of the people, and how Chairman Mao had opened their eyes and showed them that they could overthrow the despots.

We watched the young soldiers take notes of what was told them, copy the maps and diagrams into their notebooks. Each soldier had a red-covered copy of *Quotations from Chairman Mao*

Tse-tung and, at a signal, he opened it and followed while the instructor read appropriate passages. When we left they were singing like schoolboys, "The Red Army Fears Not the Trials of the Distant March."

All day we drove around the mountains. We visited villages where Mao had stayed, met old people who had seen him, spoken with him, had been his colleagues. We saw beds that he had slept in, the room in which he had held meetings and been elected secretary of the Border Area Special Committee, fields in which he had helped sow or harvest rice, pathways he had followed when running the blockade with supplies. We saw where he had sat all night writing by the light of a single string wick dipped in a dish of paraffin.

In the village at Taching we gathered up another ancient, a scrap of a man toothless, hollow-cheeked, hairless, almost a mummy. He had been with Mao from the beginning of the struggle in the mountains. His name was Chu Wen-kai and he remembered many things, but out of sequence and sometimes muddled. He remembered chiefly how he had been a leader of a Red Guard Guerrilla Group, rounding up local despots and Kuomintang spies, guiding army units, gathering recruits, finding food supplies. And then he had been elected captain of a Violence Brigade at a meeting of all the people of the five villages, and had thirty men under him to make raids on the enemy supply lines.

Years later, when Mao was the most important man in China, a message came to Taching telling Chu to go to Peking to get a medal. Mao had remembered him (the old man giggled).

"I remembered him too. Though when he lived up here with us he was a hungry man, and thin like a stick, and solemn. But in Peking he was big and strong and always laughing because there were no more despots. I was happy in my heart to see Mao Tse-tung. To hear him speak about our struggle in the mountains and how he walked about from place to place, telling everybody that they should join the revolution and overthrow the landlords. We knew that he was a clever man from the city, but he was poor as we were, and we did not think that he would rise so high. But everything he said has happened."

In Peking Chu was photographed with Chairman Mao and rode

in an automobile to the railway station. In the train he met other men who had fought in the old days, in different places. They each had been given a new rifle, made in China, to remind them how far they had come since the days when most of them had been armed with homemade guns, sometimes with none, only sticks and stones. And how Mao used to tell them, "The way seems hard, but victory is certain."

So in Taching we sat in the house where Mao had lived for fifteen months, a house that had belonged then to a timber merchant who had run away when the Red Army came.

"A capitalist," said Chu, and spat.

We sat at a rough wooden table, on benches, in a room with a stone floor, mud walls, and windows with wooden bars. A rich man's house. While the old man remembered.

Remembered how they had robbed the landlords and merchants who lived in such houses as these; had broken open their barns and given their grain to the hungry, then shared the remainder among the soldiers. They carried the grain away, back up to the mountaintop in baskets, or in their trouser legs (tying string around their ankles to keep it in). Meat was scarce then, but sympathetic townsmen in the plains gave them a little pork so that the fighters might have a taste of meat on feast days.

We went down to Ningkang through valleys crowded with cloud. Past dripping, miserable villages with chickens huddled and hunched up under balconies, and pigs sneezing.

Down to Ningkang, where Mao Tse-tung, the thin, feverish intellectual, met General Chu Teh and the remnants of the army that had taken Nanchang, then lost it again, had battled its way round by Canton and back into Kiangsi, and now came to find a resting place with Mao in the mountains. With a fraction of its men left.

They made a makeshift dais at the edge of the river at Ningkang, and both men gave speeches to the local people under a canopy of thatch. It was considered a great occasion. Now there was a fine stone staging and a paved public square known as "The Joining Together Place," to commemorate this meeting: the beginning of the red Army and its march to liberation.

Ningkang still has the look of a township that has not changed

245

for generations. Tailors sit with their sewing machines under trees in the street. Pigs, fowls, and children wander in and out of courtyards. Oxcarts trundle and grumble across the stone bridge. But in the "new" town, across the river, stone buildings begin to tower over wooden shops and houses: a branch of the Provincial Labor College, a hospital, a tourist hotel, municipal offices, a powerhouse.

The County Clerk gave us lunch and in return we took him with us back to Tseping, where he had business. Going through the countryside, he showed us what had been done since 1960, when the road came through.

Thousands of new acres had been plowed, the timber and subsidiary industry developed, sheep grazing and beekeeping introduced, the collection of medicinal herbs turned into a regular business.

"Not many people, even in China, know what life was like in Kiangsi before liberation, and fewer know what has been happening since. Many, many hundreds of years ago one of our poets wrote that in winter the people had nothing to eat but straw and seemed to live like animals up here, hiding in the forests and in caves.

"Now we have closed a door on three thousand years of oppression and poverty and have opened another that has set the people free."

Afterward we heard that of this man's immediate family, two uncles, an aunt, a brother-in-law, and two children had been murdered by the Kuomintang.

Ping wrote all this in her notebook.

Mao Tse-tung lived in the mountain for fifteen months, then gradually moved down into the plains, spreading the Communist gospel and his own reputation wider and wider, consolidating political and military strength, experimenting with administrative and mass-education methods. He took the initiative in setting up small soviet states, conducted practical exercises in recreating a nation.

Then in December, 1930, Chiang Kai-shek set out to regain control of Kiangsi. Five times he sent armies against the Reds and their soviets, losing in the process hundreds of thousands of men. In one day twenty thousand defected.

His huge, unwieldy armies with their foreign equipment were no match for peasant guerrillas on their own ground. Yet eventually, by persistence, the ruthless laying waste of the countryside, firing of the forests, and the deliberate killing of millions of civilians, he forced the Red Army to withdraw from the province. It was his final fling in a campaign which spread, in all, over four years, employed a million men, and was directed by Nazi German generals.

It seemed, then, that the Communists had now been decisively beaten. But Mao moved on. He took his vision with him and, being given full authority, led the remnants of his men deeper into China to begin again; to build another base and to wait for the day he knew must come—the day when corrupt control could no longer keep the country functioning or free.

Then the people would be ready to accept a government of any color so long as it was honest.

In Tseping, when we had rested, Kuo came to say that an old man named Lo was on the steps of the hotel waiting to take us to visit the Glorious Revolutionary Old Folks' Home.

"Now you will be able to speak to the people who lived through the terror of the Kuomintang."

Ping said, "This will be good for me also because I have not suffered enough and must learn to understand the feelings of the people."

But the old folks were very jolly and gave us nuts and tea and were happy to speak of their sufferings: so calmly, smiling, reminding each other of horrors that made Ping wince.

The matron, Mrs. Ma Hsia-chin, said that when Chiang's soldiers came she was put into prison, bound and beaten because she had been in charge of propaganda in the village soviet, and had walked all over the mountain telling every woman she met that she should work for the revolution.

She was twenty then, and not long married, and the jailors tried to make her tell where her husband was hiding, because he was a Communist and was known to be with a guerrilla unit in the hills.

247

It had hurt, being beaten across the back with iron rods, and she had cried but had not told them anything. Then her sister-in-law had come quietly and had given the jailer twenty silver dollars to let her escape, and she had walked fifty miles to her grandmother's village. She had never seen her husband again.

Now she was matron at the Old Folks' Home, living with the others who were young when she was and were members of the first village soviet committee in the Chingkang Mountains.

Then seeing Ping distressed, she fussed over her and said that she was lucky to have been born in the new China, where women are equal with men and may choose their own husbands.

Mr. Lo, who fetched us, had been the secretary of this soviet, elected (so he said) because he was the only person in the village who could then read or write.

"There were nine of us, each given a job according to his ability. The shopkeeper, Li Shan-fa, was our economist because he was good at business. His work was to collect money and to buy food and oil and salt for the village militia, which we called the Red Guard."

Feng found the highland dialect a little difficult to follow, was slow to catch exactly and translate what they said. But the old people were patient and watched quietly while I wrote.

Then when I looked up again to ask if the shopkeeper Li Shan-fa was present they all nodded strongly, beamed and pointed—all except Li himself, who, though also beaming, did not know that we were speaking about him because he was deaf.

He wore a black cotton smock and skullcap, and when the man next to him shouted in his ear that I was asking about his work on the soviet committee he stood up quickly and began to speak in a high piping voice, as though addressing a meeting, and said that he had, indeed, been the treasurer and had been very busy because the Kuomintang blockade made it difficult to buy things, especially salt, and the people were too poor to contribute much to the common fund.

Then Mr. Yu, who was a sturdy seventy-three and missing several fingers, said that he was just an ordinary peasant and had been elected to mobilize the masses because he usually took the lead at harvesting or in bringing timber from the forest.

248

He had been wounded in the third Kuomintang attack and stayed on the mountain when the Red Army left because he thought that he could serve the Party better by remaining with the people than by taking his mutilated hand on the Long March across China, though he would have preferred to do this, having no wife or children to worry about.

"We were not educated people, or rich, and had no voice or authority before Chairman Mao came to the mountain. We were the same as oxen, being led by the nose and beaten with sticks. But he showed us that we were people and that we had in us the power to change our condition. He told us that we could learn to manage our own affairs. We had never done this before. We had always done as the district officials told us, or the landlords, or soldiers of the warlords.

"When we set up our soviet we learned to have confidence and to believe that we could do anything so long as we did it together to benefit everyone. If we had not learned this, we would not have continued to fight against the Kuomintang when Mao and Chu Teh and the Red Army left us."

The Red Army left, and the Kuomintang came in and burned the villages. Those of the fighting men who were not with Mao were hiding in the hills. Members of village committees who were caught were executed. Young lads were conscripted, little children taken to the towns and sold as servants.

The rest of the village people were made to labor for the Kuomintang, mostly cutting timber for officers to sell for their private profit. Every animal was killed and eaten. This was 1935, when Japan was already attacking China and the Western World, preaching patience, was preparing for its second world war.

I took a picture of these Glorious Revolutionary Old Folks with the mountain in the background, though it was late in the evening and black clouds hid the peak. But they were pleased that I should do this and made themselves tidy, Ma putting on a padded jacket while we all waited.

Looking through the viewfinder I kept reminding myself that these were Communists; that for forty years the newspapers at home had been calling them Yellow (or Red) revolutionaries, rebels, murderers, bandits. It seemed so silly and so confusing.

249

We went to the village of Taching again before leaving the mountain, though the others seemed not to understand why I should want to do this. To ease them I said that I would like to see it in the sunlight and photograph the stone upon which Mao had sat so often in the evenings, thinking and speaking to the common people.

I said that to me this was a more historic place than the Forbidden City in Peking, more significant to the present and to future generations than any of the many other famous sights I had seen in China—this rough stone on the side of a high mountain where a fugitive man, with a high price on his head, had sat thinking about decency and justice and the happiness of mankind; making plans that, in a few years, have changed the fortunes of a quarter of the human race and may yet alter the course that civilization is taking.

They seemed surprised but satisfied, so I took my picture; and a group of young soldiers who were hanging rain-soaked tunics on a laundry line nearby hid themselves, not wanting to be photographed by a foreigner. Kuo and little Ping whispered, looking worried.

Then we got back into the car and I was glad that I had come to Chingkangshan, for to me it is not so fanciful or foolish to suggest that there may be something in the claim, though perhaps made too soon and too loudly, that Mao's thinking, if honestly applied, will affect the trend of the world's political evolution.

And if this is true, then it is also true of spiritual evolution, for the two go together, body and soul indivisible, at least in this life, whatever opinion one may have about the next—if any.

To me the debilitating weakness in Western thinking is the seeming belief that the spirit of man has become obsolete; that it is historically redundant and of interest only to poets and theologians, a vestigial part of our being which needs only occasional acknowledgment, a formal or superstitious obeisance made on holidays and official occasions in the direction of some inherited secular or religious tradition.

In this context Mao has much meaning: as a modern philosopher of international significance, a political and military strategist, a genius, a myth (many expert Western "observers" believe that he is dead). You may take your pick.

I would suggest that he has been a most successful modern missionary, preaching once again that faith and good works go together. I would suggest, too, that the achievements of his preaching and teaching present not so much a threat but a challenge to the West, and especially to Western Christianity; that if Christianity is not soon revitalized it will not long survive, for our Western world, troubled in conscience and in mind, cries out for the guidance which religion does not give, and Christ crucified is no longer justified in the works of His church.

But the Chinese believe that Mao Tse-tung has freed their spirit and given them a dignity for which they are prepared to pay with sacrifice of self and service, far beyond any that we of the West seem willing to make.

At lunchtime there were two foreign guests in the hotel in Tseping—myself and an Albanian, at separate tables. We acknowledged each other without display, but afterward, waiting on the hotel steps for our cars to come, we made halting conversation.

When I said that I was an Australian he grunted, looked glum, and shook my hand without smiling. Then he said, "We are much the same. Australian and Albanian. Few people. But we each have big brother who needs little brother to love him and tell him he is very good. It is undignified, but they pay very well." He turned away and walked to the other end of the steps.

Then the car came to take me back to Nanchang.

If, because of obvious gaps in the guidebook content of this narrative, the reader feels cheated and suspects that I have seen less of China than tourists on the usual route are able to see in three weeks, then I must admit that much has been omitted.

In Nanking our party saw and was awed by the monumental mausoleum of Sun Yat-sen and took pictures of the stone sculptures of the Six Dynasties. In Hangchow I canoed on the famous West Lake with the capitalist and my friend the professor, who spoke of the eleventh-century poet Su Shih and quoted those lines of his which equate the unadorned beauty of West Lake with that of the lovely Hsi-shih, favorite concubine of the Prince of Wu, and ultimately his undoing.

With Mr. Feng and little Ping (who perspired profusely and

was short of breath) I climbed the steep, green hills of Lushan, where emperors rested in summertime and Chiang Kai-shek built an academy for the training of secret agents to round up Communists. Here we sat in a wet cave and read eremitic inscriptions engraved on slate.

One day in the grottoes of Lungmen, near Loyang, was not enough to see the 97,000 images of Buddha, the tallest of which stands fifty feet and the smallest, little more than an inch; and the crooked pagoda of Kiukiang was disappointing, being dilapidated and unsafe for interior inspection.

But we toured for two days all around the town of Chingtehchen, which contains the oldest and most famous of all the potteries of China, a museum of ceramics, and a college for training potters.

To tell of all this at length would add words without relevance to this narrative; so let us end in Nanchang, where I went to a park set aside for children and there saw boys and girls playing at a game called "The Road of the Little Red Army." It was a kind of obstacle course.

A small boy took me by the hand and dragged me to it, anxious to show off to a foreign friend. I watched him wriggle through a pipe, then walk on all fours, cautiously, across a wire bridge six feet above the ground. He crawled on his stomach under a blanket of barbed wire and I was anxious for his pants. Then he climbed a bamboo ladder and, reaching the top, jumped to a pole and slid down to the ground (it was here he cut his hand).

He crossed a sand stream on stepping stones and finally came back, hand over hand, to where I was standing. He was excited and pleased with himself, red scarf all askew, waiting for praise. When I took his hand again it was sticky and we both looked at the blood.

He said, "It is nothing." But I shivered instinctively as we went to a peddler to buy ice cream. Feng came with the car and I went, waving back at the little boy, hearing him calling, "Good-bye, old uncle, come again."

Afterward, in another part of the park, we sat in an aviary and were greatly entertained by a quartet of black crackles, pigeon big, with orange beaks and yellow neck ruffs, each perched in a metal ring. They had been trained to maintain the following dialogue:

> "How do you do?"
> "Have you had your lunch?"
> "Long live Chairman Mao."
> "Long live the Chinese Communist Party."

I was reminded of an aunt of mine who had a parrot that could recite the rosary.

EPILOGUE

I left China because I was depressed.

Suddenly, at the airport in Changsha (where Mao, as a student, had snipped off his pigtail and pinned his first political essay upon a wall), I knew that I'd had enough. At least for a while.

After ten weeks in that huge hive of strangers I was feeling isolated, alone, and totally irrelevant. Also, I had ceased to be excited by what I was seeing and, instead, was becoming troubled, glum, and vaguely afraid: not of the Chinese, who had treated me graciously, but of the feeling that there could soon be a war between them and America; that they were expecting and getting ready for it, were almost anxious that it should begin; that it was inevitable. Also that they were certain they would win.

I came home and thought about it all, and when other travelers who had been to China came back, or passed through the city of Sydney, I sought them out and talked China until we were tired, because I wanted to be sure before writing about it that my thoughts and fears should have some sense and substance.

The professor and his wife passed through on their way to the United States and Europe, and I went to the airport to ask his opinion of the Cultural Revolution and the Red Guard movement, both of which had started before I left Changsha but had developed greatly a little later.

In reply he reminded me of the children we had seen when walking one morning in Peking; how we watched them looking up at a huge poster on which a text was written, and one of them, a Young Pioneer with a red scarf around his neck, had read it to the others:

254

"We are the children of the revolution, sons and daughters of people who were oppressed. We will make ourselves strong with the thinking of our great leader, Chairman Mao. We will follow him through storms. We will learn to remove mountains. We will learn to swim by swimming, and learn to be true revolutionaries by making revolutions."

"That," said the professor, "is the main part of your answer, and the rest follows inevitably with the pressure of events. It is, I think, reasonable to believe that China is getting ready for a war which she thinks will be forced upon her, and the Cultural Revolution, whatever its other connotations, is a large-scale ritual purification of the nation supervised by its high priests. The Red Guard movement is a concomitant and collective initiation of the millions of China's children into the status of warrior-revolutionaries. I would say, then, that China is making a declaration, telling everybody that she is prepared to defend herself and her revolutionary faith against America and the rest of the Western World, including Russia, if necessary."

We agreed, then, that Chairman Mao had inspired the Cultural Revolution, intending to make everybody in authority, every government functionary from top to bottom and in every province, openly disclose through a process of "struggle"—which is a form of inquisition followed by confession, penance, and absolution—the genuine extent of his commitment to the one true socialist philosophy preached by The Leader. This would result in mass eradication of the socialist equivalent of original sin: revisionism.

Inevitably there has been and continues to be opposition from many who, since liberation, have become comfortable and do not wish to go back to the old days of strict revolutionary discipline; from others whose private enthusiasm for their work and individualistic way of life remains greater than their interest in Mao's self-abnegating ideology; and from those with foreign experience or an instinctive efficiency which makes them impatient and even critical of the folk-philosophical system of analysis devised by Mao to help semiliterate peasants solve modern developmental problems. There are those, too, who being naturally slick and acquisitive, have been living better than most other people.

A barrage of moralistic literature, films, operas, and popular songs has been aimed at these and other ideological backsliders for the past several years, but it was not until the Red Guards came into existence (whether spontaneously or by Mao's design is still a matter for speculation) that the conflict became all-embracing and generated newsworthy outbreaks of violence.

Again there is little evidence, if any, that this conflict between Mao's dedicated followers and those who oppose the trend and effect of his

255

thinking is other than minimal. It would only be wishful to suggest that a little domestic resistance will impede Mao's aim of consolidating the nation and making it ready for a test of strength with America.

The triumvirate in charge of China seems to be comfortably in control: Mao at its head directing the minds of these 700 million people; Lin Piao at his right hand holding the army to its task of defending, helping, and politically educating the peasants; and Chou En-lai, perhaps the most accomplished politician alive, keeping the machinery of government running and the Red Guards in harness.

"This is the way I see it," said the professor, "but there are a dozen other possible ways, and without direct evidence we will not know which one is correct. All that we can say is that any nation which underestimates the strength of China and its readiness and capacity to wage a long and unrelenting war on its own mainland will be making a tragic and perhaps fatal mistake."

When a smooth voice called passengers aboard the aircraft for New York, I walked with them to the exit.

"I will be happy," said the professor's wife, "to get back to something that makes sense, to our own house and the children and their babies. I cannot understand why you men make such mess and muddle with your politics. Why don't you all keep your tongue still and get on with the fishing and digging?"

The professor shook his head and tried to smile.

Then some months after they had gone I met with a group of Australian students returning from a study tour of several Chinese cities.

In Shanghai they had been met and made welcome by a party of Red Guards and had joined their processions, some of them going through the streets clashing cymbals and beating gongs and drums for the fun of it. They were stimulated by the excitement but pulled out when the demonstrations took a personal turn, as when an elderly man was brought from his shop and set roughly upon a truck with a dunce cap on his head and a confessional placard hung upon his breast to say that he had cheated the people.

Then, in Peking, some of them had spoken to a tense young woman whose parents were intellectuals. When they had gone away for a holiday she burned their Western books and paintings, smashed recordings and foreign ornaments, and cut their Western-style clothing into strips. She called this "Cleaning the revisionist muck and rubbish out of the house."

The Australians spoke of meeting many groups of Chinese students who had come to Peking from distant cities, calling in on the way at places famous in the history of the Red Revolution. They said that an estimated 25 million of these young people were swarming all over China during the summer and fall of 1966, carrying banners, calling themselves successors of the Old Red Army, seeding machines of the new revolution, teams for disseminating the thoughts of Chairman Mao.

I have learned little enough from these fragmentary impressions gathered from travelers and students. And public news, dubious and confused, seems to be based more on speculation than evidence, or at best upon selected, excitative extracts from big character posters stuck up in the streets by any Chinese, high or low, who cares to give an opinion. Apart from these sources the only public information available for assessment is to be found in official Chinese publications, which contain as many red herrings as they do clues.

Yet in looking back on my own travels in China and assessing all that I heard, saw, or sensed, I believe that I was justified in eventually feeling depressed, and that those more expert than I who believe that the Chinese are prepared to face invasion and to fight a long and bitter war against the United States of America are right.

Furthermore I believe that not only do the Chinese have no choice but that they seem stimulated by the possibility of what they call "U.S. aggression," seeing the struggle to come as a necessary step in the direction of the socialist millennium. This is a step that only the Chinese are able to take because, after three thousand years of preparation, China itself is now ready, now good enough, pure and strong enough, to tackle what is to them the prime task of this generation—to put down, if not to exterminate, the devil of selfishness, to draw men away from the crippling temptations of capitalistic materialism, and to set them again on the road to fraternal fulfillment.

At this moment in time Mao Tse-tung does not accept, as Russia for the moment must, the necessity to compromise in the great ideological struggle which divides most of mankind, the struggle which has raged continuously since man first emerged upon this earth—the struggle to find the correct way to the unknown something that is our collective destiny.

I think that Mao sees this present moment, when the emergent masses of mankind are feeling their way towards a new way of life and looking for guidance, as a time in which all mankind might make a great leap forward, or be driven back by greed and violence into the ancient slavery.

This is all set out clearly for children to see in the big city and in the provincial museums to which they are taken: the exhibits which begin with a plaster cast of Sinanthropus Pekinensis, the Peking man who lived half a million years ago, and trace his troubled progress, his continuous double struggle against nature, and against injustice thrust upon him and his successors by upstart masters, tyrants, despots (how neatly the names fall into place), against rich and wicked people of his own kind, against hypocritical and avaricious privateers from outside.

So today every child in China mentally stands, red banner blowing and gun in hand, on the threshold of destiny, anxious to continue the revolution, to carry the struggle through to the end. (In Peking I saw housewives, with babies on their hips, giggling while they practiced in the streets, throwing wooden hand grenades at one another.)

Only against this background do I see any ultimate meaning in the Cultural Revolution and the Red Guard movement; in China's general attitude towards the rest of the world, the Sino-Soviet dispute, the recent gestures in the direction of Macao and Hong Kong, and above all in the rising tide in Vietnam.

Against the backdrop of a Chinese domestic opera we watch the ritual purification of the Party leadership, and the collective identification of workers, peasants, soldiers, students, and intellectuals with the world-wide commonality of mankind struggling upward.

So it seems to me that this Cultural Revolution and the Red Guard movement may be seen not only as a local phenomenon but as tributary streams flowing into the same wide river of history as that in which we are all swimming; that it is not possible to separate what is happening in China from what is happening to us all.

And I find myself unable to take sides, because the struggle taking place in the world today is not of nation against nation, of one great philosophical sect against another. It is a collective dilemma in which every living man, woman, and child faces the end.

INDEX

Wang Po, 73-75
Wenhui Pao (newspaper), 211
Women's Auxiliary (Nanchang), 214
Workers' Cultural Palace (Shanghai), 204
Workers' Cultural Palace and Pleasure Garden (Wuhan), 133, 137
Wu, General, 24
Wu, Prince of, 248
Wu, kingdom of, 168
Wu Pei-fu (warlord), 157, 160
Wu shu, 61
Wuhan, 129-167
   armed uprising in, 137
   Chiang Kai-shek in, 135
   industry, 140-150
   museums, 166
   population of, 131

   Red Army in, 135
Wusih (city), 229

Yangtze River, 105, 129, 131
   bridge at, 133, 139
   Mao Tse-tung's swim in (1960), 138
Yangtze River Navigation School, 167
Yellow River, 105-110, 112, 120 124
   flood control of, 106-108, 136
   length of, 106
   reclamation projects, 118
Young Pioneers, 38, 74, 138, 200, 251-252
   red scarf symbol of, 75
Yu (secretary), 245
Yung-lo, Emperor, 49

266

A Note About the Author

Maslyn Williams was born in England in 1911 of Irish parents. Orphaned early, he was reared in Australia on sheep ranches. After moving to Sydney, he became a film editor-writer for the Commonwealth documentary unit, filling in spare time as a radio scriptwriter. In 1940 he was appointed producer-writer to the official film and photo unit attached to the Australian Combined Services. In that capacity, he travelled around the world. He is the author of two works of nonfiction, *Stone Age Island* and *Five Journeys from Jakarta,* and one novel, *The Far Side of the Sky.* Mr. Williams lives with his wife in Sydney, Australia.